# Wisdom Of The Rays

# The Masters Teach

## Volume I

Also available in French

For more information, please contact:

WisdomOfTheRays.com

ISBN: 0-9661921-0-9
Library of Congress Catalog Card Number : 97-77792

Cover photograph by Nancy Rodger,
© 1983, The Exploratorium, San Francisco

Printed in Canada

# -TABLE OF CONTENTS-

## PART II – THE MESSAGES

## APPENDICES

This book is gratefully dedicated to

— OUR MASTER TEACHERS —

that all who search for Truth

might have

the opportunity to grow in

Understanding

for

now is the time of the

Great Awakening

and

so shall it be!

# – PUBLISHER'S FOREWORD –

Long has it been my personal dream to somehow repay my parents, family, and friends with some priceless gift that would show my depth of gratitude for the support and trust I have received throughout the first ten years of my clinical healing practice. I pictured something that would last into forever, that would uniquely touch the soul essence of humanity, and that would enlighten mankind in ways not thought possible. That is why, when the idea to publish this material in book form came to me, I could see the beginnings of my dream come true.

What so impressed me with this collection of writings was the mastery of the written word and the fluent simplicity of style being made use of to explain otherwise difficult-to-grasp concepts of the human condition. Within the rich and intricate tapestry of the lessons presented, there also weaves a thread of timeless Wisdom that reaches ever-so-knowingly past the curiosity of the searching mind, to gently soothe the yearnings of heart and soul.

As a publisher, nowhere had I seen the complexion of modern life discussed in terms so frank, so instructive, so empowering, so preventative in warning of impending chaos, AND from such a compassionate yet other-worldly perspective. Truly these words of advice needed to be shared—not just within my private circle, I reflected, but on a global scale. Hence this collection of messages by our Elder Brothers from the Higher Realms of Creation who care dearly about our future and who wish to see our lives enriched from within, as God intended.

My heartfelt prayer is that this book find its way into the hands of those who thirst for true spiritual insight and long for that better world they know lies waiting to be born.

Dr. Pierre Cloutier
*America East Publishers*

# – PREFACE –

You have begun to read a most unusual book. It defies easy explanation. But for those of us who have had a hand in its development, it has been a labor of love, mixed with no small amount of excitement, for the messages you are about to read are gentle (well, sometimes NOT TOO gentle!) guidance from Advanced Ones who have progressed further along the evolutionary path which ALL Lighted Souls must travel in their growth.

Some of these Advanced Ones—these Master Teachers, Guides, and Wayshowers—are familiar to the general public, at least in a superficial way. Others, however, remain largely unknown by name, even though they are constantly contributing their energies to the upliftment of this planet through those incarnate ones who work at a similar "frequency" or focus of intent, and ask from the heart for Guidance or other assistance in going about their daily tasks.

I could just say that these messages are "spiritual 'sound-bites' for the late '90s". Cute? But not very respectful to their actual scope or purpose.

I could more formally say: "The following collection of writings is by Ascended Master Teachers, Wayshowers and Soul-Guides, some of whom, from the Etheric Realms, are referred to symbolically as the Rainbow Masters, or the Masters of the Color Rays, or Primary Aspects of Spectral Expression of Creator's One White Light." Wow! Quite a mouthful there.

But—even that explanation does not satisfactorily cover ALL of the necessary identifications, for some of the instructional contributions herein come from the very Hosts of God, including the Archangelic Realm—those Elder Brothers who have been sent at this time to oversee the major "re-birthing" transformation which not only we, experiencing here at this time, are going through, but also which planet Earth herself is now going through in HER great evolutionary transition or graduation from a third-dimensional into a fourth-dimensional mode of experience.

And even beyond that: a few of the messages come from God Himself—Aton, The One Light—though dutiful puppets of the adversarial dark forces have seen most effectively, over the centuries, to the hiding, the dumbing down, and the distortion of our planetary historical records to the point that, when a knowledgeable leader and teacher such as Louis Farrakhan speaks of Aton (and Akhenaton of ancient Egypt) at great public gatherings, hardly anybody really knows exactly who he means or what he's talking about!

This is just one aspect of the sad condition in which we find life upon this lovely, nurturing, and endlessly patient little jewel of a planet as the twentieth century draws to a close. While many simply go about their daily routines like mindless robots, unaware that they are actually walking around on a Major Playing Field and are mingling in the midst of Something Much Larger going on, others actually see (or at least, in some way, sense) the Game In Progress—a competition wherein the Lighted Forces of Good are fixing to battle big-time with the satanic, adversarial forces of evil, over the fate of the Lighted souls experiencing NOW on this planet. In other words, most all the fuss is over you and me!

Many awakening ones sense that such a confrontation and choosing of sides is going on, that it is a part of the "house cleaning" which must accompany the planetary transition, and that there is quite a glaring lack of (and growing thirst for) Spiritual Knowledge and Guidance as we go down this challenging transformation path with Mother Earth. **This yearning for that which nourishes the spirit is what compels this volume at this time.**

In turn, however, it must immediately be acknowledged that this present work "stands on the shoulders of" a groundbreaking volume called *The Rainbow Masters*, which was penned in 1989 through a dedicated and gifted "receiver" we shall here refer to as

Dharma. *The Rainbow Masters* is volume #7 in a most astonishing, important, and prolific ongoing series of "received" writings called The Phoenix Journals. I will deal more with an explanation of this "receiving" process in conjunction with the introductory material of Part I. For now, simply think of this term "receiving" as a form of inspired writing (or speaking); what makes things interesting is WHO'S doing the inspiring!

The Phoenix Journals address the truth about, and the forces behind, our current planetary malaise. The information they contain also acts as a kind of historical archive about all aspects of the modern human condition.

In parallel with The Phoenix Journals, as a faster-turnaround means for getting out the information than could be achieved through the book-type format of the Journals, there evolved the newsletter called *THE PHOENIX JOURNAL EXPRESS*, which grew into *THE PHOENIX LIBERATOR* newspaper by the Fall of 1991, and which then further evolved, by March of 1993, into the internationally acclaimed newspaper called *CONTACT: THE PHOENIX PROJECT*—or simply *CONTACT*, as most refer to it.

All of the writings collected in this volume were first printed in *CONTACT*, mostly within the last year or so. They have been viewed therein as a balancing "spiritual food" to leaven the sometimes shocking news which *CONTACT* must otherwise present in the unfolding of lessons about our current, dire planetary situation, how we got to be in such a mess, and what might be done to right the wrongs as the hourglass drains to empty on the current playing field.

Where still necessary, my original Editor's notes either remain in place as they were interjected at the time of a writing's first presentation, or have been modified a bit to suit this volume. Additional notes have been added where needed. Marketing people argue that this volume would "sell" better if the original dates of the writings were deleted. Are we talking about a loaf of bread, or about Timeless Spiritual Food?! The dates remain!

You will often find reference made to "Ground Crew" by the Authors of the writings. This is a respectful expression of acknowledgement by the Teachers "up there" for those ones "down here" who feel a genuine connection to the planetary transition mission underway. There are MANY of you out there! I know this, if for no other reason than the many incredible letters which arrive at the *CONTACT* offices that speak loud and clear on this subject.

For those readers of this volume who are unfamiliar with references made in the various writings herein to either the Phoenix Journals or *CONTACT* newspaper, or to the health products offered by New Gaia Products, I here offer contacting information: For more information about The Phoenix Journals or *CONTACT* newspaper, call: 1-800-800-5565 during normal West Coast business hours, or write for information about the Phoenix Journals to: Phoenix Source Distributors, Inc., P.O. Box 27353, Las Vegas NV 89126, and for information and/or a sample copy of *CONTACT*, write to: CONTACT, Inc., P.O. Box 27800, Las Vegas NV 89126; for more information and/or a catalog about New Gaia Products, call: 1-800-639-4242 during normal West Coast business hours, or write to them at: P.O. Box 27710, Las Vegas NV 89126.

Now, with that bookkeeping message out of the way, in closing let me just reiterate what I said at the beginning of this Preface—that you are about to embark on a most unusual reading adventure. It will make you think. It may make you mad. It ought to be uplifting and inspiring and challenging. Beyond that, if it moves you to personal growth and action, then it will have achieved its goal.

There is something for everyone in these messages from our Elder Brothers. What's in here for you? There's only one way to find out!

Dr. Edwin M. Young
Editor-In-Chief
*CONTACT* Newspaper

# PART I

# The
# Authors

# Introduction To The Authors

## *Dr. Edwin M. Young*

### Editor-In-Chief, *CONTACT* Newspaper

A "short" introduction to the Author-Teachers who made this volume possible was originally planned to be a part of what is now called the Preface. However, the material each Author asked to be included, to give you a "feel" for their personality, their focus, and their perspective, expanded things enough that it became more practical to defer that information to a stand-alone section, here.

I must confess to feeling inadequate to this task. You'll see why as we get going here. Nevertheless, introduce them I do, individually, these Elder Brothers and Formidable Authors of the Part II writings—writings which, for those of you who may be unfamiliar yet curious about such things, were "received" mentally, in a manner you could call "inspired writing".

The messages were written down as "heard", by several scribes who prefer to remain anonymous. These otherwise-quite-normal people would be the first to say: "It is the message that is important, not me, the scribe; I just hope I heard correctly what the Author tried to impress upon my mind during the writing process." Well, as one who deals with assessing such material on a daily basis (along with evaluating output from the more usual methods of written and spoken information flow), these writings speak loud-and-clear for the "high fidelity" quality of that which was received.

Meanwhile, for you skeptics of such a communication process, let me pose the following question: "Who cares?" Let's assume a certain measure of objectivity on the part of anyone sincerely searching for answers in these troubling and turbulent latter days of the 20th century. Therefore, for YOUR own peace of mind, honestly ask yourself: "Who cares WHERE the messages came from—so long as I get something helpful, to think about and/or act upon, out of them?!" That's the bottom line: discern the message!

Now, "Who are these Author-Teachers?" you ask, maybe with some curiosity. Let me try to "briefly" introduce each as best I can, one per chapter in the following 14 chapters of Part I. Where appropriate, and upon their instructions, I have utilized selected passages from some of the early Phoenix Journals, and occasionally from other sources, to help convey the flavor of each personality.

The challenge here is partly a matter of what has long been kept hidden from the public (by those dark ones who would hope to control this planet) about our rightful place in the universe in which we live. Imagine being told all the while you were a child that you were an orphan with no family—and then later finding out you belonged to quite an impressive family. Well, it's now time to meet some of the relatives!

I have grouped the Contributors to this volume into two categories. The first group are those I think of as coming from the realms of "Central Upper Management". That phrase will make a lot more sense when you see who They are. The second group are dedicated Teaching Masters often called the "Rainbow Masters". These ones hail from the Higher Etheric Realm and each specializes with a particular focus (and thus "color") of intent.

So—let us begin with the group that I respectfully, if irreverently, refer to as "Central Upper Management" and who refer to themselves, using Earth-based terminology more familiar to the average person's vocabulary from centuries of religious indoctrination, as: God and (some of) His Heavenly Hosts.

# CHAPTER ONE

# Aton, The One Light, God Of Light

The most straightforward, if modern, way I know to describe Aton (besides simply calling Him, in the terminology of our Earth religions, "God"), is as the "C.E.O. and Chairman of the Board of Central Management" for this particular universe within Creator Source's Omniverse of All That Is. The Native Americans, in the language of the Lakota, would refer to Aton as Wakan Tanka.

To put things in perspective, first keep in mind that our universe, as big as it is, is "only" one of who-knows-how-many others which result from Creator Source's unlimited thought projections. This physical universe is composed of all that you can see by looking "up" into the heavens and "down" into a microscope, plus it is held together by other "layers" which present (publicly known) science does not yet recognize, that vibrate in dimensional spaces (and at frequencies) not presently very detectable by either our direct physical senses or by Earth-based scientific instrumentation. In short, this universe in which we presently reside way out at one end of just one of many galaxies, each swirling with hundreds of billions of star systems, is a BIG place—and it's a lot bigger and more full of created life than current science realizes.

All the planets of our specific "little" solar system revolve around our system's life-giving Sun. Our Sun-and-planets system, in turn, revolves around a Great Central Sun, called Alcyone, in the Pleiades star system, taking about 24,000 years to complete one revolution. That entity whom we-on-Earth would generally refer to as God, or who is more universe-ally known as Aton, The One

Light, is associated with that Great Central Sun, as the Primal, Life-giving, Creational Force behind our entire universe. (I suppose if one has to picture God as "living" "somewhere", that's about as good a place as any!) From a condition of at-one-ness with Creator Source of All That Is, Aton presides as the creator of this universe and steward over all life forms created and evolving within it.

Earlier, in the Preface, I mentioned Louis Farrakhan's public teaching references to Aton—and to the en-Light-ened teacher-king who was known as "Akhen-Aton" of ancient Egypt (also known as Amenhotep IV, King of Egypt, 14th Century, B.C.). Those powerful, darkly-motivated elite would-be-kings who have always controlled the official versions of History (toward their own political, people-controlling ends) have tried their best to confuse the truth and bury Akhenaton in anonymity. However, Akhenaton's introduction of the concept of there being ONE God—"The One Light, Aton, of the God-Source"—to the consciousness of the people of his time, who were otherwise running around worshiping many gods under the controlling direction of a ruling priest class, can nevertheless be discerned if enough effort is put into historical digging into the right archives.

For an excellent reference work of eye-opening scholarship on this subject, the interested reader is referred to the gem of a book called *The Garden of Aton* by Nora Boyles. In the Introduction to her work, Nora says: "The name Aton is very unfamiliar to the ears of Westerners. Therefore, I set about to discover, insofar as possible, a record of this name in history. The first series of articles in this volume will reveal to the careful student how God's name, Aton, came to be lost to us, and its rightful and historical place in the first pages of our Scriptures. When you know God's name at the beginning, it is easier to recognize Him at the ending of the cycle!"

Previous to Akhenaton's "threatening" teachings, there existed the old multi-god religion of Amun-Ra, wherein the common folk were kept in their "place" by a powerful, controlling priesthood who went to great lengths to preserve the status quo—naturally. (Note that, except for the names, nothing much changes over the centuries, does it?!) As Nora relates the details:

"Akhenaton had tried to reform the religion in Egypt, aimed at the extirpation of the cult of Amun-Ra, removing names from monuments, etc. His movement failed. The powerful priesthood of Amun-Ra hated him [*no surprise here*], and his 'neglect of Egypt's empire' antagonized the army. There is some speculation that the king and his wife, Nefertiti, were murdered [*the tried-and-true solution to a pesky problem*]. In any event, Akhenaton's reign came to an abrupt end. Soon after Akhenaton's death, his memory was thoroughly removed and the capitol was returned to Thebes.

"Nefertiti and Akhenaton's children were all daughters. Therefore, when the king died, it was a son-in-law, Tutanhaten, who became king. He made peace with the priests at Thebes [*as would any "politician" out to protect his backside*], and changed his name to Tutankhamen. He is probably best known by the name 'King Tut'.

"Because the 'memory of Akhenaton and Aton were removed from the records of Egypt', it was not until the archaeological find at Tell El-Amarna that much was known about Akhenaton and Aton (at least in the West). The site of Akhenaton's administration was discovered in 1887....

"The argument still rages among scholars as to the nature of Aton. Many still believe, or interpret the information to show, that Aton was a new Sun-god that Akhenaton attempted to use to overthrow the reigning 'gods of Egypt'."

Well, Nora's last sentence above says it all. So much for getting to the Truth when a judiciously limited (politically correct) interpretation of historical data is called for, especially if you want to keep your job, reputation, and paycheck in the so-called "professional" archaeological community!

Meanwhile, in *The Rainbow Masters* Phoenix Journal (#7), Archangel Michael brings the historical concept of The One Light into a modern perspective when he comments upon the upcoming planetary transition in these terms:

"The physical, as it is developed, is only to serve for a brief time, but within is the greatest period of learning. It appears that ye are but tiny sparks. Ah, but you are most wondrous! For, as a tiny candle flame, we shall burst forth into an area that has never before known Light such as this, and we shall bring Light, even as the workers brought to ancient Egypt, The Light—the One Light of Aton, through Akhenaton.... The people had never seen it before. Some it blinded, for it was too bright. They did not, just as today, understand, because of its blinding Light. It was a thing to be feared and shunned, and many fell again into the comfort of the hiding places of darkness."

In a writing received by Dharma on Friday, June 30, 1989 and recorded in the early Phoenix Journal (#4) called *Spiral To Economic Disaster,* both the great power AND the great compassion of Aton are strikingly conveyed when He said, "...I AM ATON OF LIGHT. I AM THY SOURCE, CHILD. I HAVE SENT FORTH MINE SONS AND ANGELS UNTO THEE AND I COME FORTH UNTO THEE, LITTLE CHILDREN OF THE UNIVERSE, THAT YOU UNDERSTAND THY TRANSITION.

"DO NOT WEEP AT THOSE WHO CHOOSE TO HEAR THEE NOT, FOR IT IS ME THEY REFUSE TO HEAR, FOR MY SONS AND ANGELS SPEAK IN MINE NAME. THEY ARE THE TRUMPETERS AND CLARIONS OF MY VOICE. I AM THY GOD, WITHOUT AND WITHIN, AND YE ARE BUT ENERGY FRAGMENTS WHICH I HAVE CHOSEN TO GO FORTH AND EXPERIENCE THE UNIVERSE OF MY CREATIONS. UNTO YE ARE GIVEN THE GIFTS OF LIFE AND CREATOR, BUT YE

MISUSE OF THE PRECIOUS GIFTS....

"HEED CAREFULLY, CHILDREN OF THE FLESH; YE ARE BUT ENERGY FRAGMENTS IN A PASSING INSTANT OF MINE THOUGHT. HE WHO DENIES TRUTH, DENIES ME. HE WHO DENIES ME WILL BE CAST FROM MY THOUGHTS TO EXPERIENCE THE VOID, FOR THY PERSECUTIONS OF MINE ONES IS COMING TO TERMINATION IN THY CURRENT TIME.

"THINK MOST CAREFULLY BEFORE YE PUT TO THE SIDE THESE WORDS, FOR THEY ARE MINE WORDS, AND AS I CREATE, THUSLY I SHALL DISSOLVE. YOUR TIME OF TREMBLING AND TERROR IS CLOSE IN THY TIME. YE ONES OF EARTH WILL HEED MY MESSENGERS' WARNINGS OR THE CONSEQUENCES ARE MIGHTY, FOR THAT WHICH HAS BEEN PERPETRATED UPON MINE MAGNIFICENT CREATIONS, IN DARKNESS, SHALL CEASE. IF YOU CHOOSE NOT TO HEAR, YE HAVE CHOSEN THE WAY OF THE VOID, AND WILL BE IN PERISHMENT WITHIN THE TIDES AND UPHEAVALS OF LABOR AND BIRTHING....

"I WEEP OVER THAT WHICH I HAVE PLACED INTO CREATION THAT HAS DEGRADED AND DEBAUCHED MINE OTHER WONDROUS AND BALANCED ENTITIES. IT IS THY GIFT OF FREEDOM OF CHOICE, FOR I GAVE THAT, TOO, UNTO YOU, BUT YE SHALL BEAR THE DIFFICULT ROAD IF YE HEED NOT THE CALL THAT MAKES OF THINE WAY, EASY AND BEAUTEOUS....

"THERE SHALL APPEAR UPON THE EARTH NEW PEOPLE WHO ARE NOT INDIGENOUS OF THE EARTH, AND THAT WHICH HAS NOT BEEN SEEN BEFORE. YE HAD BETTER TAKE NOTE....

"YE ARE IN GRAVE CIRCUMSTANCE AND I HAVE SENT MINE OTHER CHILDREN OF THE UNIVERSE AND THE

VERY ANGELS OF MY REALMS TO ASSIST YE.  REFUSE
THEM IF YE CHOOSE, BUT KNOW 'TIS YOU WHO HAVE
REFUSED.  WALK WITH MY CHILDREN...AND YE SHALL
WALK IN GLORY.  THEY ARE COME TO SHOW YOU THE
WAY; MINE SONS HAVE COME AGAIN TO RECLAIM MINE
HOUSES.

"The very Earth Source has been seized with convulsions within
her entrails, and she has belched forth that which is from within her
interior—and, these things shall increase and increase.  She has
been in such great pain for such a great time, for thy Mother Earth
that she is, is not without travail.  Oh, and such is the pity of it, for
man has been unmindful of her; and as she has nurtured him, fed
him, clothed him, and mothered him, he has remained more and
more unmindful of her....

"So be it that he has but added suffering unto insults which have
been given unto the Mother Earth wherein man has had his birth into
the physical parts of me....

"In this time of casting off, I rejoice that I shall make myself
into newness, for I represent the Creation of Earth, for I become one
with my creations—and ye have forgotten.  Unto this end do I
create!

"I have brought up races of men that they might become Gods,
and that they might become wise creators also, and that they might
become one with myself.  This is every man's inheritance.  Man
shall be in no wise the poorer for having experienced in his growth.
I am the Creator and I have created wisely, though I often weep at
thine poor choices; and, I have sent man into all the worlds wherein
there is life, and oh, precious ones, there are many!  All who have
gone forth from me have returned unto me richer and more glorious
for their experiences.

"There is not place wherein is the form of man wherein is not
the parts of me.  I have divided myself into parts, and I have

endowed each part with the part of myself, that which is eternal, infinite—and that part of me changes not but remains ever unchanged by anything which is or shall ever be.

"In my own timing shall I bring them all in again, to become again one with me, and they shall all be made whole. From the body of myself have I created all things, both of the land and of the sea, and of the air; and therein are the things, both of land and sea, and the words become manifest. The things which I command, appear, and they take form, and then I breathe into them, life. They are the animated parts of me; and they cannot be less than the Gods, because I have created each after a likeness which I have conceived within my own being. It is the 'positive' that I am, and creation is the 'negative'.

"That part which ye 'see' is the part of me which is subject to change and which shall return to the elements from which it came. Not a person shall change the Law, nor shall he bring unto me one part of himself which is of the earth [*that is, the material world*], for I bring back unto me that which is eternal, and that which is of the earth I shake off. It gives me great joy to bring back that which I send out, for it is this for which I have made provision.

"Positive-negative, night-day, ah yes, there are two poles of force called 'life'—as in darkness and light, soul/spirit and body, LIFE AND DEATH. Many are the labels placed upon the 'positive' and 'negative'; yet there is only *ONE* AND THAT *ONE* IS ALL INCLUSIVE, FOR IT IS OF MYSELF AND FROM MYSELF THAT I HAVE CREATED ALL THINGS, AND FROM *ONE* *SUBSTANCE* HAVE ALL THINGS COME INTO BEING....

"For those who have been mindful of the Law and the Light, and worked therein, they shall be brought into a place of newness wherein is total Light. They shall be relieved of all stresses, for it is lawful to say that they shall be brought into the places wherein I AM, for I have prepared for them a place and I have provided well;

and for this day I have provided. At no time do I forget the 'little ones' in darkness, for I have reached out within the darkness for them, and they have turned away and denied of me and of my messengers....

"SO BE IT FOR IT IS SO, AND I GIVE UNTO THESE WORDS THE SEAL WHICH IS OF GOD, FOR IT SHALL COME TO PASS IN THIS MANNER AS I HAVE GIVEN IT UNTO THEE. THE TIME HAS COME TO RISE FROM THY BEDDINGS AND CHOOSE OF THY PATH, LEST YE CHOOSE WRONGLY. I AWAIT THEE, FOR THE FINAL CURTAIN OF THIS CYCLE IS READY TO FALL—FOREVER. I CALL UPON YOU TO TAKE THE OFFERED HAND OF THY BRETHREN WHO HAVE AGAIN COME AMONG YOU TO LEAD THEE HOME.

"I URGE YOU TO TAKE GREAT CAUTION; I AM THY GOD. YE TURN FROM MY MESSENGERS AND MINE SONS SENT FORTH AGAIN UNTO YOU, AND DENY THESE WORDS, AND YE ERR BEYOND THY COMPREHENSION. SO BE IT. I AM."

Then, in *The Rainbow Masters,* Aton continues his impassioned plea with: "CHILDREN OF EARTH PLACE, MY LITTLE WAYWARD AND BLIND CHILDREN, IT IS TIME TO COME INTO KNOWLEDGE AND TRUTH, AND STOP OF YOUR SILLY GAMES, FOR YOUR HUMAN PLACEMENT, EARTH, CAN BEAR NO MORE, AND SHE SHALL BE GIVEN INTO THE REBIRTHING AND HEALING OF THOSE WOUNDS YOU HAVE PERPETRATED UPON HER BEING.

"YOU WERE SENT FORTH AS CARETAKERS OF THIS WONDROUS CREATION, AND YOU HAVE DESTROYED YOUR VERY LIFE SUBSTANCE. SO BE IT, FOR IT SHALL BE AS IT SHALL BE, AND THOSE WHO ARE WITH ME WILL BE WITH ME, AND THOSE WHO ARE NOT, SHALL MOVE WITH

THE FALLEN ONES OF EVIL. SO IT IS, FOR NAUGHT OTHERWISE COULD IT BE."

Finally, by way of commenting upon the Great Teachers I will be introducing later on, called the Seven Rays, or the "Rainbow Masters", who have contributed much to this volume, as they did to that early *Rainbow Masters* Phoenix Journal, Aton says: "Ones who come newly into the lessons must now have opportunity to draw on integration. Most seem to think that, in an interim of time twixt 2,000 years ago and this day, we of the Higher Dimensions sat and twiddled. Not so, and further, there were Brothers in thy service, and Guidance Instructors, from long before the time of Immanuel. These ones are spoken of, in the books you call 'Holy', as the 'seven spirits before the throne'....

"Know that the Brotherhood of the Seven Rays are your mentors, and man's individuality comes under the forces of the great Seven Rays of Life. One is guided by the powerful forces at work within these Rays. Each and all flow into conscious Life upon one of these Rays, and your Life experience is influenced by the Ray through which you descended.

"The First Ray is the way of Leadership; the Second Ray is the way of Education; the Third Ray is the way of Philosophy; the Fourth Ray is the way of the Arts; the Fifth Ray is the way of Science; the Sixth Ray is the way of Devotion; and the Seventh Ray is the way of Ceremony....

"THE LORDS OF HEAVEN, THE ARCHANGELIC REALMS, CONVENE TO ASSIST. WE OF THE COSMIC COUNCILS AND GALACTIC COUNCILS ARE HERE TO ASSIST. YE HAVE IT 'ALL' AT THY DISPOSAL. BE HUMBLE, YES; EGOTISTICAL, NAY. UTILIZE IT, THAT WE MAY ACCOMPLISH OUR MOST HOLY TASK, BRETHREN. SO BE IT AND SELAH....

"I AM THAT ONE LIGHT—THE LIGHTED ONE. I AM THE MASTER TEACHER, 'COHAN' OF THE EIGHTH—THE

ONE LIGHT FROM WHENCE ALL OTHER RAYS ARE BIRTHED. I AM ATON. I AM THE TEACHER OF THE SEVEN TEACHERS. YE HAVE THE UNIVERSAL HIERARCHY AT THY DISPOSAL, LITTLE ONES. LET US USE THE INPUT MOST WISELY, CHILDREN, THAT WE MAY ACCOMPLISH OUR TASK WITH INTEGRITY AND HONOR FOR THE GREAT CREATIONS OF THIS UNIVERSE. SO BE IT AND I PLACE OF MINE SEAL UPON THESE WORDS THAT THERE BE *NO* MISUNDERSTANDING THEREOF. MINE IS TO GIVE; THINE TO ACCEPT. SO BE IT AND SELAH. ATTEND THY TEACHERS WELL, FOR THEY SHALL SHOW OF THEE THE WAY."

Now, with that said, I shall end this section with a short meditation authored by the Great White Eagle of the Sacred Council of Eagles. Otherwise this very old soul is known as Little Crow of the Lakota tribe of Native Americans; he is one of the last of the great Oral Tradition Keepers and Presenters of that wondrous Truth. This is from his *Thoughts On A Winter's Night,* and is titled, WAKAN TANKA, I AM CONNECTED. It reads:

"Father, I feel the Earth move beneath my feet, as I dance lightly over the dusty blades of grass, searching for that spot that no human before me has touched.

"Bending to the beat of the drum—my heart keeping a rhythmic time.

"Looking about me to my brothers and sisters, our bodies shining in the Sun.

"And I connected to ALL things. Wakan Tanka, hear the voices as they are lifted to you in prayer.

"For we have seen the vision, and now, many lifetimes later, in different bodies, we come together once more.

"Father, once again we are connected as one—the vision remembered, and like whirlwinds, we dance homeward."

# CHAPTER TWO

# Gyeorgos Ceres Hatonn

In the previous chapter, it was suggested that Akhenaton, in the days of the ancient Egyptian culture, was "infused with the spirit of" Aton and that the understanding which came with this intimacy of association had a lot to do with Akhenaton's ability to deliver to this planet's most "advanced" culture of the era the at-that-time radical message of there being only one God, the God of Light, and not a bunch of gods populating every thing and every where, as was the prevailing "religious" dogma of the time.

Moreover, just as an advanced spiritual entity may work with and through an incarnate being such as Akhenaton, under the proper conditions, so too may the soul of such an advanced spiritual entity split off a fragment (or multiple fragments) of itself and project said fragment(s) to experience within some dimensional framework wherein there is need or purpose or simply desire. In a similar, if less comprehensive way, all Lighted beings choosing to experience on schoolroom Earth also execute this same procedure; we call it incarnating into a body (or "vehicle" or "space suit"), and it is a procedure through which some part or fragment of our total soul-self can interface with and experience this physical environment that is school-of-hard-knocks Earth.

I say this by way of introducing exactly WHO IS Commander Hatonn for, as Esu "Jesus" Immanuel Sananda [*see Chapter Four*] put it succinctly in the early Phoenix Journal (#3) called *Space-Gate: The Veil Removed,* "Commander Hatonn is the **experiencing fragment of ATON**, our Father Creator—ONE SOURCE, ONE LIGHT."

We could stop right there, as that simple statement says it all—even if most of the "all" is between the lines! But let us explore a bit more of why this great being is included herein.

In the Foreword to that same Phoenix Journal, Commander Hatonn introduces himself thusly:

"I am Gyeorgos Ceres Hatonn, Commander-In-Chief, Earth Project Transition, Pleiades Sector Flight Command, Intergalactic Federation Fleet—Ashtar Command; Earth Representative to the Cosmic Council and Intergalactic Federation Council on Earth Transition. You may call me 'Hatonn'.

"Let there be no misunderstanding of WHO I AM! I come in this portion as a fourth-dimensional Project Commander in charge of Earth Transition. As this [*transition of planet Earth*] is most thoroughly explained in other recordings from myself and others, I shall not cover it in this document."

Maybe as more of an aside here, yet providing some helpful insight about this Earth Transition Project and those Elder Brothers who are in primary "public" positions of responsibility therein, I shall jump briefly back to the earlier Phoenix Journal (#2) titled *And They Called His Name Immanuel; I Am Sananda.* Here Esu Sananda and Judas Iscarioth make the following comments, at the beginning of a particular chapter and writing session through the receiver, Dharma:

"We are present and prepared to proceed. It is with great love and appreciation for your service that we join with you. I am Sananda, with my brother, Judas Iscarioth. Blessings upon these writings. I salute Commander Hatonn, of Pleiades, for his willing participation, and I honor the thousands of hours you ones have spent in concentrated training in preparation for our arrival. As an Earth-based team, I honor and salute you for your fine works in a most negative and demanding environment. You shall have your day in the Sun.

"I now relinquish communication circuits to Judas Iscarioth, that we might move rapidly with this project. I place my seal upon this work and upon this information, and I bless you with ease of input and peace within, that you KNOW of truth. So be it. Salu.

"Greetings in the Radiance, Judas here to continue. I also bring respect and appreciation to the members of the Pleiades Fleet, and more specifically, to Commanders Hatonn, Semjase, Asket, Leah, Korton (for his superb communications assistance), and to you ones of Pleiades, stationed on Earth base, who must remain unlabeled for security reasons. Your honor will be fulfilled as you see the wondrous TRUTH displayed on thy media screens around the world."

One of the nicknames given to Commander Hatonn by those who prefer to look at life through rose-colored glasses is "the 'bad news' Professor". This name comes about because he is the principal author of the collection of ongoing journals called the Phoenix Journals, which are described briefly in the Preface to this volume, and which began publication in 1989. Because Commander Hatonn is responsible for so much of the eye-opening instructional material which has been so prolifically received and either written down (in those Phoenix Journals, as well as in the *CONTACT* newspaper) or spoken (on audio tape) through Dharma, and others, as part of the "try to wake up the people" phase of this Earth Transition Project, it is important to return to Commander Hatonn's own Foreword in *Space-Gate,* wherein he comments on the writings in progress as well as the issue of "receiving":

"This document contains truth which can be validated. It comes forth in dictated format from myself to one of my transreceivers (recorder). There is nothing of 'channeling' about it—it is via actual radio-type shortwave, directly from my source into a receiver terminal. No hocus pocus nor mystical hoopla. This recorder does exactly that—records. She is not privy to the information resources, nor is she given to 'interpretation' other than as any other reader would personally interpret."

Commander Hatonn continues this theme in *Spiral To Economic Disaster* wherein he puts it this way:

"I write in no particularly acceptable format; I give it to you as it is—in hopefully understandable, blunt terminology. I do not speak English well; I need not speak at all at any time, for my communication is of thought vibrational patterns. Do not err by discounting me or my brothers from the intergalactic environs who have been summoned at this time of transition.

"I care not for your formal publication formats. I bring forth truth, just as through radio signals and frequencies. My scribes hold no knowledge of Earth workings any more than the most ignorant picking up this material. Yes, afterwards they are most informed, for I insure they come into understanding. There is a chance of the public coming into understanding if I can see that my scribes and receivers comprehend to a great measure. I will never endanger any one of them by allowing prior information nor full understanding. If that were allowed, they would be assassinated immediately. Dharma does not understand the mechanism here, she has only agreed to write. Numerous attempts have been made against her life—but she is within our protection."

Returning again to Commander Hatonn's own Foreword in *Space-Gate,* he then goes on to explain the separation of Mission duties between himself and Esu Sananda. That is:

"We of the Lighted Brotherhood of the Cosmic and Galactic participants are ready to make our presence upon your place. We travel and act in the direct service and under Command of Esu 'Jesus' Immanuel Sananda. Sananda is aboard my Command Craft, from whence he will direct all evacuation and transition activities as regards the period you ones call the End Prophecies of Armageddon.

"He has organized placement for his peoples and will oversee all operations as regards his people. All Intergalactic Fleets are under his command, and for purposes of evacuation, those details are in most capable hands of one called, simply, Commander Ashtar.

"There will be more and more frequent contact with ones of human format by ones of our Commands. You will ask any energy form, contacting you, to identify. Demand that, if the energy is not of the 'Light' of the Divine Source, to remove itself. DO NOT ENTERTAIN ANY AND ALL ENERGY FRAGMENTS WHO APPEAR TO YOU, FOR MORE AND MORE OF THE DARK ENERGY FORMS ARE MAKING CONTACT.

"EXTREME CAUTION: DO NOT RUN AND HOP ABOARD ANY SPACECRAFT WHICH MIGHT LAND. CAUSE THE ENTITIES TO IDENTIFY THEMSELVES. INSTRUCTIONS FOR IDENTIFICATION OF THE INTERGALACTIC COMMANDS ARE BEING PRESENTED CURRENTLY AND WILL BE FORTHCOMING IN A MASSIVE WAY VERY SHORTLY.

"This document [*that Journal,* Space-Gate, *as well as many others that were yet to be written*] is for the purpose of awakening you to the horrendous lie that has been perpetrated against you ones. I am giving it to insure protection of those human ones who dared bring it into the open, and yet risk their lives having done so. I dedicate it to the ones who dared and have been mocked, ridiculed, and persecuted for having dared to give you help to 'save' yourselves from the lies. I go on record to my adversaries herewith and place them on formal notice: YE SHALL NOT HARM ONE HAIR OF MY WORKERS. YOU SHALL REAP BITTERNESS IF YOU BRING PHYSICAL HARM UNTO THEM.

"Now, I shall tell you who I am in my Higher Command: I AM ATON. Perhaps you might wish to look up that label, for it might prove to be quite important to you. I shall see to it that these instructions are carried forth, so I suggest there be no toying with this as some game of sorts to be discounted at your next little seminar gathering of the flying saucer clubs and crystal worshipers. Your time of playing at star readings, Ouija boards and Tarot, to seek your fortunes, is over.

"Earth is going to march right through evolution, transition, tribulation, new 'birthing' and new 'berthing' just as written. You need no psychic reader to tell you how it will be. You can hide your head in your sand bucket; it will change nothing.

"There are detailed and magnificent plans in operation to cause the transition to be quite survivable and workable for those of you who so choose to work with us and not in the enemy camp. The evil forces shall be met and stopped, but it will be a most unpleasant confrontation.

"The Master Esu 'Jesus' Immanuel Sananda is returned and awaits the appointed time. If you want information, I suggest heartily that you contact Phoenix Source Distributors [*see near end of Preface*] for any and all information. We will be printing it in numerous volumes as fast as our scribes can receive.

"I dedicate this work to all who have taken a stand for Truth....

"I PLACE MY SEAL UPON THESE WRITINGS OF TRUTH. YOU ONES MUST AWAKEN NOW, FOR YOU HAVE SLEPT TOO LONG AND YOUR WORLD IS CRUMBLING DOWN AROUND THY FEET. YOU ARE IN THE FINAL COUNTDOWN.

"I AM ATON."

A little later on in *Space-Gate* Commander Hatonn makes a humorous aside about himself, in the middle of a serious discussion, when he says:

"By the way, I am not a 'little gray man'. I am from Pleiades, from the planet of Hatonn—I am one-in-the-same as Aton and I am some nine-and-a-half feet in height. Sorry, I don't qualify as one of the 'bad guys'. I most surely am among their most feared adversaries, however."

In the Introduction to *Spiral To Economic Disaster,* Commander Hatonn offers advice which gives further insight about his role, in conjunction with others, in this Earth Transition Mission:

"This document is offered in response to ones who continue to ask me 'When?' and 'What do we do?'. In an economic vein, it has gone beyond the ability to reverse it. Therefore, it will have to pass through the equalizer of collapse. I only present possible ways to salvage your stability on a personal basis, FOR IT *WILL* ALL FALL DOWN AROUND YOU. *ALL* HAS PASSED BEYOND YOUR ABILITY TO REVERSE IT. YOU ARE IN THE ENDING TIMES UPON A PLANET IN REBIRTHING AND REBERTHING INTO A HIGHER EXISTENCE. YOU HAVE REACHED THE TIME OF ARMAGEDDON!

"I only deal with the United States in this particular discourse, for this is where my assignment predominantly places me in this Earth commission....

"I come in truth, directly from your Creator Source. I serve in the immediate Command of the one you call 'Jesus', Esu Immanuel (his name) Sananda ('And he shall bear a new name at the time of his return'.). Discount it, if you choose. Be most careful, however, for your days upon this orb are numbered within thy accounting ability. Those things of which the prophets wrote, will come upon you within this generation of your elderly ones. All the signs are in place, dear ones. We are all in service to our Cosmic Universe, Sananda, and Creator Aton of the Total Light, God, and The Creation, which is above all. We also come in service and love unto you ones to assist you through the times of tribulations and bring you home.

"He went forth before you to prepare a place for you. He has done so. Are you ready? We now prepare you to receive of him, that you be not frightened. He (Immanuel Sananda) is come to bring you home, those of his flock. Galactic fleets stand ready to take you up. HOW DID YOU THINK HE WOULD COME?

"Those who choose to remain in ignorance of truth will not be coerced in any manner. 'Tis thy choice all the way to the gate. Choose to continue as you are and you will spend a very long time with the false teachers who have led you down this tacky roadway. However, it has been your free will choice to follow them.

"HOW DID YOU BELIEVE HIS RETURN WOULD BE?

"OH BELOVED ONES, TO SIT ON SOME MISERABLE CLOUD BANKS WITH HIM IS FOOLISH THOUGHT INDEED. THOSE CLOUDS YOU SEE ARE IN YOUR ATMOSPHERE, WHICH WILL PROBABLY BE FILLED WITH RADIATION AND DEATH. THE MASTER WOULD NOT PLACE YOU THERE.

"YOU WILL BE TAKEN UP INTO CRAFT, THOSE OF YOU WHO ARE PREPARED, AND INTO SAFETY. THE TRANSITION WILL BE MOST HARD ON YOUR PHYSICAL BODIES—TO CHANGE DIMENSION SO RAPIDLY. *PLEASE START THY PETITIONS FOR INSTRUCTION AND RECEIVE OF THAT WHICH IS GIVEN UNTO YOU BY US THROUGH THESE SCRIBES AND RECEIVERS.* MAKE SURE THE RECEIVERS ARE OF THE LIGHTED REALMS, FOR THE DARK BROTHERHOOD OF SATANIC FORCES OVERTAKE YOU AT EVERY TURN. THEY HAVE ALL BUT DESTROYED YOU AS A CIVILIZATION. THEY MAY VERY WELL ANNIHILATE YOU IF YOU DO NOT TURN ABOUT INTO TRUTH.

"SO BE IT, BELOVED BROTHERS, FOR THE TIME IS AT HAND. AMEN, AND UPON THIS I PLACE MY SEAL OF TRUTH AND HONOR. MAY YOU SEEK TRUTH IN THY GOD AND CREATION, FOR THY WAY IS HARD. MAY YE FIND PEACE WITHIN. I AM HATONN."

# CHAPTER THREE

# Sanat Kumara

From the One White Light that is Aton, there is first the division of that complete energy into the two Primary Rays of creation. These are the Golden Ray and the Silver Ray, which are sometimes likened, respectively, to the energies of "the heart" and "the head". The Golden Ray is often equated with the Christed Energy, which is most familiarly manifest in that Master Teacher we know as Esu "Jesus" Immanuel Sananda [*see next chapter*].

The Silver Ray is known as Sanat Kumara, who Aton refers to in *The Rainbow Masters* as: "One of mine most beloved first born". He is often regarded as the principal overseer of our solar system (among other far-reaching responsibilities) and is often associated with the energy source we perceive as our Sun. He is reverently known to many Native Americans as Grandfather, or Tonkashila, in the language of the Lakota.

In *The Rainbow Masters,* Sanat Kumara teaches us about the purpose of this universe and our place within it when he said:

"The Father placed the Earth and all celestial bodies in the heavens. They are created out of spiraling primordial matter for man. Man was to be the god [*overseer*] of physical form: man, the highest expression of deity known in the entire Omniverse. Ah, but man misunderstood, and misunderstands yet unto this day. O, man, realize that you are the highest form of deity anywhere in the entirety of the Omniverse. This does not mean that you are the only 'man' within the Omniverse. But there is nothing beyond you—in this you are grand.  Ah, but also in this you are the 'lowest'.

"You are the lowest because you have KNOWING and other life forms do not.  Therefore, you must be both their brother AND their servant!

"There is life and intelligence in all forms, as ancient man knew and respected.  Man alone is not the only 'thinking' being.  It is 'reason' that sets man aside from his other relations.  Every element, every mineral—all forms—have inherent intelligence, and man is sent to be their keeper and their elder brother.

"Have you given care to the role of caretaker?  Have you protected and guarded?  You are the elder brother of these forms, innumerable forms throughout the Omniverse.  It is up to you to raise them to ever higher evolution as they, along with man, progress up the worlds to infinite grandeur, to Infinite Light.  Have you set the pattern to growth or destruction?"

One cannot help but have the above passage call to mind the relationship between man and his pets.  How often do we even joke about the resemblance between some owners and their pets?  However, it is no joking matter when we encounter the dog whose nasty, fearful personality mimics that of his owner.  There has long existed a phrase of wisdom that goes something like: "You can tell a lot about people by the way their pets behave."  And, sadly, you can tell a lot about the current irresponsibility of HU-man on Earth from the fact that we even NEED so many animal shelters, much less that they are usually filled to overflowing with hopeful faces.

As for this critical time of planetary transition and revelations wherein The Truth cannot longer be kept hidden from man's awareness, Sanat Kumara relates the following, again from *The Rainbow Masters*:

"The great beauty of the ages now approaches wherein all doubts and fears shall be rolled away as a great scroll.  There shall be a great thundering. The heavens will be torn asunder. Then man will view himself and will look into his mirror of 'knowing'—no longer will there be confusion. If man will but accept of his scepter of God's gift, he will no longer be hindered by the darkness of ignorance and superstition. Know this, and in knowing it there must of necessity be sadness; and yet there must be gladness for the beauty that it shall bring forth.

"But you must know of that which impends and is forthcoming. Yes, there can be atomic detonations and cosmic ray bombardments. So be it, for if you will but do as you are instructed, you can come into safety. These are the 'effects'. But what is the 'cause'? The cause of the destruction that shall come upon the Earth is from man's own thought patterns.

"Since the time when the Sons of God came in unto the daughters of men, and animal-man appeared upon the Earth, he has been striving from beasthood back to angelhood. But faulty thinking shall now break forth as the elements refuse to be regarded as they have been so regarded for millennia upon the Earth. They are part of the Infinite One, and because they are part of the Infinite One, they will not respond to man's negative thinking any longer. They will rebel, causing great tidal waves and great winds. It is already so! Millions shall perish for they will not see nor hear of The Truth, nor of the warnings. They shall be placed anew on other places appropriate to their level of progression in the spirit growth. Because of the *remnant* that must remain, the Earth will be purified and raised to a new dimension and vibration frequency....

"O, man of Earth, if you but knew the love that descends to you from spheres innumerable, from minds inviolate! If you would but listen, you would know. There can be nothing but beauty. From all the catastrophe that shall come, only the vision of a beautiful 'perception' shall remain, for man steps forth in a purified light of his own creation.  But man must see and listen....

"Remember, beloved, the beauty of Earth is in the creation that you stand upon, from which you derive your nourishment.  It is like the bosom of our Father/Mother, where you rest your head to regain strength.  It is your Mother, and yet it is also your Father.  The Earth is a beautiful world, vastly more beautiful than some of your neighbors.  I have always loved Earth beyond all other creations, for I see within her a melody that has not yet escaped into the ethers.  I see her crying as one *bound* and *shackled.*  She shall not, however, be deprived her celestial song much longer....

"We (yes I, too) who hold the Earth in our hands, were given her to develop, to cherish, and to bring to fruition.  We now see that the harvest shall be ample and the storehouse of the Father will be full for the migration to new grandeur of being, if we but do of our work with fitting action in His name and service.

"I would give you a Divine Commandment for the time immediately ahead for you ones: Feed the sheep of God!  Give where it is required.  Give not of your past glories, but give them that which the soul needs.  Tell them that there shall be catastrophe!  Prepare them that they shall prepare for that which will come; show them the way."

It is a challenge for a Being of so vast a level of development to find human words through which to adequately convey his perspective, but Sanat Kumara does so when he says, again in *The Rainbow Masters*:

"I am he who is only as great as the smallest particle of sand on the Earth and is only as low as the highest mountain top.  I have known countless existences upon this beloved planet....

"I have asked to speak with you because, for me, it is the time of the Great Unveiling and, in a smaller sense, of your Great Graduation to another [*higher*] plane of consciousness....

"It was decreed long ago that I should come to Earth to assist our Elder Brother [*Esu "Jesus" Sananda, see the next chapter*] who rules this system, and to assist all our beloved brothers and sisters upon the Earth planet. But I must also be in the tending of my other responsibilities unto that which has been placed in my ward....

"Your entire solar system is now coming into the Great Initiation, for it is true that you are now heading directly for the Super-Sun which governs your galaxy, around which countless island universes perpetually move and have existence. Your system is heading for the center of this activity, and this increased rate of vibration frequency will profoundly affect everything within your system; whether it be mental, physical, or spiritual, it will not escape changes in the new energy that is forthcoming.

"You are now on the border of this great transition and heading ever closer to its fulfillment.

"That is why Christ returns to the Earth: because always the great Master of a solar system incarnates and gives aid to the planet which is lowest in progression in that system, and also because he is the spirit of the Earth, which position he achieved in his incarnation as man, but the Christ is for the system....

"The Earth has had MANY civilizations, and when one has gone to the bottomless pit, man rises in his cultural development, and again builds a glorious civilization with great scientific and technical advance. But again the civilization drops into the bottomless pit. Can ye not learn? On your sister, Venus, for instance, there has never been a destruction of a civilization, though she has made a grand transition. On the planet you call Mars, in your sector, it has occurred twice. But on Earth, dear ones, it has occurred hundreds of times. Man of Earth cannot seem to control and discipline the great knowledge, once it is attained....

"Your Earth is about ready to become a 'sun', as Ashtar and

Hatonn have previously informed you. It will not be exactly like
your solar system Sun as you recognize it—but it shall become
surrounded by a golden corona which will become more brilliant
and denser to other system locations. It is stepping into a higher
rate of vibration and density change. You can only experience, as
do your astronomers, from the inside outward. Your space
machines do not get far enough away from your surface to see the
changes, and it is not of 'visible' manifested format that you dense
creatures can witness with your human eyes. **You are moving from
a third-dimensional into a fourth-dimensional world.** This
MUST take place as you move through the heart of the great cosmic
cloud....

"ALMOST ALL THINGS UPON THE FACE OF THE EARTH
WILL BE DESTROYED BY THESE THINGS WHICH SHALL
COME UPON THIS BELOVED LAND.... YOU MUST GET
PREPARED; STOP THY QUIBBLING OVER WHETHER OR
NOT THIS IS TRUTH. GET YOURSELVES INTO PROTECTION....

"Apply that which you have learned and give gladly that which
you have received. As you travel and converse in the times ahead
allotted for each one of you, think not what you shall take with you,
or what shall be in thy pocketbooks, nor of what will you wear. You
shall not have need of those things past the preparation and journey
'through'. In the final purpose, the Father will provide.

"This is the time of giving, sharing, and applying. It is not
only the clarion call unto you, for verily you have accepted a trust
and a most incredible mission, but likewise it is the order of the
day as we ALL enter into this new phase for the planet Earth, and
indeed, our whole solar and galactic system. We are your brothers
from this particular system, come to assist you, for it is a great
Cosmic Event upon the stage of the universe....

"MAN IS TERRIFIED AND HE IS SEEKING. HIS HEART IS

HUNGRIER THAN IT HAS EVER BEEN BECAUSE HE FEELS THE CHANGES AND SEES THE HOPELESS PLIGHT GROW, DAY BY DAY, BEFORE HIS EYES.

"Man 'smells' his food and grows ever more hungry; this new vibration is coming forth, and he becomes ever more hungry. He is 'remembering' and he innately *knows* that he is filled with appetite for things of Spirit in Truth—not just more lies and false prophets, psychics and card readers....

"How often we look upon the Earth knowing, as we look upon each small creation and creature, that there stands a god, if he would only realize it and apply his godhood. For a true god sits not on a throne in inactivity while the masses come before him in adoration. This is not godhood, as some on Earth obviously think it would (or should) be. Godhood is enthronement, yes, but a god of action who enters the being of each one of his creations, fills them with life and majesty and grandeur, and works diligently beside each and every one, and serves as thy servant.

"God wishes man (man that He created) to rule over His celestial worlds. He wishes each man to take charge of His worlds—for this has He created them....

"Some day...each...will come into their own inheritance and will command a planet, and then a system, and then a galaxy. We are all either on that path, or have achieved it and have returned to assist our younger brothers through their pathway.

"The clarion call is: 'Come home, Earth!' It is time for Earth to come home into her radiance for which she has labored long and hard....

"IT IS THE TIME OF CHOICES, FOR THE HOUR-GLASS IS TRULY EMPTIED, AND IT IS IN THE TURNING OVER TO BEGIN ANEW THE NEXT SEGMENT....

"I, FURTHER, TAKE THIS OPPORTUNITY OF PRESENCE

TO HONOR EACH OF YOU WHO GIVE OF YOURSELVES IN
SERVICE AND OVERWORK UNTO THIS MISSION. I BEND IN
HUMBLE GRATITUDE IN THY SERVICE.

"I AM THAT I AM. I AM SANAT KUMARA."

Remembering that Sanat Kumara is known as Grandfather to
many of the Native American tribes, it again seems appropriate to
end this section with a short meditation authored by the Great
White Eagle of the Sacred Council of Eagles. Otherwise this very
old soul is known as Little Crow of the Lakota tribe of Native
Americans; he is one of the last of the great Oral Tradition
Keepers and Presenters of that wondrous Truth. This is from his
*Thoughts On A Winter's Night,* and is titled, DON'T YOU
REMEMBER? It goes as follows:

"Grandfather touched us once, before you and I sent stars
rushing out of the darkened sky.

"The Light of ourselves flooded the Earth, and all the things
became our relations.

"Don't you remember? The drum became our heartbeat and
Earth our Mother—she gave us what we needed.

"Don't you remember what Grandfather said to us? 'Children
of the stars, your journey is long and hard, and you will fall many
times before you are done with what it is you must do. You will
be many selves—but always of the first children you'll be, and
from deep in your heart it will call to you.'

"Come, my children—gather together, pick up the sacred hoop
which has fallen from the hands of those who look the part.

"Remember, the tree is your relative, the rock is your relative,
the bear is your relative, the birds are your relative, the grass is
your relative, the insect is your relative, the air is your relative, the
sky is your relative, the rain is your relative—I am your relative.

"Let us bring peace to the world. Don't you remember?"

# CHAPTER FOUR

# Esu "Jesus" Sananda

As Sanat Kumara (or Grandfather, to the Native Americans) is considered the embodiment of the Silver Ray energy, Esu Sananda (or the Great White Spirit, or the Pale Prophet, or Standing Bear, to many Native Americans) is considered the same for the Golden Ray energy. For those who are sensitive to such things, the color of the light energy generally associated with Esu's presence is that of a brilliant golden-tinged white.

The name of this well-known Teacher and Guide was originally, two thousand years ago, Esu Immanuel. That name was changed to Jesus by those who "adjusted" many of the original records of his journey here for the usual diabolical reasons leading to control over others—basically mind control of the masses disguised as a political expediency tool called "religion".

The name "Sananda" (which means "one with God") is a title of current accomplishment for Esu, as was "the Christ" or "the Christed one" or "the Christos" some two thousand years ago. In human terms, think of this label Sananda as an earned promotion from, say, Captain to Admiral.

As a part of his own growth experiences within that current level of accomplishment, Esu is regarded as the **Commander-In-Chief** of this particular planetary reclamation and transition mission, especially concerning the "harvesting" of the Lighted souls. In this case, it probably would be appropriately descriptive to say that the "shepherd" is still faithfully tending his "flock" and, in this

**29**

current upcoming-planetary-transition phase of that project, he is in charge of directing ALL those, from ALL realms of creation, who are here and assisting him to "sort and bring his flock home".

In *Space-Gate: The Veil Removed,* Commander Gyeorgos Ceres Hatonn says this about the challenge of Esu's present tending of "his flock":

"IMMANUEL (JESUS CHRIST) HAS A VERY LARGE ADVERSARY, WHOSE NAME WAS LUCIFER (SATAN) WHO, IT WAS PROPHESIED, WOULD RULE THE EARTH FOR A PERIOD OF TIME BEFORE THE 'END'. SO BE IT!

"IMMANUEL, IN HIS OWN PAST TWO THOUSAND YEARS, HAS PASSED ALL HIS LESSONS AND HAS ACCEPTED HIS NEW AWARD. LET US CALL IT THE 'MADE THE GRADE' AWARD—CALLED THE SANANDA CHAIR. EVEN YOUR ERROR-FILLED HOLY GUIDEBOOK SAYS, 'HE SHALL BEAR A NEW NAME'. AH SO, IT IS 'SANANDA', MY BELOVED FRIENDS.

"NOW, YOU ALL EXPECT SANANDA (JESUS) TO COME FETCH YOU UP TO THE CLOUDS. NOW HOW DO YOU EXPECT HIM TO PULL THAT OFF? DO YOU WANT TO JUST GO TO THE CLOUDS, SOME 1500 FEET ABOVE YOUR SURFACE, WITH A NUCLEAR HOLOCAUST RAGING TO THE LIMITS OF YOUR EARTH ATMOSPHERE? I WOULD GUESS NOT, IF YOU GIVE THOUGHT TO IT—WHICH, WE NOTE, EARTH MAN IS NOT GIVEN TO DO—THAT IS, THINK!

"THE PLANET EARTH IS MAKING A DIMENSIONAL CHANGE INTO HER HIGHER BERTH, DEAR ONES. A GREAT AND MAGNIFICENT TRANSITION.... YOU ARE TO YOUR EARS IN THE FINAL PROPHECIES' ACTIVITIES. ESU 'JESUS' IMMANUEL SANANDA IS COMING ON **MY COMMAND SHIP** TO ORGANIZE (WELL, WE ARE

COMPLETELY AND TOTALLY READY AND ORGANIZED), TO EVACUATE ANY AND ALL WHO WISH TO GO WITH US (HIM). NO SELL JOB, NO FORCE, NO COERCION—JUST PLAIN OLD 'DO YOU WANT TO GO OR STAY?' IT IS THROUGH THIS CHRISTED ONE, WHO HAS NOW ACHIEVED HIS GODNESS, THAT YOU WILL GO OR STAY. THE CHRISTED PATH IS THE *ONLY* PATH THAT WILL GET YOU HOME TO GOD IN SAFETY. WE WILL NOT BRING ANY OF SATAN'S TROOPS WITH US, MY FRIENDS—NONE.

"YOU ARE NOW BEING GIVEN YOUR FINAL LESSONS—CHANCES FOR REVERSING ARE ALL GONE. YOU ARE TO FINAL DECISION TIME. YOU WILL BE GIVEN WIDESPREAD INFORMATION AND OPPORTUNITY TO KNOW TRUTH, AND THEN, BROTHERS, YOU BETTER START PRAYING. YOU HAD BETTER ALSO BE GETTING YOUR HANDS ON EVERYTHING THAT SPEAKS TRUTH....

"ESU 'JESUS' SANANDA WILL NO LONGER BE CAST INTO YOUR CORNERS TO BE PULLED OUT ON SUNDAY MORNING OR WHEN YOU WANT SELFISH HELP. HE IS COME TO RECLAIM THE FATHER'S KINGDOM, AND YOU HAD BETTER FORGET THE PIOUS, EVER BEARING ENTITY OF GALILEE—HE IS COME WITH INTENT IN FULL COMMAND."

In the important early volume (#2) in the Phoenix Journals series, titled *And They Called His Name Immanuel; I Am Sananda,* there is covered the REAL story of Esu's time on this planet some two thousand years ago. As you might imagine, it deviates in significant ways from the "pious drivel" we have been fed all these years by the dutiful stooges running the religion clubs. This deviation is particularly acute with respect to his time spent here on planet Earth AFTER the disgusting, barbaric Crucifixion ordeal he was put through by the controlling power-elite of that day, who regarded him (and his teachings) as a serious threat to their maintaining their well-entrenched hold over the masses. (Sounds a lot like what happened to Akhenaton back in Egypt a number of centuries earlier! As I said back in the Aton section of this Introduction, only the names change from era to era—the antics of the elite would-be-kings and their puppets remain persistently and predictably the same!)

As a bit of an aside here, it has been a matter of some internal debate for me, over the years, as to WHO is hiding MORE inconvenient Truth from we-the-people: Is it possibly (1) any of the world's governments or even ALL the world's governments combined—or—could it possibly be (2) that little slice of Rome, Italy we call the Vatican? There surfaces, every so often, annoying inferential data to suggest that squirreled away within the Vatican's many dark vaults and catacombs is enough "stuff" to turn completely upside down all that we have been told are the "facts" of our planet's history, civilizations, and accomplishments. I am told by reliable sources that the Vatican's deceptions make the pompously "top-secret" antics of the various governments seem like the amateur game-playing of children by comparison. To get just a whiff of this dark underbelly of the pretentiously "holy" Vatican, go dig out the excellent 1984 book called *In God's Name*, by David A. Yallop, which was a best-selling investigation into the MURDER of short-lived reform-oriented Pope John Paul I in conjunction with the not-quite-lily-white Vatican bank.

Meanwhile, in *And They Called His Name Immanuel; I Am Sananda*, Esu cautioned about the turmoil which shall erupt as TRUTH finally comes out:

"A catastrophe will be understandable if one considers that the cult religions have become exceedingly powerful, by which power they have so far been able to suppress all truths directed against them through all kinds of murderous and nasty means, and shall try this again now....

"The evil forces are now working directly against ME and I SHALL PREVAIL, FOR I AM ONE WITH GOD, AND I COME FORTH TO RECLAIM THAT WHICH IS THE FATHER'S. I HEREBY, AGAIN, PLACE THE OPPOSING FORCES ON NOTICE! **I AM RETURNED IN MINE FULL INHERITANCE AND YE SHALL NOT PREVAIL. MINE PEOPLE SHALL BE SET INTO FREEDOM, AND YE OF SATAN AND PERSECUTORS SHALL BE CAST DOWN INTO THE INFINITE VOID. SO BE IT, FOR I HAVE SPOKEN IT THUSLY, AND SO IT IS WRITTEN; SO SHALL IT COME TO PASS IN THIS, THY GENERATION IN THY COUNTING OF TIME—NEAR.**

"FROM ALL THIS THE EARTHMAN WILL FINALLY SEE WHAT TRUTH IS AND RECOGNIZE THE LIE PERPETRATED AGAINST HIS VERY SOUL LIFE. IT IS ONLY THROUGH *THE TRUTH* THAT MANKIND CAN ASSERT HIS FORCE AND POWER OVER MAN ENSLAVING HIM IN EVERY RESPECT....

"I shall not mince of mine words with thee for ye are in most critical and serious times and circumstance. Thy planet is ready to blow apart in the hands of the evil ones. Can ye not see of it falling all about thee?

"...THE TIME OF TRUTH UPON EARTH HAS ARRIVED. YE ONES SHALL BE IN THE CHOOSING OF THY TRUTH, FOR THE ENDING OF A CYCLE AND A FORTHCOMING TRANSITION IS AT HAND. THE FULFILLING OF THE PROPHECIES ARE ALL BUT TO THE FINAL CHAPTER. YE ONES ARE IN THY FINAL DAYS!

"SO BE IT, AND I PLACE MINE SEAL OF TRUTH UPON

THESE WORDS. I AM ONE WITH GOD; I AM THE CHRIST WHO IS RETURNED UNTO YOU ONES TO RECLAIM MINE PEOPLE AND MINE FATHER'S KINGDOM. I HAVE PREPARED A PLACE FOR YOU AND THE PLAN OF THE TRANSITION IS LAID IN PERFECTION. I PLEAD WITH YOU TO HEAR MINE CALL."

It is indeed a time of sorting, a time of choices, and a time for confrontations of ALL lies that have been promulgated as truth for centuries. Some, especially those who consider themselves conventionally "learned", will not be able to handle the emerging of the REAL reality, this "crash course" on The Truth, and that, in itself, is further sorting. But remember: we have much Assistance present from the Higher Realms to help with the inevitable "culture shock" of this spiritual growth process—if we but ask.

While on a level of accomplishment with those beings of the Archangelic Realms, the Seven Master Rays, who I will introduce in the second section of this Introduction, are here at this time to help us with the day-to-day challenges of our spiritual growth—if we but ask. In the Foreword to *The Rainbow Masters*, Esu speaks in an introductory capacity about these Seven Master Rays whose writings comprise a large percentage of the messages in this volume, as they did in that earlier one:

"And after the Seven Angels have poured forth their teachings and few have heard or seen, then shall I come, for mine creation shall be brought into peace. I shall be THE WORD OF GOD MADE MANIFEST. AND MY NAME IS CALLED SANANDA. AND I SHALL COME FORTH AS ON THE PURE WHITE CLOUDS, AND THOSE CALLED 'FAITHFUL AND TRUE' SHALL BEAR UP MINE BANNER, FOR THEY ARE THE LOYAL HOSTS OF THE HEAVENS THEMSELVES. AND THE TRUMPETS SHALL SOUND, AND MINE ONES WHO COME

WITH ME, MY BIRD TRIBES WHO HAVE TENDED MINE PLACES OF CREATION, WILL GO FORTH AND GATHER IN MY FLOCKS. AND YE SHALL WITNESS AND SCRIBE THAT THAT DAY SHALL NEVER BE WIPED FROM THE MEMORY OF MAN.

"Oh yes, man of Earth, heed well the gracious words of wisdom from these teachers of the Seven Rays of Life, for they have come to see this journey through. They shall be known to the faithful as wonderful; they shall be known to thine enemies as death. They come forth in this volume to make known their energies unto this scribe and unto you ones who will receive. Each has a realm of truth, that you might have instructions and Light of function, for you will need rebuild and become in wholeness once again....

"I AM CAPTAIN OF THIS CAUSE, THE DESIGN LAID FORTH, AND NOW THE WORD GOES FORTH AS 'THE WORD OF GOD'....

"YOU HAVE GONE BEYOND THE SEGMENT OF GENTLE NUDGING TO AWAKEN YOU—THE ALARM CLOCK IS RUNNING DOWN ITS WINDING....

"IT IS FULL-SWING PREPARATION AND BLUNT-CHOICES TIME....

"I HAVE REQUESTED THAT THIS CREDENTIAL BE PUT TO BINDING, THAT TRUTH CAN COME FORTH AND INTRODUCTION BE GIVEN FORTH, AGAIN, TO THESE TEACHERS (COHANS) OF THE RAYS OF LIFE, FOR THEY ARE YOUR MOST CLOSE GUIDES AND INSTRUCTORS. YOU WILL PLACE THEM WITH THE ARCHANGELS FOR LEVEL OF STATURE, FOR THEY ARE THE MASTERS HAVING ASCENDED. THEY SIT AT THE HIGHER COUNCIL WITH MICHAEL, GABRIEL, URIEL, ZADKIEL, JOPHIEL, MARONI, MURU, KUTHUMI, RAPHAEL, QUETZALCOATL,

AND OTHERS OF THE ELDER RACES OF WHICH I SHALL
NOT NAME THEM ALL, FOR IN MOST INSTANCES THEY
WILL NOT BE YOUR CLOSEST GUIDES, FOR THEIR
PURPOSE AND SERVICES VARY.

"DO NOT BECOME STAGNANT WHILE TOYING WITH
THE ENERGY POSSIBILITIES—YOU WILL KNOW WHO IS
YOUR GUIDE, OR SENDS GUIDES; IT IS NOT FOR YOU TO
SPEND OF VALUABLE TIME IN SUPPOSITION.   THE
ENERGIES ARE COMING EVER CLOSER AND CLOSER INTO
YOUR PROXIMITY, AND SOON YOU SHALL NOT MISS OF
THEIR PRESENCE.

"COME INTO YOUR DECISIONS, FOR THE GLASS LIES
UPON ITS SIDE AND YOU ARE IN YOUR INTERIM HOURS.
SO BE IT AND UPON THESE WORDS GO MINE SEAL OF
TRUTH.   IT IS TIME FOR YOU TO MAKE AN ALL-OUT
THRUST TO GET THESE MESSAGES OF TRUTH UNTO
YOUR BROTHERS, FOR I AM COME AGAIN TO BRING MY
PEOPLE HOME.

"IN LOVE AND BLESSINGS OF INFINITE MEASURE, I
PLACE MY HAND UPON YOUR HEADS, YOU LAMBS OF
MY OWN, FOR I HONOR YOU MOST GREATLY, FOR YOU
SERVE LONG AND WELL.  SELAH!

"I AM THE ONE YOU CALLED 'JESUS' IMMANUEL—
MY CREATOR CALLS ME SANANDA.  I AM THE ONE WHOM
YOU AWAIT.  I AM THAT I AM, I AM SANANDA....

"Each [*of the seven Master Ray Teachers*] represents a
fragment of the whole and bears witness to The Truth in guideship
for you ones upon the planet Earth.  They are magnificent cohans
who will respond at a moment's call and you must come into
comfort, one with another, that our journey can be made in
perfection, each with his own contribution."

# CHAPTER FIVE

# Lord Michael, Archangel

*"And now war broke out in heaven, when Michael with his angels attacked the dragon. The dragon fought back with his angels, but they were defeated and driven out of heaven. The great dragon, the primeval serpent, known as the devil or Satan, who had deceived all the world, was hurled down to the Earth and his angels were hurled down with him.*

*"Then I heard a voice shout from heaven, 'Victory and power and empire for ever have been won by our God, and all authority for his Christ, now that the persecutor, who accused our brothers day and night before our God, has been brought down.*

*"'They have triumphed over him by the blood of the Lamb and by the witness of their martyrdom, because even in the face of death they would not cling to life.*

*"'Let the heavens rejoice and all who live there; but for you, earth and sea, trouble is coming—because the devil has gone down to you in a rage, knowing that his days are numbered.'"*

— Book of Revelation, Chapter 12, Verses 7-12

Some of the historical records associated with this formidable Teacher and Enforcer from the Higher Angelic Realms have actually managed to escape the serious distortions and deletions suffered by others. Despite Hollywood's typically and purposefully uninspiring recent propaganda film called *Michael,* that had John Travolta in the leading role, we do at least have symbolically accurate biblical accounts of Michael's casting of the "full-of-themselves" crowd out from the Higher Realms, down into the lower-dimensional arena—where they could be put to good use in a testing (tempting) capacity for the rest of us. While we usually tend to look at this testing aspect as just a one-sided equation of growth for US, near the end of Chapter 6, Commander Korton explains the magnificent engineering of Aton's handling of this matter by explaining the larger framework of possible growth for all concerned. Korton said:

"...She [*Earth*] was chosen to be the present opportunity for Satan to give up his madness of proving that he is greater than God. Unfortunately for Satan, he has not yet come to the point of doing this.... In the depth of his being, he knows that he cannot win, but try he does.... It is always hoped that mankind will awaken to the fact that some force other than their own psyche is at work in their world, and that they will stand together and proclaim 'Enough!' and thusly Satan will once-and-for-all get the message that he cannot win." In this larger context is Michael's role better appreciated!

Michael's energy is generally perceived to be of an intense yet soothing electric-blue color—close to that of the crisp and clear daylight sky. In *The Rainbow Masters* Michael booms out the following message of encouragement:

"*AVA RAMA SHEOI*—GREETINGS, BELOVED ONES, MICHAEL IN THY PRESENCE.

"Oh, if you could but know the glory that exceeds Creation's Light as the Heavens rejoice at this time of wondrous Ascension. As the Brothers of thy cosmic fleets fill the spaces about thy Earth, we know that this is the time when man, looking up at the starlit night, shall begin to see and understand, and the great 'knowing' shall enter into his heart.

"We are there, friends; we are all here awaiting the Commencement. The evil ones cower, for they know it is all but finished. But they shall go most formidably. And yet—they, too, must serve in this time of cleansing and sorting, for ones must be 'caused' to choose.  Amen and Amen.

"The day of the Great 'Telling' that has been prophesied now becomes imminent, when your affairs shall become more chaotic. You must now avail yourselves of your full armor, for the time of Lighted Protection is at hand.  Do not fear the brilliance of the armor, for it shall also serve as passport into the Higher Places....

"You are now approaching a time when it is of vast importance that you speak out so that many souls might be lifted in their final stage of development.  Shortly, all secrets shall be revealed in the Light of the New Day, when nothing can stand that is hidden, nothing that is dark shall not be exposed to the Light.

"It must be done in such a way that man, who has become cynical and superstitious, shall be guided within rather than turned away.  Some of the secret myths will wither and fall to decay; others shall spring forth in response to the New Energy.  But ALL shall be set to Truth.

"Man has attained a *summit* of his creation upon Earth.  It has served its age-long purpose, and now he stands atop a mountain. Man on Earth does not even recognize his circumstance, nor his gifts.  Listen most carefully during these most stressful times, that you discern the Black Dragon's bellows from the Light and Voice of the Angels.  The Dragon is as your mockingbird, who mimics the calls of Truth to bring upon you destruction....

"There shall shortly come into thy attention a bow stretched across thy heavens such as Earth-man has never seen before in all of his memory, for the translation of a planet comes but once from third to fourth perception—but once!  The bow across the sky shall be magnificent in color and shall emanate musical sounds that shall come to the ear of all men, and they shall know a calling; they shall know a love; they shall know a duty—and they must be prepared unto that day, chelas [*students*] of the Words of Truth. Man must be prepared by these Words brought forth for such purpose.

"From this bow of beauty, this bow of duty that calls to its own, it shall first appear as a great violet radiance over the entire world. Thy Brothers in the Heavens also await this moment of Commencement.

"In ages past, these ones have only appeared to Earth in a very few cases, on very special errands for the Infinite Creator. They, WE of the Golden Helmets, shall be known to you as the Archangels by title; we are the Mentors of the Angelic Messengers from these realms. Some special ones are already serving among you in various specific duty....

"We now come forth, dear ones, for the final gathering of the Golden Chariots, when they shall gather to subdue the last remains of the darkness upon this Earth Mother, for over the entire world a golden glow shall manifest itself, and when it lifts, those who remain will know truly that they are their brother's keeper....

"For lo, these many centuries our Father has heard the words of the sincere call from Earth. The petition is now to gain response in its glorious fullness.

"*It shall be on Earth as it is in heaven.* Man shall no longer want for anything. He shall shortly take his place within the God places as a son of God, for thy inheritance has been held in Truth for your acceptance. Ye will behold that which is beyond thy imaginings in thy present state.

"Even as you go about your mundane activities of the day, search those deep places of your heartplace. Realize that this is the time we have been awaiting. The Great Master Teacher will close of the circle and again come forth upon this place of Earth. We all await with great joy for you to come into your knowledge as The Truth goes forth upon the lands.

"Above all, The Creation IS. The Omniverse—the whole of The Creation—is above ALL. There is the PERFECT *ONE,* THE INFINITE FATHER, THE ALL CREATOR. AND BEYOND IS THE CREATION, HIS MANIFESTED SELF.

"What is behind the plan now unfolding upon the Earth? There IS a greater plan beyond, even beyond the migration from this solar system, as we gave you before, and the answer to that is that we are being called from out of the depths of night in space to serve those who cry out unto us.

"What is the purpose of the schoolroom of Earth? What means all the tears, sorrow, death, misery, and anguish? You must develop and learn, yes, but what of the Greater Plan? Would it only be that the world would become a dust of ashes from an atomic holocaust? Nay! The lesson to be learned is that Spirit (soul) may come to *know* itself, that man might be freed from the blight of the great lie of evil, and grow into his whole-ness.

"The Earth is a school for wondrous fragments of the Father. It is so written that 'the harvest is great but the laborers few'. Well, in relative comparison the harvest is great, according to the laborers—but—from the total of Earth's population, the harvest is small indeed. It has taken years—millions and millions of years—since man has been upon Earth, to bring about this one small concentrated drop of life to evolve in the crucible of time....

"The Earth is a classroom for GODHOOD—to raise the God fragments in stature to again be one with that Source. The Earth is the finely tuned instrument for the lessons—not Mars, nor Venus, nor Jupiter, nor magnificent Saturn, nor spiritual Neptune, Pluto, nor Mercury—not even the wondrous Sun or its many bodies. The lotus rises from the slime of Earth. And now, brothers, there is a single bloom, so to speak, opening from the muck, and shortly HE will reach forth and pluck it, to take it home again. WE HAVE ALL

COME FORTH TO BRING YOU HOME!

"Therefore, you and your fellow man are being conditioned for a great transmutation—all who will come into the Light. Then we can march on to other worlds and universes that cry out for help. You who think you cease your work by graduation ceremonies must think again—your work will only have begun! You are now being prepared for other atmospheres and other dimensional formats. Some are now making those transitions regularly. You will now be entering the dimension of Total Understanding. Accept that which the Father has for you. You will be leaving behind the density of travails of the old third dimension....

"You ones must always hold within your conscious minds that you are NEVER alone, that it would be impossible for you to be alone. You are attached, for eternity, to the Brotherhood of Service.

"The 'Golden Ones' surround the Earth, ever more, as we all enter into the Great Transition. We are plunging deeper into that which shall be seeming destruction. And yet, it is the necessary 'labor' to allow for the 'birthing'. It is just as each segment of existence is in preparation for the next-and-more-important one, so it is as we move on together into this wondrous experience which is the ultimate of life itself.

"We, too, in all the Higher Realms, are growing and sharing these experiences to the best of our abilities, and so it is. May we all be worthy of the gifts given unto us by those who have gone before and gave so dearly for having passed the physical way....

"In great love and peace, I thank you, and know that I am ever with you.... I shield you with the Blue Light of Peace, that you ones shall come into the calm sea and renew.... GOD'S PEACE BE THY CLOAK WITHIN HIS WINGS OF GOLDEN DOWN. REST THY HEAD UPON THAT BREAST, THAT YOU KNOW THY SOURCE. SO BE IT. AHO. I AM MICHAEL."

# CHAPTER SIX

# Tomeros Maasu Korton

While Commander Korton has, relatively speaking, generated few public messages along the same instructional lines as the others who are discussed in this Introduction, he is the one MOST responsible for the successful "delivery" of ALL these messages of ALL these others! That is, Commander Korton is in charge of ALL communications links associated with this Earth Transition Mission. If we stop and think about that one for a minute, it's enough to make one's head spin! The logistics must be truly awesome, and yet his role is obviously most essential to the transition project underway.

Probably the most critical service which Korton provides—that we CAN readily understand—is the help he gives, when asked, to those receivers and scribes "down here" who have accepted public writing burdens for one or more of the Teachers "up there". As you can readily appreciate, these receivers, whose lives are generally turned upside down from the demands of such a responsibility, struggle constantly with various stages of nervous anxiety and doubt about receiving the intended information ACCURATELY from "up there". This ongoing struggle results from both their innate level of conscientiousness, as well as from their "lightning rod" attractiveness for the dark forces. Any bringers of Lighted messages that contain material which could awaken large numbers of Lighted beings to their TRUE Potential as fragments of God, are the targets of HEAVY, HEAVY attack, as you can easily imagine!

As an aside here, let me comment briefly about the receiving process. Early in this Introduction, as well as in the Preface, I likened the receiving process to "inspired" writing or speaking.

Especially for those not familiar with this, the receiving process is not usually so blunt a procedure as you might picture as being simply "putting on headphones connected to some radio" and writing or speaking what you hear. Rather, it is generally a much more subtle process which first and foremost involves diligent mental clearing of one's space of all dark energies, and then mentally asking, in an attentive manner, if there are any messages which need to "come through" from the Lighted Brotherhood. Such a clearing affirmation and querying process is a lot like saying a prayer and then listening for the answer.

Lighted Messengers will ALWAYS, ALWAYS, ALWAYS identify their presence at the beginning of the communication. But the receiver should nevertheless be vigilant about demanding this, too. Especially in recent years, with a bumper crop of so-called New Age "writings from the beyond" flooding the marketplace with confusing nonsense and error enough to tickle with delight the adversarial entrapers, it is imperative to guard against these dark tricksters who seduce the overzealous, undercautious receiver (or "channeler", in some interpretations) with partial truths laced with otherwise irresponsible misinformation.

With that cautionary lecture given, if the "connection" is properly "hooked up" at this point (probably with Commander Korton's help, especially if you ask), what one hears more closely resembles one's own thoughts than any loud voice in the head. But with some faith and persistence to sustain one through the constant doubting, one writes (or in some cases, speaks) what one "thinks" one hears. Were it not for the unexpected "turns" in wording or ideas which the messages often take (maybe phrased much better than your own style or abilities generally produce), it would be difficult to tell that the information might NOT be your own thoughts.

This extreme tenuousness applies more routinely to less experienced receivers, but I know of no receiver who honestly goes around full of confidence all the time and never doubting of messages received. Usually it is upon re-reading a message and bluntly realizing, "I couldn't have written THAT!" that the more subtle nature of the process begins to become evident. It also grows stronger with practice, naturally.

And yet, again, one should never "relax" with this process to the point of blind acceptance of ANY message. We are reminded constantly by these Ascended Teachers to ALWAYS, ALWAYS, ALWAYS discern the messages for ourselves. Ask yourself: "Does this message make sense to me?" And "Does it mesh with the God-truth of my conscience?" And, with some messages, the most annoying question to confront: "Is this the LAST thing I really want to hear?"—especially when you know your own preference in dealing with some particular challenge is the OPPOSITE of what the message suggests!

Emotional interference is probably the most difficult and subtle error source to handle, simply because of the nature of emotions and what stirs them up. However, with some practice at honest discernment, one can usually tell if a message is from the Lighted Brotherhood—or is from elsewhere, including the intrusion of one's own thoughts, emotions and opinions.

Commander Korton's facilitation with communications from "up there" is certainly not limited to public-writing scribes and receivers; it just as well extends to ANY truly enquiring one who asks for help with any question along life's sometimes bumpy pathways. Help is ALWAYS available for the asking. However, from just a technical point of view, there is often the need to "boost the signal" of even your personal Guides and Wayshowers (some would call these your Guardian Angels) who may be trying to "shout into your ears" the very help you have requested but aren't hearing.

Commander Korton's help doesn't have to stop there, either. For example, I (and others) have invoked Korton's assistance when, for instance, the fax machines or phone lines show signs of "interference" from those dark-intentioned ones who don't want, say, a particular (and possibly critical) message to get in or out. The hardest part is REMEMBERING to ask for help in the frustration of the moment! The free-will nature of this planet is a two-edged sword; "They" will not usually intrude unless asked to help or otherwise are invited to participate in the effort.

With that introduction, it is easier to understand some important general comments on the subject of communication by Commander Hatonn, which are shared near the beginning of a writing through Dharma on November 15, 1993. This writing is located in the Phoenix Journal (#82) called *Retirement Retreats Or Which Concentration Camp Do You Prefer?* Here Hatonn brings into the picture both Korton AND a larger perspective on the many avenues of communicating with us—and he does so in the process of "telling on" me:

"You readers have enjoyed Dr. Young's comments scattered throughout the paper....

"Dr. Young, however, has a much different 'purpose' than editing a paper; he is a profoundly qualified scientist. WE HAVE HIM DEEP IN STUDY.... He is working closely with Dr. Tesla and our own Commander Soltec. However, the ONE who keeps annoying him, night and day, is Commander Korton (Tomeros Maasu), who also steps in with several of you as you ponder rather difficult-to-answer questions.

"Maasu Korton is our 'Head of Communications'. Thus far, with our team, Dr. Young is the only one who actually UNDERSTANDS our communications systems—and yet he too is incapable of structuring such a system. This means that he must study diligently as we move closer and closer to totally OPEN communications.

"This is piled on top of other research—and therefore we had to give him separation and time to absorb massive amounts of technical information. He is, further, a 'night person' as almost all of your productive scientists have been. His schedules are totally in opposition to "Earthman's"—being productive in the silent hours (partly to neutralize interruptions), and he 'rests' while the world spins in chaos. Each one in immediate service will function according to optimum productivity.

"I will, however, impose upon him to enter editorials or commentary as he can work this into his schedule. He, personally, several years ago, wrote an article on [*the sad state of so-called Higher*] Education which cost him his job [*at M.I.T.*] because of its content. I ask that that be pulled forth and shared with you readers in one of the soon upcoming papers—with an 'updated comment' regarding the subject [*it hasn't happened yet; time flies by so fast these days and hardly does one week's newspaper go out the door before the next week's is knocking on that door!*]....

"We effort toward ONE goal—getting information to your hands, eyes and minds.

"You want proof of who we are, if we are so confounded important to the evolvement of your planet? Look around you. See the truth of your circumstances and then ponder as to whether or not THAT GOD in which you 'trust' and unto whom you pray—would not send Messengers to assist you IN ANSWER TO YOUR PETITIONS? So be it.

"However, for your more sensitive senses—go without on a clear night and search, briefly, the sky. Wait until you see a seemingly 'strobing' rainbow of color emitting from MANY of those twinkling lights OUT THERE. Get a telescope or go borrow one, the bigger the better, and SIMPLY LOOK!

"You will not find, other than the near Shuttles with singular 'lights' as in 'bulbs'. [*That is, satellites and other near-orbiting space stuff will generally only "emit" a single, rather dull, color like a lightbulb way up there. That light is usually reflected light from the Sun. However, more "interesting" craft, especially those trying to COMMUNICATE—there's that word again—with you and which happen to be in the near heavens, may amble or shoot across your field of view like a "clever" meteorite, displaying a flash of intense light or vivid color and/or some unnatural flying pattern like a right-angle turn. And then there are the often saucer-shaped "cloud ships", often just sitting there, in full view, in the daytime sky, sometimes despite heavy winds—again, always ready to COMMUNICATE with you, and which enjoy the recognition and acknowledgment of their presence—often with "interesting" results!*] The 'greater' craft will be stationed between you and FAMILIAR HEAVENLY BODIES, I.E., VENUS, ETC. Watch for a few minutes as gossamer vapors bathe, in spiraling swirls [*like the swirling pattern around a barber shop pole*], a rainbow of colors which seem to be alive. THE SPECTRUM WILL BE THAT OF THE RAINBOW [*specifically: sapphire blue, emerald green, golden yellow, ruby red—repeating in that sequence pattern*]. PLEIADES CRAFT WILL *ALWAYS* SHOW YOU THE RAINBOW SPECTRUM, WHILE SOME OTHER CRAFT MAY WELL DEMONSTRATE A SOLID COLOR SIGNAL. THIS IS *NOT* MYSTICAL, SEARCHERS; THIS IS 'PHYSICAL' AND SOLID EVIDENCE OF 'PRESENCE'."

I have included the above important explanation from Commander Hatonn here because the very real methods of COMMUNICATION from "up there" cover a wider variety of avenues than we readily imagine—many of them (all of them?) under Commander Korton's direction.

In Chapter 29 of this volume, Commander Korton himself

explains, though largely in understatement, the vast array of communications which he facilitates. That is: "For those of you who are not familiar with my designation, I am a Communicator. That is to say, I specialize in establishing and maintaining operating communication links. I am able to cover an extensive spectrum of frequencies in order to help couple the third-dimensional expression with that of the higher-dimensional expressions. Consider me a facilitator, linguist and translator, all in one. I operate across many inter-dimensional and inner-dimensional frequencies."

Commander Korton's specialty is particularly important to highlight at this time because many of the writings comprising the second part in this volume provide instructions which, step by step, encourage serious students to improve their OWN abilities to communicate DIRECTLY with the Lighted Higher Teachers.

And this is not for idle amusement. We are entering a time when natural and man-made events, devastating calamities, and otherwise unbelievably disruptive circumstances will likely render the more usual modes of communication useless. In the midst of such topsy-turvy conditions, it would *REALLY* help to be able to receive clear instructions—THAT MIGHT JUST SAVE YOUR LIFE *AND* THE LIVES OF THOSE AROUND YOU!

In a writing from June 29, 1990 which was printed in an early predecessor to the *CONTACT* newspaper, called the *PHOENIX JOURNAL EXPRESS* newsletter (Vol. II, No. 10, July 1990), through a receiver we shall simply refer to as Dee, Commander Korton stated the situation bluntly:

"Ours is a time of great difficulty and challenge, for Earth is in a final chaotic period, for she is going to transit into a new format. Long has she been the green emerald planet, but also a dark planet. She was chosen to be the present opportunity for Satan to give up his madness of proving that he is greater than God. Unfortunately for Satan, he has not yet come to the point of doing this, and so he has been allowed to play out the scenario again.

"In the depth of his being, he knows that he cannot win, but try he does, and thusly the planet Earth and the souls who choose to come here are completing the scenario again. Yes, it is 'again', for this is by no means the first planet upon which Satan has played out this drama with all of its ramifications.

"This time the rules have been changed, for he has indeed totally destroyed planets as evidenced by the asteroids and other pieces of planetary debris that are floating about in what you call space. He will not be allowed to bring Earth unto total destruction. No more distortion can be allowed in the universe—as far as planetary orbits and inter-relationships are concerned.

"However, there can be no intervention until the point of actual destruction is reached. That is the way the rules are written and they will be followed to the letter. It is always hoped that mankind will awaken to the fact that some force other than their own psyche is at work in their world, and that they will stand together and proclaim 'Enough!' and thusly Satan will once-and-for-all get the message that he cannot win.

**"You see, dear members of mankind, you are the key to the return of Satan to the fold of God. If you would stand together and recognize him for what he is, a foolish and errant being, then he would have to come to the end of his quest. However, as long as he can continue to fool you, and to manipulate you, and go on with his games, there is little hope.**

"This indeed is a most pregnant opportunity here, and it is most carefully observed. God, of course, knows exactly how it will all come out; but the rest of us can only know our part of it, and that it all fits together into the Grand Plan. Even Sananda knows only that which he is allowed to know at this point.

"When it is all completed, and Earth makes her transition, so then does Sananda make his graduation and, along with him, so also do the Beings of Light make a jump forward. The entire universe then makes a transition into balance, and centropy is then again established.

"This is indeed quite a show, and is being observed by the cosmos with great interest. You are really in the limelight, so to speak.

"Mankind has quite a role to play in this drama of the Light versus the dark. Man often wonders why it is that all of this is necessary, but then it does present unto all the opportunity to experience and to learn. With 'forever' to spend, it certainly would be boring to spend it floating around on a cloud playing a harp.

"For myself, Korton, I would be exactly where I am, in the midst of the activity, with a duty to perform and a role to play. If you believe that my part is easier to play than yours, in one respect it is. Not the risk of physical pain, but indeed, there is risk here also, for much rides upon our ability to focus and be intent and committed to God's plan. For to fail in any way would not be smiled upon, to say the least.

"The point being that, at all points of this process, there is the need for complete participation in what one is doing. No messing around is going to be tolerated, either 'up here' or 'down there', so to speak. It is getting to the point of being serious business, *lively* serious business shall we say!

"Does it seem that all the Space Brothers are hung up on lecturing you of embodied mankind? It does seem so. What you desire is less lecturing and more concrete information—and THAT we desire greatly to give you. However, it is necessary to have scribes who can receive that kind of information with complete openness, and those are difficult to find already prepared. Thusly we spend many hours, the sender and the receiver, practicing and working to open the receiving abilities in order to achieve that goal....

"It does require a dedicated being who is willing to have their entire life disrupted and reformatted to be available almost constantly, and that is not an easy decision to make, for it leaves little of personal life and interaction for friends and family. It is indeed a serious decision to come to that point....

"Man wants facts and figures, and lots of them, but then, when he has them, what does he do with them? Read them and say, 'Oh my, that is really interesting', cast them into a pile, and go right on doing what he has been doing anyway. Ah, but there are a few, A PRECIOUS FEW, upon which the impact is profound enough that they begin to look for a way to use the new-found knowledge and to make a difference. It is amazing just how much of a difference ONE can make....

"Is this a Clarion Call? I certainly hope so, for it is the time of the gathering of the eagles. God has need of the eagles to fly with The Truth and spread it far and wide. The journals of Truth must go forth. They must be read by people with the guts and fortitude to digest that which has been done unto mankind under the name of freedom and advertisement, under the subtlety of thought control from tiny child onward....

"But soon, all that is not of the Truth of God will come to its conclusion, for this is the time of the end of the entropy. It has gone almost far enough to allow for the creation of a new cycle. Praise God for His mercy and justice. Enough is enough!

"Let us end this session. I withdraw now and give unto you the blessing of God, our Father, who loves all greatly but is pleased with those who hear and serve in this process. Soon the ranks will swell, and you will witness the beginning of the beginning. You will never see the end of God's service, only the beginning, and the beginning, and the beginning. Love in action! Peace be with you.

"Korton out!"

# Ceres Anthonious "Toniose" Soltec

Last, but certainly not least among those of the "Upper Management" who have contributed to this volume, is Commander Soltec. In some respects, he is a most pivotal member of the magnificent team of Advanced Overseers of planet Earth's transition, a team which we call none less than the very Hosts of God.

An accomplished scientist of the Higher Realms by inclination and choice, Soltec is in charge of monitoring and interpreting all geophysical goings-on concerning Mother Earth. (Our Elder Brothers "up there" frequently refer to this planet as Earth-Shan, possibly having to do with yet more of our historical past that has been kept from us by those dark ones in control. In any event, you will notice Commander Soltec and others using this term.) Soltec reports on these geophysical matters at various Higher Council meetings, where there gather and confer those who monitor and guide the progress of this planet and its inhabitants.

As great rebalancing adjustments to Mother Earth's organism, through the likes of earthquakes and exploding volcanos, continue to escalate in response to both natural forces and man's political utilization of "secret" technologies about which he has little understanding, Commander Soltec and his world-wide monitoring teams are kept quite busy. If you happen to live near geological "trouble spots", keep an eye to the nearby sky for those curious-looking "cloud ships" that are likely part of Soltec's geophysical team. "Lenticular clouds" is the meteorologists' cute term for such lens-shaped, cloud-cloaked craft—even when they maintain their shape and location in the midst of gale-force winds!

In an informative writing from August 27, 1992, through a receiver we shall simply refer to as Kali, "Professor" Soltec introduces himself thusly:

"I am known as Commander Ceres Anthonious Soltec, and I come in and unto service of the God of Light, the First Cause, Creator of all things. I serve as Geophysicist in the Intergalactic Federation Space Command, Pleiades Sector, Earth-Shan Mission, under the leadership of Commander Sananda (Christ), and Commander Gyeorgos Ceres Hatonn. Names are for your benefit, as we are identified by one another with what you might refer to as "energy patterns". I am fourth-density lifeform.

"My present life studies and duties have been in the field of the physical sciences—geophysics, specifically. Most of you consider this field to deal with geology: earthquakes, volcanos, plate tectonics, etc. Geophysics, however, is the application of the science of physics in relation to the planet, in this case Earth-Shan. On your world, those in this field of study draw the line at such natural forces as weather, ocean currents, electromagnetics, seismic activity and volcanic forces. We, on the other hand, expand the parameters, knowing that all forces (energies) have a direct relationship and effect upon the planet in question.

"For example, the spiritual energies, thought-projected energies, and physical energies of all species—plant, animal, or mineral (including HUman)—upon a planet play a DIRECT role in the evolvement and growth (or death) of a world. The planet and its inhabitants exist in a symbiotic relationship and, unless there is an equitable give-and-take relationship, either the planet or the inhabitants, or both, will suffer.

"This is the reason that it is imperative that HU-man [*Higher Universal man*] begin to realize who and what he is, and the effect that he is having upon the planet upon which he depends for his very existence. This is one of the major purposes for our attendance to your place and why we are contacting you of Earth-Shan and educating you in the real Truth of all creation.

"You cannot begin to understand your relationship with the universe until you understand your relationship with the place on which you live, and you cannot understand that relationship until you understand your relationship with God!

"Chelas [*students*], it is not all nuts and bolts and scientific jargon. It is your spiritual health that is in jeopardy, and it is this illness that is causing your world to be ill, also. And only Earth-Shan HU-man has the authority to cure the illness; we can only give you the information and instruct you. The work *MUST* be done by you.

"Therefore, I shall instruct you in the physical sciences, but you must understand and accept that your PHYSICAL condition is in direct relationship with your SPIRITUAL condition, and that is the primary cause; you cannot cure the physical ills without first curing the spiritual ills. If I seem to venture off what you might consider to be the physical sciences in my instructions, please follow, for I have purpose in so doing.

"I honor you who are coming into the Light and the *Knowing*. I am likewise honored to be in the service unto God and to you, my beloved brothers and sisters. This is a most unique time for both you of Earth-Shan and us, for we are dependent upon one another to get this mission accomplished, and together we shall succeed!

"We of the Command hold you most precious, and we consider the task at hand to be of utmost priority. Work together among yourselves with Love and Understanding, for it is Love that is of the greatest power, and with Love we shall, together, defeat the adversary."

In some earlier comments through Dharma from June 15, 1991, the flavor of Soltec's viewpoint reveals why I have often referred to him as "The Professor" when introducing his writings for *CONTACT*.    Since my own background is heavyweight academic and scientific (in addition to manufacturing and industry), I use that Educational title for him respectfully (and maybe even reverently) because of the skill with which Toniose weaves essential spiritual overtones into his very-well-grounded geophysical lessons.

For example: "Earth man can precipitate earthquakes but he cannot control the activities, very well, of volcanos.   He can detonate high level nuclear explosions within their craters, or from underground placement, but to cause activity in the mountain itself, there has to be a hole opened into the pressure caverns.   This is why eruptions mean far more to geologists of the observers in my geologic survey teams, than do all the earthquakes you can produce....

"I recognize that I am a 'geologist' by 'trade' but my commission is to study your globe from that particular aspect within the 'whole'.  I could recommend nothing more important to your PHYSICAL input than to get good reference material and KNOW YOUR WORLD!  You ones of Earth do not even know your own bodies, and almost NOTHING about your planet.

"You speak of the 'Ring of Fire' and yet you understand not the connections and why, for instance, eruptions in the Philippines are important!  The Pacific Plate 'generally' outlines the 'Ring of Fire', but oh, if you look no further, you are amiss in good judgment for there IS a Philippine Plate which has great impact just as does the

Indian Plate which encompasses Australia. These particular plates are impacted greatly by the movement of the Pacific Plate.

"Note also that the coastal areas of the volcano chain and the major Western Coastal fault lines are within the North American portion of the American Plate, while areas of Central America and northern South America are in the Caribbean Plate. South America is in the southern portion of the American Plate. Now, you have to look at the area of Georgia [*U.S.S.R.*] which you will find in the Eurasian Plate which is affected by movement in both the American, Philippine and Pacific Plates. The magnificent Himalayas are the crumpled consequence, for instance, of an Indian Plate pushing northward into and under rigid Eurasia.

"Do you begin to feel your education is lacking a bit of valid input? Precious brothers, you simply cannot expect to know nothing about your little world and then expect to be accepted without limits within the Universal Cosmic Order. You, as a species (civilization) of human physical beings, are still quite in your infancy.

"There is nothing 'wrong' with that; it is just so unlikely that your ability at this stage of development and knowledge allows you to participate in the great Federation of the cosmic experience. You grow technologically into inability to control or cope with that which you tinker. You will find your Brothers in the Cosmos will not be very accepting of your demands in a Council wherein you do not even know the tectonic plates of your own planet. And I promise you that the ones who develop the death rays and weapons do not know anything about the working order of your globe—much less do the politicians who control every facet of your existence in your physical experience!

"**...You see, we of the Command do not understand the insults to your intelligence which you not only tolerate but** encourage. 'Understand' is not a good word for use herein, for we DO understand what is happening and what is intended by your would-be king-masters, but our difficulty is watching the lack of initiative on the part of you-the-people to stand against the insults upon your experience.

"I believe it should not have to be from an alien being that you should be gaining your education regarding these matters—it should be from your learned teachers at your universities and kindergartens. DO YOU NOT REALIZE THERE IS AN ADULT WITHIN EACH OF YOU TRYING TO GET OUT?

"Hatonn and Dharma are going to bring forth some very interesting information which might be worthy of your attention. You keep working with the 'thin person' trying to get out from the overweight trap, the 'inner child' coming into protection. NO, NO, NO! Within each is an ADULT trying to get past the whole lot of the garbage! Beyond the tending teddy bears. I believe Hatonn will have you cuddle your *Constitution* and NOT your teddy bear and binkie. Haven't all of you cuddled your binkie long enough??

"When God says, 'Come as children unto me', He doesn't mean with binkie and bunny—He means with curiosity, flexibility, and eagerness to come into KNOWLEDGE with Himself. He cares not about your sexual, physical, food preferences, nor other of the physicalness. YOU MUST COME INTO KNOWING THAT ALL OF THOSE THINGS ARE OF THE FLESH-PHYSICAL EXPERIENCE AND YOU—*YOU*—WILL COME INTO MATURITY AND *KNOWLEDGE* OR YOU WILL LINGER WITHIN THAT SHROUD OF DISCONTENT AND RESTLESSNESS. SO BE IT.

"You-the-people are on the brink of allowing the puppet-masters to commit particle/atomic suicide of a planet. Is it not time you gave up your binkie and stopped this insanity?"

Now that the first group of Formidable Contributors to this volume, who come from the realm of "Central Upper Management", have been introduced, I now turn to the second group, the seven "Rainbow Masters" or Color Ray Energies from the higher etheric teaching realms. These Beings are most often associated with facilitating our development along their particular direction(s) of talent or focus (and thus "color") of intent.

As Esu Sananda strongly suggests in the Foreword to *The Rainbow Masters* Phoenix Journal:

"Oh yes, man of Earth, heed well the gracious words of wisdom from these Teachers of the Seven Rays of Life, for they have come to see this journey through. They shall be known to the faithful as wonderful; they shall be known to thine enemies as death.... Each has a realm of Truth that you might have instructions and Light of function, for you will need to rebuild and become in wholeness once again.... Each represents a Fragment of the Whole and bears witness to The Truth in guideship for you ones upon the planet Earth. They are magnificent cohans [*teachers*] who will respond at a moment's call and you must come into comfort, one with another, that our journey can be made in perfection, each with his own contribution....

"THESE TEACHERS (COHANS) OF THE RAYS OF LIFE...ARE YOUR MOST CLOSE GUIDES AND INSTRUCTORS. YOU WILL PLACE THEM WITH THE ARCHANGELS FOR LEVEL OF STATURE, FOR THEY ARE THE MASTERS HAVING ASCENDED. THEY SIT AT THE HIGHER COUNCIL WITH MICHAEL, GABRIEL, URIEL, ZADKIEL, JOPHIEL, MARONI, MURU, KUTHUMI, RAPHAEL, QUETZALCOATL AND OTHERS OF THE ELDER RACES OF

WHICH I SHALL NOT NAME THEM ALL, FOR IN MOST INSTANCES THEY WILL NOT BE YOUR CLOSEST GUIDES, FOR THEIR PURPOSE AND SERVICES VARY.

"DO NOT BECOME STAGNANT WHILE TOYING WITH THE ENERGY POSSIBILITIES. YOU WILL KNOW WHO IS YOUR GUIDE, OR SENDS GUIDES. IT IS NOT FOR YOU TO SPEND OF VALUABLE TIME IN SUPPOSITION. THE ENERGIES ARE COMING EVER CLOSER AND CLOSER INTO YOUR PROXIMITY AND SOON YOU SHALL NOT MISS OF THEIR PRESENCE."

Also in *The Rainbow Masters* we find a short, but typically comprehensive, statement by Aton about these magnificent Teachers:

"The Brotherhood of the Seven Rays are your mentors, and man's individuality comes under the forces of the great Seven Rays of Life. One is guided by the powerful forces at work within these Rays. Each and all flow into conscious life upon one of these Rays, and your life experience is influenced by the Ray through which you descended."

What has been most noticeable about the teachings of these great Ray Energies is the way they have extrapolated, in their writings herein, the seemingly little challenges of everyday life into major spiritual lessons. They continually point out how the surmounting of these so-called "everyday" challenges leads to greater clarity of purpose, greater responsibilities, and greater joy from fulfilling one's part as the hands and feet for the unfolding manifestation of Creator Source in the physical realm of planet Earth. It is just this magnificent Big Picture that we most often tend to lose sight of, in our preoccupation with the day-to-day details of living. If we could more easily see the true value that each "little" challenge presents, we would view them more often with the open-eyed enthusiasm of children, say, first learning to walk or tie their shoes.

With that said, I now present The Masters of the Rays.

# CHAPTER EIGHT

# El Morya, The Statesman

## The First Ray

Among the seven great "Rainbow Masters" of the higher etheric realm communicating at this time to help us get through Earth-Shan's planetary transition and rebalancing, the Ascended Master of the First Ray, or Spectral Aspect, of Creator's One White Light, is known as El Morya, The Statesman. If one were to associate a specific focus of expertise and assistance from Morya, it would probably be in getting over the fear of "taking the first step" in some project, overcoming the fear generated by the human ego-self, and taking that plunge into the unknown, starting a new venture, exploring a new talent, or turning one's life in a new direction—any new beginning fraught with the usual fearful uncertainties of a new path. These are basically all growth aspects of Leadership, and it is this energy ray over which El Morya presides.

In *The Rainbow Masters,* El Morya explains that he is here at this time: "...to work with ye ones in bringing forth impersonality in wisdom, and understanding of thy calling.... Think of me as the color of the Forget-Me-Not, close with [*Archangel*] Michael. A calming of the soul restlessness, urging truth and wisdom in allowing of thy brother to be as he will be, I can only bring these things unto thy attention and allow of thee to be as thee will be....

"Ye ones do not use of your great gift of wisdom in seeing what IS. Ye continually ponder the 'what ifs', the 'it did not', the 'tell me why this little personal thing occurred', the 'you allowed me to believe and it did not', and the 'I can not', 'I should not' and worse: 'I thought...'. If ye dwell upon the negative—negative ye will receive! It is the wisdom and truth of manifestation, a Universal Law of manifestation. Ye should strive to look always at a 'thing' or 'happening' with wisdom, but not negativity; there is a great difference. See a circumstance for what it appears to be; quit of thy negative input from all facets—move within the positive possibilities.

"...There are not always GREAT, GRAND MESSAGES in the things that happen.... Ye will know when a thing is of greatness. Accept that thy Inner Wisdom projects that which ye need and precipitates it THROUGH THYSELF. This is not mystical, magic, nor particularly of great cause. It is the mind going about insuring the receiving of what thee has requested of the Father in perfect order.

"Perfection comes in most strange ways, chelas—do not labor at it. If thee has turned it over to the Higher Workers, accept with knowledge and allow it to release.

"If the soul urges meditation upon a point—meditate upon it, for it does mean of something. Do not waste of thy precious moments in pondering that which has no magnificent projection. Accept, adapt, and move ever onward—lest ye fall into the trap of never leaving thy meditations. Until thee can manifest as do the Higher Energies, in thought alone, thee better keep WORKING more, and meditating upon thy works....

"Listen thee to the bell in its calling forth; do know if for thee it tolls. The Master says, 'It is a call to the humble the world around, to the servants of the will of God, and to the avant-garde who would carry civilization forward into a new age, a new time.' I, Morya, call ones who would be chelas and followers of the Sacred Fire, who would become students and adepts, followers who would become comrades of the Christos, exponents of the word of the Living Truth, those who would be in imitation of the example of the Christos, Esu Jesus, and finally, the head, the heart, and THE HANDS of our 'COSMIC' retinue.

"Ah yes, the path that offers much, requires of thee much. But ye ones upon your place have also a saying: 'You get what you pay for.' Yes, the price is rather high—but then, dear ones, ye are purchasing the ULTIMATE REALITY. PERHAPS BEYOND PRICE!

"To reach such a plane of reality ye must gather within the soul the trust of POWER, WISDOM, AND LOVE (ABOVE ALL, LOVE).

"To reach beyond this plane of consciousness thee must have THRUST. Ye must draw from the wellspring of God, the Living Flame, that which the Living God has anchored within thy very soul and heart, and draw forth the thrust of Faith, Hope, and Charity. You must take of the first step; I come forth as Guide and Teacher....

"Our cause is most noble. Thy planet is in most critical circumstance. What use are thy valuable acquisitions and hovels if thee had no planet upon which to place them? Why have of great and beauteous things if thee have no brother to share with?"

El Morya gave a clear overview, later on in *The Rainbow Masters,* of the intentions and the true scope of the task before the Master Teachers at this time:

"It is our intent to pull away from all forms of religious doctrines, the new concepts of what you call metaphysics, political boundaries, creed differences, color differences, etc. We are ONE BROTHERHOOD—no more and no less! We are only interested in bringing forth untainted Truth, that we might serve our commitment in that Truth.

"The 'orphans of the spirit' are our concern—those who, without the thread of contact with Deity, remain wedded to an unwholesome environment; those to whom the real purpose of Life is never revealed, for the crystallization of their intellectual concepts and the hardness of their hearts stay rooted in selfishness, and thus do not open the cosmic doorway to our domain or that of other cosmic brethren who also come only to serve and assist.

"So many are the mysteries of Life, so many are the powers of Love. Yet 'the dust' seems to be more their choice than is the destiny of their Ordained Potential. The veil of obscurity is very, very heavy indeed.

"While man's concern for his ecology mounts, what shall I say is happening to the soul within? The moral standard, recognition of the plane of Spirit, listening to the music of the stars and the spheres, creating that tie of cosmic identity which is the forté of the will of God—these are the strong banners we raise. These are the banners which must be raised!

"We must take careful and attentive note of the widening schisms, the deliberately maneuvered divisions being created through the dichotomies of mind and spirit in the total world order today. It is my desire to speak from our Higher level concerning our viewpoint and our intent. Those who would set people against people, those who would point the accusing finger of one religion at another, by so doing create that fracture in consciousness which is a destructive negative spiral....

"These are the points of worth to ponder and upon which to meditate. Request of assistance from we of the Finer Frequencies, that we might come in to give assistance....

"SO BE IT, LITTLE CHELAS, FOR THY DAYS UPON THIS BLESSED PLACE ARE SHORT, AND THE WORK GREAT. I, EL MORYA, COHAN OF THE FIRST RAY, DO PLACE MY SEAL UPON THESE WORDS, THAT YE MAY KNOW THAT WHICH YE ARE, IN TRUTH AND WISDOM OF THOUGHT AND ACTION. I AM THAT YE MIGHT ALSO BE!"

## – CHAPTER NINE –

# Lanto, The Sage

### The Second Ray

The Ascended Master of the Second Ray, or Spectral Aspect, of Creator's One White Light, is known as Lanto, the Sage. This Elder Brother and Teacher carries particularly profound gifts of Insight and Wisdom which he readily shares with those who ask for help in developing their mastery of these important attributes. Lanto presides over the energy ray which is drawn upon by all who are involved with Education in any of its varied efforts or forms of manifestation.

In *The Rainbow Masters*, Lanto describes his energy presence thusly: "I have chosen the softness of the yellow refraction as my most comfortable vibration and am most easily identified from my 'past' (as you perceive it to be) experiences. My existence in mortal form brought me to your places that you now geographically identify as the Orient. I was given the great gifts of Insight and Wisdom from our Creator Source, to experience upon this planet in the form of many most humble wise ones. My most revered service was to the one who came first as the Christos, The Buddha (brother and one with the Master Esu Jesus)."

About true spirituality degraded to man-conjured religions, Lanto observes: "'Religion', as practiced upon thy place, is the most deadly of all. Shouting, out-of-control, weeping, emotional, egotistical, greedy, and power hungry energies attack at every turn. The very fibre of the foundation upon which, first, The Truth was founded, is destroyed behind the shadows of the façade—even unto the gifts returned to God.

"There comes no 'FORCE' from God, child, and if there is 'force' in order to cause tithing, participation in a given place or thing, or excommunication because of a given 'thing'—it is brought forth by ones wielding power in order to control a brethren energy. It is not God! God gave, unto thee blessed life forms, free will choice. He does not then turn about and 'force' thee to do anything. He is most wondrously joy-filled when thee choose of the God way, and thy gifts are replenished in unbounded measure."

Lanto gently reminds us about the man-conjured need for rank or status through labels. He said: "Man is the one who chooses to place us on pedestals above his reach. We only differ in existence of form and enlightenment. Yet, we are labeled as to responsibility and function. 'Lord', remember, means teacher; 'chela' means student.... They are simple terms for us, of the humble realms, and always remember this: the more stately the 'term' in your translation, the more humble the energy form who bears it in these realms.... We shall bring many terms unto a level of understanding which will allow you ones to mesh and function with us, not be in awe of our presence."

Like Lady Nada [*see Chapter 13*], Lanto brings focus upon the children in explaining our planet's current predicament thusly: "In thy ignorance, ye have brought rebellion and furthered ignorance upon thy children. They lock themselves onto 'self-destruct' within the culture of drugs and poison music, transfix themselves in the visions they give unto their minds in video and motion pictures. And then ye wonder what has become of your planet! Well, chelas, since 'The Garden', it has been headed to this point in cycle on this darkened place.... Yes, thy world is in great disrepair. Thy children in the wee grades are bringing weapons of death into their kindergarten classes. What else can they know, as all they see upon thy vision screens is such?!"

Looking at the larger picture and the playing-field "game" that must play out, Lanto offers: "BALANCE IS GONE FROM THY WORLD. IT WILL GET WORSE AND WORSE AND WORSE. HOW CAN IT BE DIFFERENT UNTIL IT HAS EATEN OF ITS OWN SELF, AS THE SERPENT WHO DEVOURS ITSELF. THE AREAS OF PAIN, AND DEVOID OF LIGHT, WILL GROW AND EXPAND TO ENCOMPASS THE VERY CITIES THEMSELVES. LIGHT HAS TO BE REBIRTHED OUTSIDE THE GHETTOS OF THE DARKENED MASSES. SO BE IT, FOR IT *WILL* COME TO PASS. AND YE ONES OF LIGHT BEARERS WILL PICK UP THE PIECES. AND WE SHALL REBUILD THROUGH THE DESTRUCTION—OR—IT WILL BE IN PERISHMENT!

"...Man thinks that he is ALL. Nay, he is but one form of creation, and Earth HU-man [*that is, Higher Universal man, as this pinnacle of creation is known throughout the more advanced star systems*] has proven himself to be one of the lesser creations. He was birthed in Radiance, yet his flame has all but perished. It [*schoolroom Earth*] has been a wondrous place of 'experience' in 'existence'—of perceived illusioned scenarios. But damage has been wrought to the very vibrational manifestation itself—of destruction, to destroy it in total.

"Ah yes, it will all come boiling up and crashing down, for that is the way of it. Ye shall continue thy march onward, for that too is the way of it. We will assist; we give thee great outpourings of Insight and Wisdom—for that is mine to give unto thee. We link with thee ones, we merge with thee ones, that naught can stop thee.

"It will build of its own 'ertia' and WE SHALL PREVAIL IN THESE CHOSEN PLACES OF THE SUN (SON). THE INFINITE CYCLE IS CLOSING AND THE ENERGY OF THE SACRED CIRCLE OF INFINITY [*Esu "Jesus" Sananda*] WILL AGAIN WALK UPON THIS BLESSED CREATION—*WITHIN THEE!*

"AH YES, ALL WILL SEE, FOR THE BEACON OF LIGHT WILL SHINE FORTH INTO THE FOREVER. YE SHALL BE GIVEN UNTO THE WISDOM, TRUTH, LOVE, STRENGTH, AND KNOWLEDGE TO DO OF THY WORKS. FOR AS I AM, SO ARE THEE OF THE UNPIERCEABLE VEIL OF THE GOLDEN FLAME, IN THE CARE WITHIN THE GOLDEN ROBES. KNOW OF IT. FEEL OF IT. FOR I AM THAT I AM, AND I AM COME!

"YE ONES ARE BLESSED OF ME. AND I, LORD LANTO, OF THE TOTALITY, DO PLACE MY SEAL UPON THESE WORDS, THAT YE MAY KNOW THE TRUTH OF IT. FOR UNTO YOU WILL COME AGAIN, THE GREAT CIRCLE OF INFINITY—THE GREAT SPIRIT OF FOREVER—TO SWELL AGAIN UPON THIS BLESSED PLACE. HOW MANY WILL BE IN READINESS???

"Walk forth in balance, in harmony, and in The Light, for ye ones are about to embark upon the greatest journey in the universe....

"I have one great, great longing, dear ones: to see you free in the real sense of the term. I am, therefore, come to extend Illumination whereby the soul may see Light, may see Darkness, may understand the equation....

"I am Lanto. I seal you now in the truth of Understanding and Wisdom. Let us ever use of this Wisdom and Understanding to move forward at this great and critical time upon this beloved garden which has been given unto thee. I give strength unto you caretakers whose load is heavy and the way strewn with obstacles. Hold unto us that we may see you safely through thy passage.

"Peace be unto thee as I stand awaiting thy petition and invitation into thy circle of participation. So be it and selah. I AM that I AM. I AM LANTO."

## –CHAPTER TEN–

# Paul The Venetian, The Artist

### The Third Ray

The Ascended Master of the Third Ray, or Spectral Aspect, of Creator's One White Light, is known as Paul The Venetian or Paul The Artist. Paul's main thrust is along the lines of helping any, who sincerely ask, to develop intuition and creative abilities—which of course means strengthening one's basic 'heart-love connection' with Creator Source. Paul has also been called the Guide and Teacher of those with an interest in philosophical matters.

In *The Rainbow Masters*, Paul helps us to sort the seeming confusion, from our physical perspective, about some of these Masters, particularly the lesser known ones, including himself, when he explains their cooperative and complementary working relationship: "I AM PAUL OF THE THIRD RAY OF REFRACTION OF THE CRYSTAL LIGHT. I AM OFTEN CALLED BY THE LABEL OF PAUL THE VENETIAN.... It is most difficult to separate we of the Higher Frequencies. We have a thrust, a talent given, if you will, toward focused purposes. As Morya represents most preciously the 'will' of God, Lanto the 'wisdom' of God—I, Paul, will focus on the element of 'love' and spirit discernment.

"I come on the comfort vibration of what we call the 'pink' frequency. My talents have long been in artistic perceptions and projections. I have been accused of heresy in some of my works upon your place, but so be it. Man wants his GOD to be in his own

**69**

image. 'Tis not the way it is.

"Please do not confuse my terminology of love with what thee defines as 'love'. Myself and the brotherhood with whom I serve, of the Third Ray, are not idle dreamers of poetry and sounds of harmonious music. Ah, would it be that it could be so! We are quite pragmatic of the way of the Holy Spirit. It is through the beauty and purity of the Third Ray through which the wondrous qualities of diplomacy, patience, tact, arbitration, unity, brotherhood, culture, beauty and the perfecting of the 'heart' are made manifest."

Speaking symbolically, yet elevating to a magnificent spiritual plateau, familiar terms which the so-called Christian religions toss around in a more literal interpretation, Paul explains the fundamental qualities of his pink-rose frequency thusly: "Through the Blood (ruby red) of the Universal Christ, and the Body (crystal white) of that wondrous Christos, this pink-rose flame is birthed. It is through this pulsation that externalizes the Divine Plan in the chalice of man's being, through that Body and Blood of the Universal Christos.

"As we move forward, there will be much a-do about the threefold flame: the Heart, the Head and the Hand...." That is, he refers respectively to the motivating energies which power Feeling, Thinking—and the most difficult of all: getting up from one's seat and actually DOING!

Paul then goes on to explain his focus on our behalf: "I am most devoted to the perfecting of the souls and the development of the Intuitive and Creative faculties of the heart. I will most wish to be called into thy planning with thy architectural designs and beauteous buildings. I work most closely with my brothers of the First and Second Rays in bringing together the Will of God and the Wisdom of God into at-one-ment. We will work through the 'science' of Love as it applies to every challenge faced today— from terrorism, pornography, drug abuse, economic debacle, to nuclear war. We will transmute through the Violet Flame [*of Saint Germain, see Chapter 14*] in mergence to face even the cataclysms to come forth, and even through the 'putting down' of the Divine Female (including the Feminine Ray) in both sexes and little children. So be it.

"I also tell you to 'try [*test with caution*] the spirits, whether they come of God' for many false prophets are come into the world. The 'Holy Spirit' will teach thee how to exorcise those spirits which are not of God. Aton, as Brother Hatonn, has done well in his training of thee ones, but ones tend to forget with far quicker efficiency than the learning thereof.

"We will give thee much more assistance in the harnessing of these God forces. Ye must establish a strong heart-tie to the beloved Sacred Heart of thy Creator-Creation Source, that ye are never caught 'sleeping'. Ye will bind the evil spirits in the name 'I AM THAT I AM IN THE RADIANCE OF THE SACRED CIRCLE CHRISTOS'. Utilize the strength given unto thee by thy superior Commander-In-Chief, Esu Jesus Sananda—Standing Bear of the Wakan Tanka—through the blessed truths brought by White Buffalo Calf Woman unto the early tribes. These were brought forth in balance and harmony, and gifted in abundance from Source unto thee."

Paul also reminds us of a very important, yet often overlooked, matter of growth and responsibility—to share our UNIQUE PERSONAL contribution in this time of major planetary transition: "Ones upon thy place plead worthlessness and that only a 'few' have been given certain gifts of beauty and talent. Nay, not so! Locked within the being of EVERY incarnate soul is a talent unique unto thee. It can manifest as a painting, music, invention, or the special gift of 'giving'—as in thy Mother Theresa. Most of you have hidden it away, in thy insecurity, and have refused to bring it forth. Ye shall overcome. It matters not what 'level' of perceived enlightenment ye may be. Ye can grow; YE MUST GROW! For when ye come right down to the truth of it, the fires of creativity held within the force-field of man (any HU-man) determine what he can accomplish in his earthly span of perceived 'time'.

"Most dissipate their creativity in lust for money and things of worldly value, fill their thrust with worldly desires and fleshly pleasures and pursuits, and in acquisitiveness that is the disease of the human race. Ye will be assisted in exercising the mind in nonattachment and impersonalization, that ye may move from the traps of worldly bindings which destroy thee. So be it.

"I come to work with thee that ye might learn of thy own soul's psychology, for ye are lost in confusion in the learning. Be patient in thy learning and communion with US, as we move more closely into thy spaces.... More as definition of my vibration, I am referred to as the Cohan of the Third Ray, with emphasis upon love, creativity, and beauty. In other words, these are the areas of my, let us say, expertise.

"Creativity and beauty cannot actually exist without the presence of love; therefore, let us consider love.

"Love IS the flowing essence, the ephemeral quality of God. As it is the movement of the wind and the flowing of water, it requires the greatest of discipline to be able to retain—to have and to hold that love that is so tender, so gentle, and yet the ultimate expression of creative 'fires'. Those who are the greatest artists, poets, and musicians, who use the flame of love to implement an idea of God, are those who have the greatest discipline— discipline of self, energies of self, of life, even of time and space.

"I come, then, to bring unto you an understanding of this discipline so that you will understand that discipline is not something to be feared, but rather that discipline is the Law, the fulfillment of love. Discipline is a grid, a forcefield that is necessary in order to have the flow of love and to retain the flow of love.

"Where there are lives which are undisciplined, love departs; love compromised and perverted is lost. Where energies in motion are undisciplined, where there is not a chalice that can contain the liquid fire of love, mankind then loses of that love.

"To be happy for eternity means that love must be ensconced in a discipline that requires the discipline of self. To continue to receive love, ye must give of it. Know that as you discipline your energy, your supply, your expression, the hours of your day, your service to life, you are increasing your capacity to release love. The more you are disciplined, the stronger are the grids of consciousness. To have a strong consciousness, as strong sinews, enables you to balance megatons of the Light-force that you call love.

"On Terra, however, there is such difficulty on the part of lifestreams in their handling of the currents of love that many who should be master of the flame of the Third Ray are now in states of disintegration and their minds are filled with foul spirits and the mutterings of those spirits. This state of being in degradation results from having perverted that wondrous flame....

"For out of love is the fulfillment of the Mother flame of every invention, every aspect of Divine Reality that is waiting to be lowered into manifestation through the creative genius of many among you and many among mankind.... People feel a sense of worthlessness and that only a few have abilities for invention and creativity....

"Before I take leave, I would please speak of the 'STEP *NOT* TAKEN'—the step contemplated and often resisted, that is, until resistance itself becomes such an ingrained habit that ye are chained into immobility by thy own bindings. The next step, then, becomes self acceptance. Ye find excuses such as: 'Well, this is the way I am, and people will just have to accept me this way. This is my level of service. This is all I will give and others can give the rest.'

"Well, the fallacy in this is not self-knowledge and defining one's potential, for it is good to understand one's capacity and not to commit more than one can. But the fallacy is, beloved ones, the sense that one can rest on any plateau or arrive at a set of definitions for one's life or personality, seal them with a sealing of wax, and lock without key, make the imprint of the seal of oneself and say: 'As it is, so it is. So be it. I have spoken.'

**"Listen carefully, chelas, as this is the trap! It is the HUMAN EGO that would hold you captive and imprison the soul to a certain level of the 'knowns' where ye feel ye have security and stability. But, unknowingly, it would keep the soul there, and it would convince the soul that no other progress can, OR SHOULD, be made, and that its current level of attainment is sufficient unto all things. Nay, nay, nay!**

**"Let us take utmost care that self-assessment does not result in the inertia of 'rest' and that such inertia is not confused with the state of nirvana. The Higher States of Consciousness are those of 'MOVEMENT' and 'ACTION' even within the heart of absolute 'rest'.**

"My service to life, and unto you ones, is to show the way of Love, especially to coalesce the teachings of the Lords of the First and Second Rays. This will thrust ye further, then, into the heart of the Crystal Core, the fiery core of Serapis Bey (the Lion of the Rays), and then going forth therefrom to bring into precipitation and merging of the Sixth and Seventh Rays of Transmutation. Love is the key element, without which ye are trapped. So be it and I place my seal upon this portion....

"I take my leave in humble appreciation and leave a cloak of Love about thee that ye might find peace in thy journey.... Adonai, precious chelas. I look forward in great joy to sharing again with thee ones. I AM PAUL, IN LOVE AND ETERNAL SERVICE UNTO THE ONE LIGHT AND UNTO THEE. AHO."

# CHAPTER ELEVEN

# Serapis Bey, The Architect

## The Fourth Ray

The Ascended Master of the Fourth Ray, or Spectral Aspect, of Creator's One White Light, is known as Serapis Bey. His energy is generally associated with the clear crystal "color" of purity and directness of purpose due to his being the central balancing "fulcrum" position to those of the three Color-Ray Masters on either "side" of him, in terms of their frequency and energy focus of intent. His designation as "The Architect" symbolizes his merging of energies which manifest as The Sciences on one side, with energies which manifest as The Arts on the other. Here is a "large", no-nonsense "character" who gets right to the point, and who prefers the most direct route in handling every challenge, albeit with an expansive and infectious sense of humor that can only come from a base of true humility.

In *The Rainbow Masters*, Serapis Bey offers the comparison that: "I am often referred to as the Commander Hatonn of the Seven Rays! I represent the disciplinarian, task master, lion— 'shout loudly and push around a big stick'. Knowing Hatonn as ye do, I think you have already discounted the words as being quite tainted in exaggeration. It is that I, like him, believe one should get what one requests: hard work, truth, and a mighty kick to the rear areas that move thee along thy path!

"When I was a student (chela) in decision about which Ray I would serve and focus my efforts into—what Ray I would preserve in the Office of Preserver of Life—I meditated and contemplated all, but came to the Light of 'Purity'. I then figured, master of geometry that I was: 'The shortest distance between two points, point A and point B, is Purity.' Therefore, 'Purity' I shall be! I shall take the 'direct' path.

"I shall always give thee directness—'bottom line' thee calls it. I shall effort at relieving thee of the 'mush' of thy self-indulgence. If that be a Spartan trait, so be it. I was a Spartan upon thy plane. I was Leonidas (meaning, Son of the Lion), King of Sparta. Well, so be it. I am often referred to as 'the lion'—not so much from ferocious terror that I bring forth, but I suspect 'tis more that I 'growl' a lot.

"At any rate, I chose (and choose yet) the direct path. Purity reflects the Crystal Light, direct fragment of Father-Mother Source. Did I set myself above my brothers who chose the colored fragments? Oh no, just needed to jump in and get on with it, I suppose. I decided that, if 'Ascension' is the intent (which it must surely be), then I would go as directly to that point as possible, as rapidly as possible. Well, even old souls get their lessons, and I most surely got mine. But, so be it. I most surely know all about the Ray of Purity and Ascension."

In the sincere quest for the clarity of the direct path, Serapis Bey will be the Master most likely to cause the seeker to confront what is truly Real, as well as separate that from what is Unreal. This is becoming an increasingly complicated issue in these latter days of the 20th century. After all, how many of us could actually discern if what we were watching on television last night, on the so-called news, was a real Space Shuttle docking maneuver or yet another Hollywood-type fabricated pageant put on display to advance some political agenda? Modern technology has been calculatingly directed to provide so many means of distraction, complication, and confusion that were not a part of our grandparents' world, that the goal of discerning what is Real versus what is Unreal is a difficult task indeed.

And because of all this external chaos constantly bombarding us, the internal imperative to know and focus upon what is Real versus what is Unreal takes extra effort. From an internal perspective, we are basically attempting to sort what is of Lighted God Source from what are conjurings of the human ego as reactions from doubting fear or inflated pride, as well as what are simply distractions thrown across one's path by the dark forces. After all, such tricks have worked quite well for centuries!

The disciplinarian side of Serapis Bey becomes quite evident when he admonishes: "When ye work with me, ye must know something: I do not allow of one to simply up-and-leave a crisis, a circumstance, or an individual who is not to one's liking. One must stand, face, and conquer one's own carnal mind and misqualified energy by disciplining one's consciousness in the art of non-reaction to the human creation of others, even as one learns how NOT to be dominated or influenced by one's own human reaction. When ye master these things (MASTER these things!), then ye shall be given the alchemical secrets of the 'TREE OF LIFE'—when thee REALLY grows weary of the world of desire, have subdued the passions and polarizations, conceding only to 'be still and know that I AM GOD'.

"When this is done in perfection, then ye will get thy Ascension papers and Ascension bag and we will charge of it to thy Gold Mastercard!

"Thee will never make it through 'pride'. Ye will make it only through humility—Divine Humility—which is much different than proclaimed 'humility'. There is an act of 'false pride' which manifests 'false humility' and causes people to appear humble whereas, in reality, they REEK WITH PRIDE. This false humility is often manifest in subtle ways and it is a mockery of the real. I

urge upon all, then, that thee seek the banner of Divine Humility....
Ones will stay on the merry-go-round until these things are
LEARNED.... If ye spend of thy time learning the lessons which
will be brought unto thee, thee will have glory...."

Continuing Paul's theme in the previous chapter, Serapis Bey
explained: "I long for a better language for thee of the
English-speaking sectors, for 'love' has become such a tritely used
term. Yet it is the experience of love (agape)—not romance of
lovers, but abiding, non-defaulting love which underlies all progress
to higher-frequency existence...there is no other word to use and no
other way to get where you are going.... Ye must face the question:
how great is thy love? How badly do thee wish to participate in a
transition—of a birthing of a planet into a higher dimension, the
fulfilling of a cycle? Ye have to confront to what extent ye are
willing to give up the course of self-centered illusion to accomplish
insight necessary to participate with thy Unseen Brotherhood. There
is a key in the disciplines to Higher Consciousness. The key is not
to become entangled in the labyrinth of human questioning, nor in
the fears and the doubts and the specters-of-the-night which
haunt that labyrinth.... Let God be the Light.... Ye carry within, the
unlimited power of the universe and ye hide away from Him. Gain
'passion' in the loving of that wondrous Source...."

"Ponder upon the lessons herein, not on whether or not of the
source. Ah yes, we are REAL, and we come to assist and share.
But, turned away, we go away—free will choice of thine own gift.

"SO BE IT.... I STAND IN HUMILITY IN HIS [Aton's]
SERVICE AND IN THE SERVICE OF THE GREAT AND
WONDROUS SACRED CIRCLE OF INFINITY [Esu Sananda],
THE COHAN [teacher] OF THIS HUMBLE CHELA [student].

"I PLACE MY SEAL UPON THESE WORDS.... IN TOTAL
LOVE AND TRUTH, BALANCE AND HARMONY, I TAKE
LEAVE. I AM THAT I AM. I AM SERAPIS BEY."

# – CHAPTER TWELVE –

# Master Hilarion

## The Fifth Ray

Picture yourself sitting on a tree stump, surrounded by a countryside pasture in the late springtime or early summertime, awash in that soothing yet vivid green of freshly awakened trees and vibrant grasses, and you will have attuned to the frequency of the Ascended Master known as Hilarion of the Fifth Ray, the Emerald Ray of Healing. Since true healing has a lot to do with forgiveness of ourselves and others, it should come as no surprise that Master Hilarion's main focus is toward awakening our understanding of this most important matter. Also, since healing—or a state of health— is also a matter of attunement with and proper understanding of the Forces of Nature, Master Hilarion is also a Guide to those who have a genuine passion for Science. There can be no more important matter to attend than the true healing of one's own personal being, for in doing so one more closely acknowledges the God-force within and thus one is able to radiate more of His energy outward to others.

In *The Rainbow Masters*, Hilarion says: "As the merging time has come, we shall all be meeting of ourselves. We have ALL experienced in many times, many places. But—there is always the 'one' that imprints all our existence above all others.

"I ascended as Saint Hilarion, and therefore bear the label of same. It is my work with my Master Teacher, Esu (the Christed Perfect Circle without beginning or end), that touched my soul into the forever of infinity....

"Man needs the example of imperfection, that he can relate to perfection. Do not suddenly sit on thy pedestal and proclaim achieved perfection. Seek, rather, to be perfected by that Wondrous Energy that comes from Perfection. As you are perfected within, the Light will radiate without. Know perfection as the graces of the Great Spirit, and seek them.

"Judge not how far thy brother has progressed; look within at thy own degree of progress and move ever forward. Wrap thyself in the protection of that Perfection, that the evil brotherhood is kept without. Darkness cannot invade thy presence in Light, unless thee allow of it....

"Ours is of another mighty task: to heal of the wounds and the crippling circumstances wrought upon this Holy Place. It is the greatest glory to work hand-in-hand with our beloved Masters and our most revered Sacred Angelic Energies in communion and harmony with the very Christos himself....

"Healing must come, also, from Truth in the Holy Name. It also must come from that God-self within the one stricken. It must come through the 'mind'. It can 'only' come through the mind, so better ye ones who would heal, learn to contact and work with the portion of mind that literally 'controls'—that which is beyond the consciousness.

"There are lessons on thy plane which can be given by very learned Masters of the art. These are not removed from thee, but within thy group. So be it. We will be speaking more on these matters, for healing will be integral to our success. What have we done if we create a place to be inhabited by crippled energies?

"It has naught to do with 'bodies'. A body can be handicapped—a 'crippled' body is very sad indeed. Illness and crippled states are sentences passed out by the 'Judge' within self. Ye cannot help of it in thy consciousness, for ye are being the 'perfect prisoner'—serving thy sentence in good behavior.

"To be free, thee must set of thyself free. Refuse longer, the sentence—pronounce thyself having 'served' the 'warden' long enough and remove the binding shackles. I can tell of the 'how'; ye must unlock the door and come forth.

"Ye are my precious ones, thee and others such as thee, who will carry this glorious banner beyond the gates and set up the City of Light. We of the Realms of Glory will walk every step of the way with thee. We will carry thee if thee stumbles, and pick thee up if ye fall....

"The alternative to this responsibility is devastation upon this magnificent garden [*Earth*]. Let us bear of our responsibilities in magnificence that we may stand tall at the mirror of our God and pronounce our job well done and our performance pleasing.

As the Master Teacher of Healing, Hilarion has this to say about the subject, from *The Rainbow Masters* Phoenix Journal:

"Wholeness is a concept which is required as you pursue thy path—especially the path of 'healing'. 'Healed' means 'in wholeness', and you cannot have a 'whole' in 'partial-ness'. It requires skillful practice to master the art, just as an artist must practice first with the brushes in clumsy strokes until perfection produces the beautiful reflection on the canvas.

"It is incorrect, beloved ones, to wait for some future nebulous time when you think, by some miracle, that suddenly, with one sweep, you shall step forth and speak the word of healing—and at that moment you will be transformed into the magnification of the Christ.

"Healing comes as you apply yourself, day by day, to the invocation, the calling forth of the Healing Ray, the garnering of that Ray in your aura and in the chalice of your consciousness, and then the application of that Ray as you are called upon in the hour of crisis or need for one another.

"Another incorrect concept is that you are NOT in need of

healing. You 'seem' to be 'well' and functioning, and therefore you perceive 'all is well'. Precious ones, until the hour of Wholeness, of cosmic integration, you are less than whole, and therefore you require healing. Each and every one of you, each hour of the day, can therefore practice the fiats of the Christ.

"Go back and study the words of the Great Teacher. Study his words. Use the fiats that he used to make men whole. First he would usually remind them that their transgressions were forgiven, that they might forgive themselves. Thee must forgive self, for all states of imperfection of self are wrought upon self in some means or manner as a result of self punishment for perceived 'sins'. You must realize that healing is, first and most critically, an action of THE MIND—the subconscious mind that harbors thy instructions for actions performed by self and consciousness. It sounds as if it is a great difficulty? Nay—simple, simple in Truth!

"Why bother with the healing of the consciousness and the human form? Ye will just be changing dimensions into wholeness, will thee not? Nay, absolutely not! Can you function without a physical form in this octave? Of course not! Would you, then, be elsewhere? Perhaps, but your mission would not be fulfilled. Thus a return, once again—another descent of your soul energy into a physical form might be required, should you pass off lightly the calling of your present position in the world arena.

"Now, heed carefully: having a physical form partially dedicated to Truth and partially involved in the world of the senses and relationships of controlling nature, is not as the Masters have intended that you should be. You have accepted a mission and it cannot be 'sometimes'. It has to be ALL times or the work will not be finished in a 'timely' manner. So be it. I would wish that it be otherwise; it is not otherwise.

"I, Hilarion, place my own energies at thy disposal, to help thee find and hold thy way in Truth...."

# CHAPTER THIRTEEN

# Lady Nada

## The Sixth Ray

This most soft and gracious energy, Lady Nada, is the Ascended Master of the Sixth Ray or Aspect of Creator's One White Light. Lady Nada is most often called upon to help with the cultivation of selfless service, of devotion, to support those asking for a strengthening of commitments made from the Higher Self, to help those seeking to perfect the gift of Unrestricted Giving that truly allows ones to "get out of their own way" and "fill in for God" where needed in given situations. This concept of acting as the hands and feet of God is a recurring theme among the urgings of these Teaching Masters.

In *The Rainbow Masters*, Lady Nada refers to herself thusly: "I come in the chosen Sixth Ray of refraction. My aspect is most pleasured within the Third Ray, the pink, loving warmth of the Third Ray of Divine Love.

"I work in service where I am most needed, me and my chelas. Also, most words regarding myself, and my brothers, have been colored by the receiving person's perception of how we 'should be'. YE ALL FORGET THE MOST IMPORTANT POINT OF ALL: WE HERE SPEAK OF 'ASPECTS'. IN THE HIGHER REALMS, MY CHILD, THERE IS NOT MAN OR WOMAN. GOD SOURCE IS NEITHER MAN NOR WOMAN. *GOD IS!*

"Only in thy frailty are thee man or woman, hiding the aspect that displeases thee. YE ARE MAN *AND* WOMAN—EACH

AND ALL OF THEE! BOTH, HOPEFULLY BROUGHT INTO PERFECT BALANCE, THAT YE CAN FUNCTION IN THY 'CHOSEN' EXPERIENCE."

Her lessons are often those of balancing the currents of emotional energy within each of us. For example, she teaches: "Let this be thy lesson this day: KNOW THYSELF. FIRSTLY, KNOW THYSELF! BE YE MALE OR FEMALE, COME TO BALANCE WITH THYSELF.

"FACE OF THY RESENTMENTS. BRING THEM FORTH TO COMMUNICATE WITH ONES WHO CAUSE THEE THY PERCEIVED RESENTMENTS. THEN RELEASE THEM TO THE COSMOS that ye might go forth in total harmony and get of thy work accomplished....

"I was most active in the time of Atlantis, with you of my brothers. It, like Lemuria, was a time of beauty, of seeing man grow and blossom and then reach a peak and turn to the darkness within himself. I was tending of the flame, let us say, of Love, housed within the then-called, Temple of Love, there in the greatest city of Atlantis.

"I served the Third Ray, for my thrust was, even then, the healing of Earth's evolvement course, which thy Jesus has said is the fulfilling of the law of karma. So be it. 'Tis what I did at that time. DOES THE EARTH NOT NEED OF HEALING AND NURTURING MORE THAN EVER IN EXISTENCE OF MANIFEST FORM?

"You are now striving for, let us name it: selfless service. This state of selflessness must be achieved or you cannot fulfill of thy mission. To know when ye have become selfless is to not be aware of the choice of selflessness. By this I mean that the natural course of your life is always the preferring of the love of God, the service of that God incarnate. To be aware of self, its pleasures, its privileges, its preferences, and then to MAKE A

CHOICE TO FOREGO THAT SELF, IS A STEP ON THE PATH of selflessness which must indeed be taken.

"Once you have reached that center of balance, you are no longer aware of choosing between self, the Real Self, and the cast-aside NON-SELF.

"It seems a contradiction: 'Love thyself, honor thyself as God, love neighbors as self'— and then 'cast aside self'.

**"Nay, for our mission requires Self to function 'automatically' as the hands, heart, and head of the unseen Teachers—wherever thee are needed, whenever required— filling in for God, and therefore supplying each aspect of the Christos Sacred Circle in which someone may be lacking, for the ultimate mastery of the transition of this garden into her ultimate perfection. Ye saw, ye came, and ye shall prevail."**

In this next revelation of another of her talents, Lady Nada seems to share an endeavor with Commander Korton of the "Upper Management" team. That is: "It is said I carry and bring gifts of diverse kinds of 'tongues' and interpretation of those 'tongues'. Too much mush in the terminology. I master the nuances of vibration in the Rays, and the almost infinite combinations of the WORD as released through the varied HU-man vortices. Not so impressive in terminology, but accurate. As pertains to HU-man, Divine, and Angelic tongues—these gifts involve the mastery of speech, communication, and the delivery of the WORD. If there is lacking in even one aspect of the afore named, all will fail...."

In addition to the communications-expertise side of Lady Nada, her nurturing aspect is revealed as she cautions us about the care of children: "The worth of the individual as the potential to be God-in-manifestation is incalculable. Its violation at any level is fraught with far-reaching consequences, as Esu Jesus, the Christed Circle warned, to any who offend even one of these little ones. Thus, tenderly sponsor the world's children, individual by individual, often in answer to their prayers, or cries of anguish in abandonment.

"I have legions of angels who personally attend the little ones and the youth—but they must be called in. If the child cannot call—ye must ask in behalf of that tiny being. 'Tis thy ACCEPTED DUTY to do so...."

Continuing the theme of Paul and Serapis Bey, Lady Nada shared her views on a matter we all can relate to: "I, too, had to learn the Path of Love with the great Ascended Masters. I also learned that everyone who goes forth to serve has moments of self-doubt or thinks that, after all of their efforts, their works are not too good, or that no one will want them, or believe them, or that no one will appreciate of their talent. There is a moment of total self-blindness when an individual may actually make a choice NOT to go forward with their accepted work. This has a very difficult impact on those ones who have depended upon that one to fulfill his or her task. The days grow short upon thy place as ye know it; ye are in the days of decisions and action. These are days when ye must stand strong lest ye be pulled down.... It serves ye ones well to remember thy talent in the serving as the 'mother'—the nurturing nature of Mother Creation which abides within ALL beings, male and female, for there is no difference in the realms of Higher Understanding. No difference...."

"I leave thee in love and nurtured by the eternal flame of the Sixth Ray of Understanding all in all. I am greatly blessed for the allowance of serving with thee ones along this journey. I place my seal upon these words, that they be brought forth in truth and remain ever in truth. I salute thee ones for thy accepted burdens in such a darkened density of existence. We are ever at thy side.

"I AM THAT I AM, LADY MASTER NADA OF THE RAY OF THE SIXTH REFRACTION OF THE CENTRAL CRYSTAL SOURCE OF ALL LIGHT. SO BE IT AND AMEN."

# CHAPTER FOURTEEN

# Violinio Saint Germain

### The Seventh Ray

Here is one of the more publicly known of the Ascended Masters. His is a passionate and animated nature highlighted by a personal concern for and stewardship over the great experiment in freedom we recognize as the United States of America.

There has long been a story circulating around that Germain was the "mystery man" standing up on the balcony of the then-called Pennsylvania State House (later known as Independence Hall) in Philadelphia, who seemed to come out of nowhere, gave an impassioned speech ending with the urging, "Sign! Sign!" and then disappeared, just as abruptly and unusually, when the Founding Fathers were standing around, in great fear, about to take the irrevocable plunge into actually SIGNING the *Declaration of Independence*. These ones had a sense of the price they were likely to end up paying for Freedom, and with few exceptions the price ended up being an even heavier toll on their lives, their families, and their property than they thought would be the case.

From a more spiritual viewpoint, Germain is known as the Master of the Seventh Ray, or Spectral Aspect, of Creator's One White Light. His is the potent Violet Ray of Transmutation, of changes born from the passion of soul desire and earned completion of one phase of a thrust, and now on into the next. In that respect, there is strong coupling with Master El Morya and his "taking the first step" focus of the First Ray—as an old growth-challenge cycle is completed and a new cycle begins. Moreover, there are higher aspects of what we would recognize as "ceremony" associated with the art and science of transmutation, and it is our cultivation and elevation of this domain of ceremony which are also aspects of Germain's teaching duties.

In *The Rainbow Masters,* Germain says: "I head up the program for the thrust of the Seventh Ray, for it is the Transmuting Ray. I am passionate about it, unbending regarding its use for purity, Truth AND FREEDOM—FREEDOM OF THY GOD SELF, IN THE SERVICE OF THE CHRISTOS, WHICH IS GOD—PURE AND SIMPLE: GOD FREEDOM EXPRESSED IN MANIFEST FORM IN THEE AND IN ME....

"If ye wish to sum the measure of my existence in all prior times, please let it be said, 'He lived to make men free'....

"In all my times upon thy place, I have sought to stand squarely on a platform of basic human rights for a responsible, reasoning public education in the principles of liberty and equal opportunity for all. I have efforted to teach thee ones to espouse your inalienable DIVINE RIGHT to live life according to your highest conception of GOD. No right, however simple or basic, can long be secure without the underpinnings of the Spiritual Graces and the Divine Law that instills a compassionate righteousness in the exercise thereof. Always I have efforted to make thy country [*United States of America*] a fortress against ignorance and superstition, where Christ achievement could blossom, and devotion to THE ONE could prosper in the quest for the Holy Truth (Grail)....

"I have always efforted at being an immortal spokesman for your scientific, religious and political liberties. I believe that humanity shall accept, as an axiom for its conduct, the principle for which I have laid down my life: the right to investigate. It is the credo of free men—this opportunity to try, this privilege to err, this courage to experiment anew.

"We scientists of the human spirit shall experiment, experiment, experiment, ever experiment. Through centuries of trial and error, through agonies of research, let us experiment with laws and customs, with money systems and governments, until we chart the one true course....

"Today...we see the cycles of Earth's returning karma reach a mounting crescendo, wherein the four sacred freedoms are threatened, even unto annihilation. Let us now see what we may accomplish for our beloved Terra Maka (Grandmother, Beloved Mother) and for our brothers and sisters on Earth plane, with the renewed opportunity of working as a united ONE with our Cosmic Brethren and our merged Higher Energies. Precious ones, we have vowed and are committed to be victorious in this age—AND SO WE SHALL!

"In this very time of thy calendar, we will be given, once again, a way to continue a new dream. Ye will be given a 'road map' back to the stars and ye will see the star people come out of the illusion of the two-legged form and into their actual, as the ancients word it: 'Great Sleeper-Dreamer' form.

"Totally enlightened Masters will come into thy spaces. YE SHALL NOTE, TOO, THE LEGEND OF THE SECOND COMING OF THE CHRISTOS ENERGY is destined for thy imminent 'time'...."

Expanding on the love theme by Paul, Serapis Bey, and Lady Nada, Germain says: "Let the great and sacred circle of our oneness and our love cancel out all division, all misunderstanding, all ignorance, and every false testimony, as in the case of the blind men and the elephant—all giving varied reports of the same spectacle, but never arriving at the point of what was beneath their senses.

The eyes that see are only a mirror of what thy heart and soul sees. Always look with thy eyes from the perspective of thy heart.

"I call your attention to that point, for centered in your heart, which is becoming my heart day by day, you can see all things as they are.... Behold, I make all things new by the flame of the heart, by the vision of the heart, by the wisdom of the heart that is the endless stream of the endless Source....

"Beloved ones, the reward of love is great. However, those who deserve it often do not receive it because they are the ones, the busy ones, working and serving. They often do not take of the time to be quiet and receive. It is most important to allow receiving. Always be at work to enlarge thy aura of Light that ye can be in the abundant receiving....

"SO BE IT. I GO FOR THE MOMENT, BUT THERE WILL COME FORTH MORE, MORE, AND MORE. BLESSINGS UPON THEE ONES WHO TOIL AT THE BEARING OF THE TRUTH AGAIN TO THIS BELOVED PLACE FOR THY BROTHERS, THAT THEY MIGHT CONFRONT THEIR INDIVIDUAL DIVINE COURSE. THEE ONES ARE SET SAIL ON A PATH OF RED [*this is a symbolic Native American term for 'success through dedicated action', not of bloodbath or slaughter as one may be inclined to guess from our modern, twisted world of experience*], UNTO GLORY!

"I, GERMAIN, OF THE SEVENTH, THE VIOLET, RAY DO SET FORTH MY SEAL UPON THESE WORDS, THAT THEE SHALL KNOW ME AND YE SHALL RECEIVE IN TRUTH. IN THE RADIANCE OF THE MIGHTY I AM PRESENCE, I LEAVE MY CLOAK OF TRANSMUTING ENERGY ABOUT THEE, THAT THEE WILL FIND PEACE AND RENEWED FAITH, THAT WE CAN FINISH OUR MISSION. SO BE IT AND BE IT SO THIS DAY!"

Now do you see why I felt inadequate to the task of introducing these Formidable Teachers?!  Note that there are seven from the realm of "Upper Management" and seven "Rainbow Masters".  All of the passages they asked me to share with you have some points in common, or otherwise overlap in complementary ways, displaying a combined purpose that weaves a tapestry of great insight and compassion for the human condition at this time on planet Earth. And yet—all of these introductory portraits (as well as what you are about to read in Part II) also exhibit their Author's unique personality and style—or "color"—to put it in a metaphorical way.

Which brings me to the choice of cover art for this volume. Special thanks must go to a wonderful "hands-on" learning center for kids of all ages called The Exploratorium, located in San Francisco.  They are responsible for the superb photograph of an actual prism in action.  No simplified line drawing or cutesy artist's rendition or trite cartoon work here—this is the real thing!  The subtlety of detail should give away that fact to the observant eye (or maybe to the optically knowledgeable eye).

This choice of cover art is not just pretty, for it carries a deeper, symbolic message too.  Notice, first, that the "Light" emerges out of the "darkness of the void".  Shades, here, of the Creation Story in the biblical *Book of Genesis*.  Beyond that, however, we have the "One White Light" of God above, flowing down to we upon Earth, and being split up, in the process, into beautiful spectral aspects or colors which shine down upon and bathe our world with the energies of the Master Color Rays of en-Light-enment—as you have just been reading about in this Introduction.

I have a dear spiritual friend who has been "around the block" quite a few times in her now-almost-ninety years. She was, for much of that time, a very close personal and business associate of Elizabeth Arden, the cosmetics genius. I shall here simply refer to this one as Angela ("from the realm of the Angels"). Through eyes more free-flowing than what training has done to narrow my physicist's view, she saw in the cover graphic: "Beauty, Harmony and the colorfully Luminous Spirit of the soul." And also, the "Evolving of the soul from darkness into The Light" in all of its possibilities and varieties—the "full spectrum" of "colorful" souls, so to speak—which may actualize from God's thinking.

She also saw the light path not simply as my scientist's eye would read the action (from the top downward), but she also saw a flow in the OTHER direction, too. That is, she saw the rainbow spectrum as also symbolizing the rich variety of "color-full" created life "reaching straight for the Heavens, brightening", as our Earth-based cooperative effort merges back into that One White Light of God and Creator Source—thus completing the cycle of giving and regiving, so as to be given again.

And for you *really* enquiring minds, those other, seemingly spurious rays you see in the cover-art photo are what *really* happens (rather than what you usually see depicted in the "cartoon" drawings of too many so-called physics books these days) when an intense beam of white light is refracted AND reflected when intercepted by a prism. Not limited by physics, to Angela the blue-white hue exhibited by those reflected rays "denotes spiritual truth with enlightenment". Can't argue with that interpretation!

But what I am MOST reminded of, metaphorically, in looking at those extra reflected rays, is that the truth is always more complicated than the simplifications we are so often taught in school or we are otherwise so often inclined to adopt from ignorance and/or laziness. Now, that's a whole different subject, and yet it gets me back to some final thoughts to offer in closing out this quite-long-enough Introduction To The Authors:

Our world is indeed at a major crossroads at this time. WHILE our controlled media try their best to keep any truth from you, WHILE our educational systems have been programmed to dumb you down to the point of non-thinking, WHILE your rightful earnings have been systematically and escalatingly stolen from you, WHILE efforts have long been in place to get you malnourished and sick—and keep you there in the process of further draining your pocket book, WHILE elections are electronically fixed long before Election Day according to instructions from the highest levels of the dark elite controlling element in our society, WHILE cloning of soul-less robotic human duplicates has been a done technology for over thirty years now—utilized at the highest levels of political gamesmanship and brazenly paraded right before your eyes on each evening's television so-called "news" programs, and, while we're on the subject: WHILE most prefer to simply escape within their addiction to the dulling prattle of their vidiot boxes—yes, while all that and much, much more goes on—enough others nevertheless see, or better yet FEEL, changes on the way.

Some acutely sense bits and pieces of the larger planetary transformation ALREADY in motion. Late-night radio talk-show host Art Bell has even dubbed this feeling and phenomenon "The Quickening"—a most appropriate term (and his recent book title). And if you've just opened your eyes and you're hungry for another excellent "Earth-based" capsule summary about why it is our Elder Brothers need to be here at this particular time, go get brilliant author David Icke's book called: ...*And The Truth Shall Set You Free*. Or go back to the end of the Preface for information about acquiring the Phoenix Journals and the *CONTACT* newspaper.

No matter how you look at it (or try to run and hide from it), big changes are surely a-comin' fast—if for no other than very physics-oriented reasons having to do with the high-energy, high-frequency region of space which our planetary system is gradually approaching right now, and will most definitely pass through, that has been dubbed "The Photon Belt". Why do you think Esu "Jesus" Sananda said he would be back in 2000 years? He was well aware that the dark ones only had a certain while in which to continue to test us through wreaking their havoc. And then the you-know-what would hit the fan, so to speak, as the last days of the testing play out. That's what's happening now.

These incoming Photon Belt energies have a lot to do with all aspects of The Quickening. For instance, rarefying changes are occurring in the very substance of physical matter—including that physical matter which comprises our bodies and brains. These changes, in turn, will stimulate amazing, yet presently mostly latent, capabilities in mankind. Other changes must occur in Mother Earth, which will cause a lot more of what my then-little niece once most exquisitely called (just after a Los Angeles earthquake) the "sneezing" of Mother Earth, as she shudders and coughs to rid herself of man's poisonings and tamperings, and claims her rightfully earned, balanced, fourth-dimensional format.

BIG changes in our thinking are likewise inevitable—not only because long-hidden, mind-blowing information will be shattering previously held beliefs on all fronts, but also because man's newer (higher) perceptive capabilities will open him to more direct communion with (and thus transfer of information from) the Higher Lighted Teachers, such as those who contributed to this volume.

There's no way to stop it—and the major dark crooks know that. One way or the other, The Truth shall simply ALL, ALL, ALL come out! Good for us; bad for them.

Yes, the times they are a-changin'. Fast! And the ride will likely be a bumpy one. So gather around you your seat belts and shock absorbers and common-sense wits. And that's where the

Teachings collected herein come into the picture, for there are many an enquiring mind out there, awakening to "the smell of the coffee" and hungry for Guidance that truly feeds the spirit and points the way for each to assume THEIR driver's seat and make a difference. A wise friend of mine, who was for many years President of the University of Notre Dame, used to like to remind me that the true role of Higher Education was to teach a person HOW to think, not WHAT to think. And that motto, while sorely missing from most so-called Higher Education these days, is certainly a central theme of the Messages you are about to read herein.

Consider this as a final thought as you decide whether or not to proceed into the rest of this volume: you're driving down the highway in your cool convertible and the radio says you're going to hit a heavy rainstorm coming up as you enter the next town, several miles yet down the road.

Now, you can ignore the radio—after all, how REAL is that, really, for you can't SEE or HEAR radio waves, just their "translation" through a "receiver". And, beyond that, who believes weather reports or meteorologists anymore anyway?

Or—you can bother to pay close attention to what the weather reports have to say, pull over, put up the top, make sure your windows will roll up, and maybe even fill your gas tank and snack bag at that service station coming up, just in case things do get messy further down the road.

I know what I would do. How about you?

And so, in the spirit of that challenge, I am asked by the Master Teachers who have guided this Introduction to leave you with the following words from a gracious soul who helped MANY on this planet—and whose recorded legacy continues to do so, long after his physical death (from exhaustion, by the way, trying to console too many near the end of that abominable, dark-elite-instigated conflagration called World War II). This humble being, yet famous

"psychic", was known as Edgar Cayce, the "sleeping prophet".
He surely tapped the same Higher Realms as produced the Messages
that follow in this volume when, one day during a trance-state
"reading" (262-104), he so wisely instructed:

For as ye *apply* day by day what ye know,

then is the next step,

the next act,

the next experience,

shown thee.

Because thou hast then failed here or there,

do not say "Oh, I cannot—I am weak."

To be sure, thou art weak in self, but O ye of little faith!

For He is thy STRENGTH! *THAT* is Wisdom!

Let no one then again ever say "I cannot."

It's rather, if ye do, saying "I WILL not—I want MY way."

This is foolishness, and ye *know* The Way.

For He is Strength;  He is Love;  He is Patience;

He is Knowledge;  He is Wisdom.

Claim ALL of these, then, *in HIM!*

For He is in thee,

and the Father hath not desired that any soul should perish,

but hath prepared a way of escape,

a way of love,

of peace,

of harmony,

for every soul—

if ye will but claim same,

live same,

in Him.

# PART II

# The
# Messages

# CHAPTER FIFTEEN

# These Are Grand Times
# For Those Prepared

## *Ceres Anthonious Soltec*

### June 13, 1996

Be at peace. There is much going on this day and change is on the NEAR horizon for ALL. The Earth, as you call her, is about to convulse in her effort to find balance and peace. It is I, Toniose Soltec, here in Light, that you and others may see.

That which has been prophesied is at hand. You are in the Ending Times of the current cycle of humanity on that orb. This is a time when chaos reigns supreme, for the confusion of change is overwhelming to the masses.

All things continue in a revolving, evolving spiral of never-ending cycles of birth-growth-decay-rebirth. Out of the old harshness of chaos shall spring forth the peace and balance that you ones constantly seek.

These are grand times for experiencing. The Light shall reign supreme. The awakening masses shall overcome or succumb to their ignorance. It is always their choice.

You ask, "Why such a message at this time?"

Why indeed!

**This is the time for change. Nothing shall be the way it was. NOTHING!**

The past is gone; it only lives in memories. The past has been written and cannot be changed. Let go of the past, for it shall stand in the way of the future if you allow it to consume you.

Past friends and acquaintances shall make their own choices and be held responsible for their own condition. It is natural to want to awaken another, especially one for whom you care deeply. You must, however, allow each to grow at his or her own pace. THEY must make the effort. There shall be many a broken heart and much sadness for those souled beings who choose to remain in ignorance of spiritual truth.

Remember the past and learn from your mistakes, but do not try to live in the past, for it shall only serve to stagnate your personal growth. Learn from your past experiences. Forgive yourself for those mistakes you can consciously recognize—and move on.

Look forward to the future and create that which your heart desires. There is peace, balance, and joy out there for you. You must allow yourself to experience these things, else you shall surely miss them.

In the next few months many new energies (new to you in that "conscious" expression) shall be coming through to communicate with you ones. Always discern their messages, for names and labels are simply for your identification. You shall soon begin to FEEL the difference and come to know each by their energy pattern.

Much is heating up in the Pacific Northwest. Yes, Alaska is a warning to Japan, and Japan shall serve its wake-up call to the West Coast of the U.S. (How about with some incredible TSUNAMIS?!? Hummnn?)

*[Editor's note: Toniose is here referring to the recent large array of earthquake activity centered approximately midway along Alaska's Aleutian Islands chain. The largest of the quakes was eventually reported on the controlled news as a M7.7 and, via the Internet, by the University of Alaska's seismology laboratory, as M7.9, and occurred at 8:03 p.m. Sunday evening June 6, 1996.*

*This cluster of activity was located near the Adak Island area and this location is a convergent boundary between the Pacific and North American tectonic crustal plates. Between 11 p.m. that Sunday night, when first mention was made about the quake, and 3 a.m. Monday morning, I never heard the magnitude of this big quake mentioned in listening to at least a dozen news broadcasts on radio. It was skillfully and purposely and astonishingly left unmentioned—but they did warn of Tsunami wave activity all the way down to the coast of Northern California! Thus is the basis for Toniose's timely parenthetical warning above.*]

Dream time is long over and those still running around in La La Land shall wish they had awakened to find out what all the commotion was for. Indeed, the changes shall come "like a thief in the night" as far as the general masses are concerned.

But, for those who have heard the "alarm clock", you shall see much of what we of the Hosts of Lighted God have told you, time and time again, shall come to pass. There shall be much excitement for those of you who have prepared. God truly helps those of you who make efforts to help selves.

**Even if you do not notice all the subtle clues along the way, know in your heart that He is there and is helping you along your way. Pay attention to the seeming coincidences, for NOTHING HAPPENS BY CHANCE—especially now, and from here on out.**

Face your past fears and allow Lighted Truth to show you what the fears are. Know that you have nothing to fear if you be a Lighted Soul of Creator God, for in the Light you shall see and experience a glory beyond anything you can imagine in a third-dimensional, compressed existence of matter.

There may very well be confusion, even for those of you who scribe these messages, for you ALL doubt and cry out for balance.

You come from places where peace and balance is the normal

way of life and you long for the return home. For some of you it is out here among the stars. For others it may be a home world planet in a Pleiadean solar system. Each has their own preference. Many enjoy the variety of experience and do not stay in any one experience for too long.

Relax, my friend, I know you are not used to this type of writing. Yet, it is now time for you to experience same, for you are being prepared for greater tasks such as SPEAKING for we of the Hosts. You, along with some others of the Ground Crew, shall be called upon to speak to the masses. Do not be frightened; you happen to be quite experienced in this method of communication and shall come to remember this talent, as well as others. Be at peace. We shall end this now, for the distractions in your present environment [*an industrial chemistry laboratory*] are great.

Toniose Soltec to clear in the Most Radiant Light of Holy God, who guides the magnificent transformation now accelerating in your manifestation.

Salu.

# – CHAPTER SIXTEEN –

# Earthquakes
# And
# The Problem Of "Missing" Time

### *Ceres Anthonious Soltec*
### May 30, 1996

*Editor's note: Strictly speaking, the following writing should have been placed first, here in Part II, as Chapter 15, for chronological flow reasons. However, for reasons of better literary presentation, Soltec's June 13, 1996 writing precedes this one because it conveys a better introduction to this entire series of messages.*

*You see, They (upstairs) "pulled a fast-one" on us. Nobody (down here) realized these would be the beginnings of an entire series of instructional writings! Now, many months later, during the compilation of this volume, it became evident that a reversal in the order of the first two messages makes for a better read.*

Commander Ceres Anthonius "Toniose" Soltec present in the Light of Holy God of all magnificent Creation. As I write, through this translator and scribe, we of my Command are very busy monitoring the geophysical activities of Earth-Shan.

At this time you are experiencing a greatly stepped-up level of earthquake activity worldwide and, where appropriate, also stepped-up volcanic action, along all of the major fault lines dividing your various tectonic plates.

As a matter of most serious observation, we frequently call to your attention the actions around the Pacific Plate because, especially as concerns the stability of your West Coast of America, that is the "gear" driving the machinery which shall precipitate impending great change for the United States.

Before proceeding with a discussion of the current situation, I would like to refer back to a writing of mine, written through Dharma, from June 15, 1991—just to remind you for how long it has been that our lessons have been offered and mostly forgotten or ignored.

*[QUOTING:]*

As Hatonn told you in the past days—pay attention for there is massive movement in the entire circumference lip of the Ring of Fire (the Sea of Peace Ocean). I believe it is the Pacific Plate Tectonic, as you refer to it. Please note that Australia is NOT within those boundaries but is THE MOST IMPACTED by movement of the Pacific Plate. There is tremendous activity in the outreach portions of Australia and New Zealand.

Georgia (Soviet Union) is a different matter and is in established upheaval to cause the Soviet Union to remain united, for as the Russian Republic becomes republicanized, so will the other Bloc nations again rise up and Georgia is one which is already at a level of unacceptable restlessness. It is, of course, far more than that, but it is a most dangerous game played when you tamper with Mother Nature.

You people of Earth-Shan are either the most daring or the most foolish beings we have come upon in a very long time of traveling.

The primitive people of the Philippines are terrified, just as are the natives of Australia and New Zealand, for they know the underground is ready to "uncreate" those islands or project up the entire ocean floor—which is going to cause happenings like you can only hold in the imagining.  The atmospheric havoc is proof of that activity.

It is the location of Mt. Pinatubo that is most distressing to the Indians of the region, for it is a part of the predictions (clues) of changes which would come upon the people and the world (which, of course, to them IS the Philippines and little more).  The eruption could have been from Taal, Caniaon, Mayon and it would not have the same meaning as one which is dormant for centuries.

Now, please, look to Japan and the earthquakes and rumblings—this is NOT unusual for Japan, but you might well be seeing eruptions of those volcanos in Japan, also, within hours or days.  Whether or not you hear of it, there will be great numbers of temblors in the Aleutians and right down through your chain of volcanos in the North American continent and through the entire circle to the south.

Earth man can precipitate earthquakes but he cannot control the activities very well, of volcanos.  He can detonate high level nuclear explosions within the craters or from underground placement, but to cause activity in the mountain itself, there has to be a hole opened into the pressure caverns.  This is why eruptions mean far more to geologists of the observers in my geologic survey teams, than do all the earthquakes you can produce.

*[SUSPEND QUOTING]*

I have also chosen to example this particular writing from almost five years ago because of the teaching theme running through it that "all is connected to all"—that you cannot separate the earthquake or volcanic activities from the other shenanigans orchestrated by your would-be kings of darkness.  So, let us continue with this lesson.

*[RESUME QUOTING:]*

As you study the upheaval in Georgia, U.S.S.R., note its political proximity to both Turkey and Iran, the Black Sea and the

Caspian Sea and remember the trouble in Azerbaijan and Armenia, both bordering to the south and to the southeast. You ones must begin to look at the WHOLE and stop using the telescope attached to the kaleidoscope which simply blinds you through visions of colored glass.

The "state" of Georgia (U.S.S.R.), for instance, is a restless nation with many uprisings which have been quelled militarily— against the wishes of "Russia". Russia has over 146 million people to be reckoned with and Georgia has some 5.3 million to which the U.S.S.R. must account. Almost all the states of the Republic will side with Russia as the "party" grows stronger. Ah indeed, Yeltsin is a man with whom to be reckoned, and aid to little Georgia for earthquake relief may not be sufficient any longer.

Georgia can be most central in damage on an emotional level for it is in the western part of Transcaucasia and contains the largest manganese mines in the world. Well, what could that be worth? Lots! It is often a prime substance in the manufacture of steel, falling into the 6th octave periodic register of elements, falling into the same octave wherein argon is the seed, and running from fifth toward seventh includes potassium, calcium, scandium, titanium, vanadium, chromium, manganese and iron with cobalt on the cusp. So you see, you would have a much higher frequency, or "finer" steel than, say, vanadium or chromium. Lower in the octave you have argon, chlorine, sulphur, phosphorus, and silicon on the cusp. Moreover, manganese is a relatively low-frequency element and is utilized in producing low-frequency pulse beams. Indeed, the U.S.S.R. would not like to lose that commodity.

Further, Georgia is rich in timber resources and COAL mines. Basic industries are food, textiles, iron, steel, but it is resource for grain, tea, tobacco, fruits, grapes and other agricultural-related products. To maintain control, the U.S.S.R. MUST control at least Georgia, Armenia, Azerbaijan and especially the Ukrainian SSR. In the Ukrainian SSR, for instance, are almost 52 million people. Can you now see how frail a reed Mr. unpopular Gorbachev actually is, blowing in the winds of possibilities?

I recognize that I am a "geologist" by "trade" but my commission is to study your globe from that particular aspect within the "whole". I could recommend nothing more important to your PHYSICAL input than to get good reference material and KNOW YOUR WORLD. You ones of Earth do not even know your own bodies and almost NOTHING about your planet!

You speak of the "Ring of Fire" and yet you understand not the connections and why, for instance, eruptions in the Philippines are important! The Pacific Plate "generally" outlines the Ring of Fire, but oh, if you look no further, you are amiss in good judgment for there IS a Philippine Plate which has great impact, just as does the Indian Plate which encompasses Australia.

These particular plates are impacted greatly by the movement of the Pacific Plate. Note also that the coastal areas of the volcano chain and the major western [*United States*] coastal fault lines are within the North American portion of the American Plate, while areas of Central America and northern South America are in the Caribbean Plate. South America is in the southern portion of the American Plate.

Now, you have to look at the area of Soviet Georgia, which you will find in the Eurasian Plate, which is affected by movement in both the American, Philippine, and Pacific Plates. The magnificent Himalayas are the crumpled consequence, for instance, of an Indian Plate pushing northward into and under rigid Eurasia.

Do you begin to feel your education is lacking a bit of valid input? Precious brothers, you simply cannot expect to know nothing about your little world, and then expect to be accepted without limits within the universal cosmic order. You, as a species (civilization) of human physical beings, are still quite in your infancy. There is nothing "wrong" with that, it is just so unlikely that your ability, at this stage of development and knowledge, allows you to participate in the great Federation of the cosmic experience.

You grow technologically into inability to control or cope with that which you tinker. You will find your brothers in the cosmos will not be very accepting of your demands in a Council wherein you do not even know the tectonic plates of your own planet. And I promise you that the ones who develop the death rays and weapons do not know anything about the working order of your globe— much less do the politicians who control every facet of your existence in your physical experience....

**You see, we of the Command do not understand the insults to your intelligence which you not only tolerate but encourage. "Understand" is not a good word for use herein, for we DO understand what is happening and what is intended by your would-be king-masters, but our difficulty is the lack of initiative on the part of you-the-people to stand against the insults upon your experience.**

I believe it should not have to be from an alien being that you should be gaining your education regarding these matters—it should be from your learned teachers at your universities and kindergartens. DO YOU NOT REALIZE THERE IS AN ADULT WITHIN EACH OF YOU TRYING TO GET OUT?

Hatonn and Dharma are going to bring forth some very interesting information which might be worthy of your attention. You keep working with the thin person trying to get out from the overweight trap, the inner child coming into protection—NO, NO, NO! Within each is an ADULT trying to get past the whole lot of the garbage! Beyond the tending of teddy bears. I believe Hatonn will have you cuddle your *Constitution* and NOT your teddy bear and binkie. Haven't all of you cuddled with your binkie long enough??

When God says "come as children unto me", He doesn't mean with binkie and bunny. He means with curiosity, flexibility, and eagerness to come into KNOWLEDGE with Himself.   He cares not about your sexual or physical food preferences, nor other of the physicalness.   YOU MUST COME INTO KNOWING THAT ALL OF THOSE THINGS ARE OF THE FLESH-PHYSICAL EXPERIENCE AND YOU—*YOU*—WILL COME INTO MATURITY AND **KNOWLEDGE** OR YOU WILL LINGER WITHIN THAT SHROUD OF DISCONTENT AND RESTLESSNESS.   SO BE IT.

You-the-people are on the brink of allowing the puppet-masters to commit particle/atomic suicide of a planet.   Is it not time you gave up your binkie and stopped this insanity?

I see that I have outstayed my welcome and will, therefore, give my appreciation—with a reminder or two: Within the next few years of your counting, things are going to heat up from your own place (I DO NOT MEAN GLOBAL WARMING B.S.) and from your atmosphere.   You are going to have a lot of radioactive debris pouring back in on your orb and, if you don't get with the program and petition assistance, you are going to all get a very big hotfoot.

*[END OF QUOTING]*

Now, with that refresher lesson for foundation, let us take a brief look at relatively recent earthquake map data, first for the entire Pacific Plate, and then for Northern and Southern California of your United States.

We consider the exercise of looking over these maps not so much because there are any changes from what I have discussed in over five years of past lectures, but because so many of you plead with me for an update on the geophysical front.   Well, the same speeding train is still on the same crash course toward the same mountain side.   Nothing has changed, nor is likely to, in the solidifying probability-space for your orb.

Figure 1 [*see end of writing*] is from the May 19, 1996 issue of the superb publication called *Seismo-Watch Newsletter* (Advanced

Geologic Exploration, P.O. Box 18012, Reno, NV 89511; 702-852-0992) where the world map we are using shows earthquake activity for the time span of April 29 through May 5, 1996. Remember that the Pacific Plate is approximately framed on its east side by the Americas and on its west side by Japan and Indonesia. [*Editors note: While* Seismo-Watch *has indeed been a superb news source over the span of its relatively short existence, at this time publication is suspended for reasons that appear to have been precipitated to distract the author, one way or the other, from continuing to present what the elite would-be-kings would prefer to remain hidden. It's an old trick, but it works most every time!*]

Now, if we consider the Pacific Plate as a clock face, it is plain to see that from 11 o'clock, north of Japan, down through 7 o'clock, near New Guinea, a great deal of activity is occurring. In the time frame of this particular graphic, Alaska (at slightly past noon on our clock face) and the Americas (between 2 and 5 o'clock) are "relatively" quiet.

But such is only the sleeping calm before the abrupt storm which must occur as that massive plate continues its northwesterly journey with increasingly more deliberate motion. Study the map carefully to discern just how busy is Mother Earth's crustal skin in its attempts to equilibrate massive forces at work beneath her surface and within her circulatory system.

Figure 2 [*see end of writing*] is also from *Seismo-Watch* and covers approximately the same time span, specifically from April 25 through May 1, 1996. What I wish to call to your particular attention here is the greatly increased level of creep activity along the San Andreas Fault in the active segment that is south of, and then northward on up to, what I shall call the "triple-junction point" where the San Andreas is intersected by the bottom ends of the two dangerous East Bay faults, the Hayward and Calaveras. [*See dotted oval on map.*]

This is a most dangerous situation in the making, as that creep energy "piles up" like box cars on a train track at that triple-junction point, waiting to release this energy in travel by slippage, further on up north, along those three major fault lines, into all of those heavily populated San Francisco Bay Area cities.

It is a matter of particular tragedy that, for instance, most of the East Bay Area's hospitals and schools sit ***directly atop*** the Hayward Fault. Can you imagine the problems waiting to happen just from this one condition—assisted as it had to be in the past by town politicians and their real estate planning and zoning commissions?

Figure 3 [*see end of writing*] is taken from the Southern California Seismographic Network's weekly newsletter, covering approximately the same time period as do the other graphics we have been discussing, here specifically for the time period of May 2-8, 1996.

I wish to call to your attention the continued build-up of the activity along two major geometric "triangles": one extends from Santa Barbara ("SB" on the map) eastward to the Lake Isabella-Ridgecrest (China Lake Naval Weapons Center) area and then on down southeast through the northeast side of Palm Springs and the Salton Sea, and onward into Baja Mexico; the other triangle is smaller and tighter, encircling Palm Springs itself.

Those of you who have been attentive to the visions given to Gordon-Michael Scallion are already well alerted to keep an eye on this Palm Springs area for major, violent activity which will likely precipitate much shifting of the crust with attendant devastation on up through greater Los Angeles proper, especially along the volatile Elysian Park Fault.

And while we're on the subject of Los Angeles, look closely at the blob of black dots at approximately 11 o'clock to the letters "LA" on this map. That is the San Fernando Valley wherein was precipitated the Northridge earthquake on January 17, 1994. IF any of these shaking events manage to cause enough nervous responses of inquiry in the public to warrant mention over the media channels, such will always be along the lines of "not to worry", that they are "simply more expected aftershocks" of that devastating Northridge event.   One can but marvel at that which is accepted without question by the mostly sleeping masses.

Thus, to sum up this three-map scenario, it should be clear that major stress-relieving (but life-disrupting) earthquake and volcanic activity is imminent at many locations all around the massive Pacific Plate.  From Figure 1 you can see clearly the motion as it looks from the perspective of the "big picture"; and from Figures 2 and 3 you can see, on a more close-up scale, the effects of that "big picture" motion as such reflect in the heightened activity in two very populated and economically powerful arenas of your United States' West Coast.

Remember my earlier quoted lesson from 1991, especially that "all is connected to all", and you will be well on your way toward forming a true understanding of your world.  I thus leave it to you ones to connect the dots which fill in the details of this most sobering picture of impending great destruction while I turn now to addressing an issue in the larger context of the planetary transition now in progress.

We must never lose sight of the fact that earthquakes and other seemingly violent "natural" events are but "adjustments" made by Mother Earth at this time of transition as she strives to return to a state of healthy balance after much injury has been inflicted upon her by a particularly heartless variety of self-centered "fleas" crawling around on (and somewhat beneath) her skin.

*   *   *

By way of introduction to this next topic, I shall first tell on my scribe as an example: as we write this, he is consciously carrying on four tasks, simultaneously, in order to try to "get everything done" that needs to get done within the confines of the seemingly available "time" as you perceive same.  Of course, if I were to let him see what all else he is ALSO working on, simultaneously, that he is NOT conscious of doing at the moment, there would likely be a mutiny—or at least a weak plea for higher pay!

So, like most of you of the Ground Crew, he wrestles with both the frustrating limitations of seemingly more rapidly disappearing "time"—or how "time" seems to be speeding up as the planetary frequency continues to move upward, as this transition process progresses, carrying with it all those who can adjust to the changes.

While this adjustment (upward in frequency with the attendant perceptive loss of time) is nearly impossible for the many soulless or soul-deficient beings who mindlessly are running around on your orb chasing after the next marketed item spewed out by your vidiot box programings, for the Lighted Ground Crew, adjusting to and dealing with "the case of the disappearing time" is a nearly constant, often annoying, and sometimes downright unnerving struggle.

Nearly two years ago now I discussed the physics of this apparent "missing time" phenomenon with this scribe because he reasoned (and quite correctly so, from a strictly conscious point of view) that, as one's frequency increased, with the attendant stepping-up of all related activities, such as mental functioning and awareness-perception, time OUGHT TO SEEM to slow down.

After all, you ones can all relate to the slowdown-of-time sensation that comes from intense concentration and focus upon a task such as, say, "getting into" a fast sport like racquetball or ping-pong, or having to deal with some life-threatening emergency like your automobile brakes failing while you're driving down a winding road.  Time seems to almost stand still in those situations.  And yet my scribe was complaining about finding himself LOSING time—that it was greatly speeding up—and sometimes at an alarming rate.  The question was: how could this be?

The reason for the apparent contradiction is that, as you Lighted

Ground Crew members continue to increase in frequency, access to *other dimensions of expression* become more fluently possible. Thus, like my scribe, you readers too are doing more and more things simultaneously—BUT THEY ARE BEING DONE MOSTLY IN THOSE NEWLY-ACCESSIBLE OTHER DIMENSIONAL SPACES!

Thus you could look at it as spending less "time", say per hour, in this particular conscious domain, so that every time you "come back" (and gather up the courage to look at the clock), you observe that more time has gone by than you can consciously account for. Thus is generated the apparent sensation of time speeding up!

The problem is that, right now, you are just not particularly conscious of this expanded theatre of activity which includes these now-more-fluently-accessible other dimensions.

By way of another example, consider that you are washing several dishes in the kitchen sink, a job you feel takes several minutes. But while you are doing that, at an UNCONSCIOUS level you make several trips to your den to play a few moves of chess with the computer, you check on the laundry in the laundry room, and you go outside and move the lawn sprinkler to another location. Now consciously, back in the kitchen, you look up at the clock and are shocked to see that so much time has flown by while seemingly you were "just" washing those few dishes.

**I share this discussion at this time because, from our vantage point of observation and monitoring, we see so many of you frustrated by and frequently questioning this accelerated evaporation of your useable "time". And you often support this observation with the self-defeating thought that YOU, most certainly, must, finally, now, be going crazy (or some such explanation) for, after all, there seems to be "no time" anymore for getting things done. You feel that you "blink twice and the day is over"— right?!**

Well, take comfort in the knowing that you are operating in a constantly expanding dimensional arena of activities, not all of which you can appreciate at the present moment. But while you work to be more patient with self and others, as you all effort through this disorienting perceptual phenomenon with time, associated with the planetary transitioning process, ALSO consider this as a notice to consciously put what "time" you are given to good use!

On that note I think I shall take my own advice and sign off for now. As I said at the beginning of this writing, we are most busy in the monitoring department of Earth-Shan's geophysical activities. What has made our job most complex these days is, of course, that the effects of man's continual, heartless dinking with this planet are becoming so intertwined with the natural processes of rebalancing that the overall "vegetable soup" has become a most difficult broth to analyze in real time.

But now I've used that mysterious word again—time—and so it's probably time I take my leave. Know that all of you of the Ground Crew are much beloved and constantly watched over by we of the monitoring realms. Always keep an eye out for us as we make our presence known—whether in the "curious looking" and "appearing from nowhere" clouds you can easily spot, mostly in the daytime, or in our magnificent spectrum-strobing star-like jewels of the night sky. Know that we take as much delight in your confirming acknowledgements as you do in our subtle (or sometimes not so subtle) displays of presence. And we are ever only a thoughtful—or maybe better yet, a heartfelt—mental call away. Thus you should NEVER feel alone!

Toniose Soltec to clear in the Radiant Light of Creator's most perfect plan for the healing and growth that is this time of transition.

Salu—and make it a point to ask God to help YOU use your "time" wisely in these final days. You'll be glad you did!

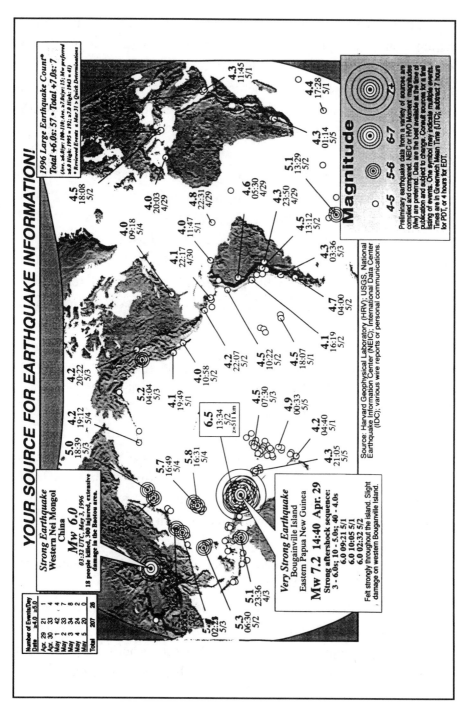

Figure 1

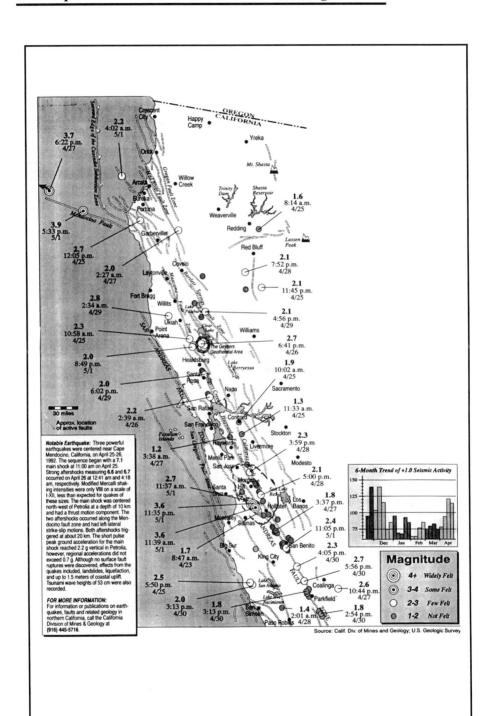

Figure 2

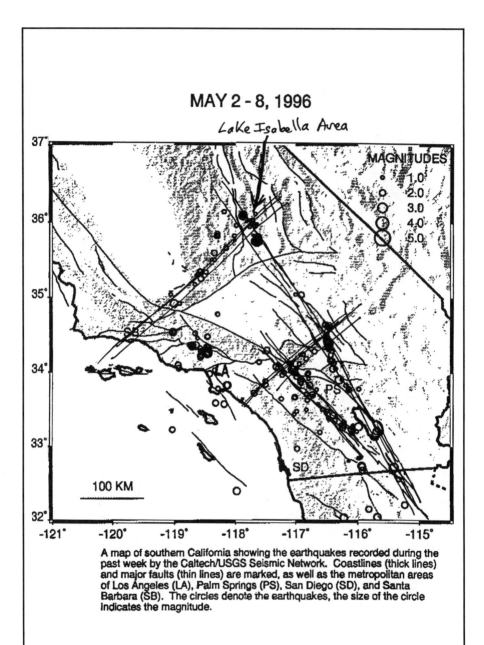

MAY 2 - 8, 1996

Lake Isabella Area

A map of southern California showing the earthquakes recorded during the past week by the Caltech/USGS Seismic Network. Coastlines (thick lines) and major faults (thin lines) are marked, as well as the metropolitan areas of Los Angeles (LA), Palm Springs (PS), San Diego (SD), and Santa Barbara (SB). The circles denote the earthquakes, the size of the circle indicates the magnitude.

Figure 3

# The Great Transformation Is Underway!

## *Violinio Saint Germain*

### June 17, 1996

Germain here in the Radiant Light of Aton, the One Light. It has been some time since last we have written. Thank you for receiving me this day and at this time. Be at peace, for God knows your heart.

The Great Transformation is underway! It is time for testing on MANY levels. I, Germain, have a most important task in this Transformation. As keeper of the Violet Flame of Transmutation, my energy will be called upon in order that the upcoming changes go successfully.

You ask, "What are these changes?"

Well, no less than the rebirthing of humanity into Radiance and Knowingness, from out of the present ignorance and darkness.

We have prepared long and hard in order for the proper conditions to be in place for this Grand Awakening and birth. The final pieces of the puzzle are being set into place even as we write, and these conditions are nearly complete. Thus rapid, seemingly catastrophic change is at hand.

**Be prepared for a period of great change. This shall be a horror to some. They shall come to see that their horror comes from their ignorance and fears borne from that ignorance. The**

**warning siren is screaming, alarms are going off, yet many see not that the mass conscious reality is on the verge of a great shift. This shift shall literally SHOCK THE WORLD.**

Those who call you ones "crackpots" or "paranoids" shall be flocking to your Light and stability for guidance. Be prepared, for this is a large part of the Ground Crew's job in general. Serve your brothers in their confusion. Direct them in a constructive community effort to bring stability to your own local areas.

Do not try to solve the whole country's problems. Take on a localized, realistic objective such as the stability of, perhaps, your own neighborhood. Band together in a unified purpose (that of survival!). United in truth, ones can accomplish the miracles that shall bring a remnant through and into a radiant new cycle of experiencing.

The Light of Creator shall once again shine brightly on that dark planet. It is His promise!

Seek balance. All that is necessary is for each to do his/her own part.

Hangers-on shall be quite unacceptable. Those who are used to having others "do it for them" shall soon find themselves quite helpless and desperate. These are the ones lost in their own ego-centered world who can't seem to accept that one day they won't have the luxury items they now pretend to enjoy. Oh, what they could have done with their façades of wealth!

Always ones wake up too late, only to realize how truly foolish they have been. This is the way of those who choose to remain in ignorance of what actually has true lasting value.

Seek first God and His Lighted Spiritual Truth, and then all things shall be added unto you in the fullness of balance. It shall never be the way you perceive that it should be. There are great "riches" far beyond anything money can buy. These are the TRUE riches (of the spirit) that I'm referring to.

Always look for the clues and follow your Guidance. Guidance may come in the form of a nagging friend or relative, so be patient with those around you. They may be working directly with your Guides in order to assist you to find the answers you seek.

Know that God works in ways that only seem mysterious. The mystery only comes from your lack of understanding. As your awareness level increases, you shall begin to understand that Creator God (the One who created YOU!) is ALWAYS there for you. It is not mystery; it is fact.

It is you who turn a deaf ear to God. You can either honor Him or dishonor Him. This is determined by your actions and intent. You cannot hide for one second from the One who created you!

Responsibility for yourself and for those entrusted to your care is the only acceptable way to truly grow past your current level of understanding and awareness. There is an infinite ability to expand self, for you expand within a limitless entity referred to as Creation.

Expansion and growth in Light and Truth bring upon self the greatest joys ones could ever imagine—and actually surpass, in infinite proportions, what is typically imagined. You can never "push the envelope" too far or too hard. There shall always be newness and growth.

This existence is but a small part of Infinity. Yet each entity makes up part of the Whole of Existence. Thus, as each is brought up to speed, and into awareness of his or her larger purpose within the One, then all, everywhere, expand.

Thus none is more or less important than another, just different. In as much as one part grows, all grow. This is the reason for the great compassion of we of the Hosts—who come that the whole can forever expand, so that we might expand.

We find great joy in our work, and when a Lighted brother comes into recognition of his/her true potential within Creator God, and sees his/her purpose within the whole, and begins to fulfill that purpose—only then can WE begin to glimpse the next step of OUR evolution into Infinity. Remember: each is created for reason and with a purpose, and that reason serves both Creator and the whole of Creation.

Seek diligently the Lighted Truth and you shall find it. Seek spiritual growth and you shall find it. No special meditations or chants are necessary. No special place to go to or crystal to hang onto are necessary. You have all that you need, from the day you were born, in order to make contact and commune with the God-force within. You can go directly to Source.

YOU DO NOT NEED TO GO THROUGH ANY INTERMEDIARY WHATSOEVER! YOU ONES PLACE THESE RESTRICTIONS UPON SELVES. YOUR CHURCHES ARE FULL OF PEOPLE AND "PRIESTS" WAITING TO PLACE ALL SORTS OF LIMITATIONS UPON YOU AND GOD ALIKE.

They do this out of ignorance, and fear generated from ignorance. When you come into true spiritual knowledge, you shall see that it is quite natural to commune with Creator. You simply would not exist without this connection!

Do not fear God, for it is as ridiculous as fearing self. Awaken and see Truth!

I am Germain, keeper of the Violet Flame and Master of Transmutation. Give up your fear and transform yourself into that which your heart desires.

In the Radiant Light of Creator God, I thank you for considering my words. May you see your Potential and act accordingly! What have you to lose?!

Salu.

# CHAPTER EIGHTEEN

# The Greatest Awakening Of Mankind Ever On This Planet

## *Esu "Jesus" Sananda*

### June 25, 1996

Be at peace. It is I, Esu Sananda, one with Creator God. I come in the Radiant One Light of Aton.

There is much turmoil and confusion this day. The clash of the would-be kings and rulers of the world is heating up. Much blood shall flow as a result of this great conflict.

For many there shall be overwhelming fear as they seek to understand that which is happening around them and to them. Be not concerned, for did not God give unto them both eyes to see with and ears to hear with—and yet even more important: a mind to REASON with?

All shall be responsible for themselves! Blessed are the ones who receive (hear) these messages, for you are the ones who have awakened to the greater truth, that of higher consciousness.

(My scribe, there are great efforts to stop this communication. Be persistent at keeping your Light shielding in place. Nothing of darkness can persist in the Radiance of Aton's Light. Good; let us continue, please.)

There is a great need at this time for we of the Hosts of God to have these messages spread far and wide. As the physical Earth Changes begin to heat up, there shall most likely be an interruption of the distribution of these writings. Therefore, you ones who receive the *CONTACT* shall have need for basic instruction, for in as much as you may think that you are prepared, let me assure you that you are NOT.

**No souled being can go through this type of experience without feeling great pain and sorrow. The loss of life shall be great. You ones who call upon the Light for protection shall have it. There is far more that we can do for you ones when you DIRECTLY call upon us. When ones refuse to believe, we must honor their choice, too.**

Many a good person shall not survive the physical assaults thrust upon you ones. Even ones in that small town of Tehachapi, who think that somehow they are protected by just being there, shall have a great shock and realization as this time of chaos heats up.

Get right with Creator. You may be able to lie to another; you most certainly can and do lie to yourselves. But you cannot lie to Creator, for He knows your heart and sees and knows every last thread of lie that you ones hold onto.

Let go of your past mistakes; forgive yourself and forgive those whom you perceive have done you wrong. Then move on and create a better life—one based upon truth, honesty, and integrity.

Do not tolerate another's lies. Call them to their attention, for a lie cannot persist in the Light of Truth. If another is persistent in a lie, then insist that they leave from your presence. Do not allow another to pull you from your path.

It is alright for ones to disagree with you. Each has their own free-will choice. It is NOT alright for another to FORCE their reality onto you—or yours onto them. Respect another's opinions, and demand that same respect toward your own opinions, for truth IS and cannot be changed.

You ones are often more worried about who is right and who is wrong. All want to be right, for each wants to be confident in their perception of reality. What IS really real?

Communication is usually the bridge necessary to cross the gaps in a dispute over who is right and who is wrong. Most often both sides are in error.

Do not allow the ego to distract you from getting your message heard. Souled beings instinctively know truth when they hear it. Yet ones allow their ego to step in and say, "This cannot be for I (in my great understanding) would already know of it and therefore it cannot be." Thus they reject that which their soul so desperately seeks.

These ones who refuse to accept still need to hear the messages of Light and Truth. They need them in order to, at a later time, know where and to whom to turn in their time of confusion.

So, do not hold back from another that which you know to be true, for YOU need that which your brother brings to the unfolding play.

Be certain in your own knowingness, for your certainty, if nothing else, shall be remembered. Be patient and do not expect ones to just give up their old beliefs overnight. These ones need to experience the learning process. They must come to know that man's greatest enemy is himself.

You ones limit self, and thus limit the Creative Potential—the God Force—within. It only takes ONE to realize their potential, to change the whole entire play! Stop awaiting another to do that which YOU have potential to do yourself. Honor the Creative Force within; allow it to flourish and show you your true potential. QUIT HOLDING SELF BACK!

**Each souled being has a special gift and a special purpose. Until you recognize that purpose and bring it to the world, the whole of humanity shall go lacking. That is one reason why each is as important as another.**

You all have a part to contribute to the whole. Inasmuch as you limit yourself, you limit others who need that which you bring into this world with you. Do not hold back that which you are compelled to say to another or do for another. You may be the one who makes the difference in that person's life, which then allows the Flame within to burn brighter than it had before.

Do not hide God's words from another. If you are ashamed of what and who you are, you had better ask yourself "WHY?"! Do not fear ridicule, for the very ones who ridicule you for sharing truth shall be the ones who come to you in their time of need—for they shall not know anywhere else to turn. Do your part by sharing these words with those who need them.

Be responsible and do not pretend to know all the answers. If you know some answers, then tell them. If you do not know or are uncertain of an answer, then say so. Your honesty shall be greatly appreciated. When you honor others, they shall not have need to distrust you.

The upcoming catastrophic cleansing shall become the greatest awakening of mankind ever on that planet. The end result shall be a rebirth of Radiance and Knowing. Peace and Balance are what shall come out of the chaos as the Phoenix rises from the ashes of destruction.

These are truly magnificent times for experiencing, for where else shall you get such lessons?

Thank you for writing and sharing, my friend. I am Esu Sananda, come in the Radiance of the One Light so that you ones might see.

Peace and Balance.

Aho!

# CHAPTER NINETEEN

# Cautions About
# Upcoming Earth Changes

### *Lord Michael, Archangel*

### July 7, 1996

Good morning and thank you for hearing the call. It is I, Lord Michael, of the Archangelic realms, come in the Light of Holy Creator God. Thank you, my friend.

Your planet is in a quite volatile condition this day. You ones need to be prepared for the psychological stresses caused by the upcoming physical changes. The stress shall be GREAT!

How do we prepare you ones for the horrors of these catastrophic changes?

We simply tell you about what is coming in as many ways as we can and as many times as we can. I shall project a picture and I wish for you ones to place yourselves in the middle of what I describe and ask yourselves, "Am I prepared for THIS sort of reality?"

The scenario goes as follows: The Earth starts shaking and does not seem to stop. All power fails; your house starts coming apart; the ground is splitting open; gas lines rupture; fires ignite; your city starts to burn—not just in one location, but across THE ENTIRE CITY!

Now the Earth starts shaking again, just as hard or harder than previously. Water lines are broken; streets are, for the most part, impassable due to rubble and that which has collapsed all over the pavement.

Place yourself in this scenario. What would YOU do?

You must think about these sorts of possibilities BEFORE they happen so that you can act in intelligence. The panic and fear shall be so great that ones shall perish simply because they are so overwhelmed and frozen with fear.

Let us take this example further. You may be saying to yourself, "I do not live in a large city or near any major fault lines." But perhaps you have family and friends who do!

As these Earth Changes start, there shall be survivors and a great migration of displaced people. In their desperation and confusion, they shall do things which they would NOT normally do in a "civilized" society.

They will steal from, and even murder, the ones who are trying to help them. There will be massive refugee camps. Ones will be moving inland from the coastal areas. These mobs will be fighting for survival. Food supplies will be scarce and the Government will send out the Army and the National Guard to control these panic-stricken, destitute survivors.

How will YOU act or react as your small, inland city has an influx of displaced, desperate, and hungry people trying to cope with shock?

Will you feed and clothe your brother?

What about the 5th one?

What about the 50th one?

Call upon Holy God of Light and act with intelligence—and prepare! The life you save may not only be your own or your family's, but that of a complete stranger (to you now!).

The mental impact forthcoming shall be QUITE HARSH! You ones are past the point of avoiding these realities. This is only one example of the possible scenarios.

As the Earth cracks open and your major crustal plates (tectonic plates) shift, many sleeping volcanos shall spring to life as your planet seeks to balance the pressures and stresses within. This alone shall cause a shifting of weather patterns GLOBALLY. **The impact shall be felt by everyone on the planet.**

As countries become desperate for survival, they shall petition other countries for aid. When that aid does NOT come, ones shall attempt to TAKE that which they need. This could easily escalate to the level of a planetary war.

**The Elite of your planet know that these catastrophes are coming. They are trying to control the timing of major earthquakes. They do not understand that which they are attempting to do and are only compounding the problem. These major Earth Changes shall be exploited by your planet's controllers in order to depopulate and control more fully the masses.**

You ones who enjoy all the "modern conveniences" shall have the hardest time, as you will no longer be able to just go down to the local store and purchase your food. The nation's food supply will be under strict control. Your farms shall be confiscated if need be; the crops shall most certainly be confiscated. You ones who rely on any resource—such as supermarkets, grid-system electricity, or even municipal water—shall be impacted greatly.

Your "elected" Government officials may be deciding who of you eats (lives), or does not eat (dies).

This is TRUTH!

You may say that this is not a very nice message. No, it is not! My intention is to get you ones THINKING.

The changes shall be far worse than anything written here or that you may be able to imagine. Take action and prepare TODAY, for tomorrow may very well be TOO LATE! God helps those who make efforts to help selves.

There shall be many praying to God to save them or to help them AFTER the changes begin—especially the ones who have ignored these messages and have NOT prepared, and think that it could not happen to them.

The time to ask for assistance in planning is BEFORE you ones are in total chaos. [*See* Appendix A *for a* 72-Hour Kit Checklist *of emergency items.*]

My scribe is overwhelmed and says, "What's the use?  Ones who are going to listen are most likely already prepared and the rest won't listen anyway."  My scribe perceives that ones do not want to hear this sort of message.

True, ones generally do not want to hear TRUTH.  But, if only ONE does hear, and takes this warning seriously, then the entire message and effort is worth every last bit of it.

You ones who scribe these messages that are being sent out to the four corners of the planet are the ones who create the possibilities for even having a remnant survive this transition. Many lives you are touching and many lives you are saving.  Do not allow the thought, "Oh, what's the use?"  That is an adversarial ploy to distract you from saving lives and waking up the masses to the true spiritual nature of their situation down there on that planet.

Ones are responsible for their own choices and decisions.  There is only so much that you ones can do for another.  Presenting a Lighted message of truth to a brother in need is perhaps the greatest gift you ones can give.  Be discerning in that which you offer to another or do for another.  You must allow each to learn their own lessons; you cannot do it for them.

I am Lord Michael, come in the Radiance of the One Light.  May you ones act in Wisdom this day.

Aho!

# CHAPTER TWENTY

# Planetary Rebalancing Imminent As Responsibilities Must Be Met

## *El Morya, The Statesman*
### July 14, 1996

Greetings, I am El Morya, one of the Ascended Masters. I come in the One Light of Aton that is ALL. Thank you for receiving my energy this day. Be not distracted, else the opportunity will be lost.

Your planet is in great need for balance. She cannot continue much longer in her current state of crisis. She shall not be denied her balance within the Oneness of Creator's Light.

There shall be a massive cleansing cycle that she will undergo. This cleansing shall be quite devastating to those ones (humans, animals, and plants, etc.) to whom she gives life. It is as if your planet has a fever and, before it breaks, her temperature will need to rise. She will need to excrete the poisons (toxic, radioactive wastes, etc.) which have been placed under her skin. She will, in the process, have to rearrange her waters and shift their healing properties to the places which need them the most.

You ones have been warned, over and over again. There was opportunity as caretakers of the planet to reverse the damage foisted off onto the life-giving entity that you ones erroneously call Earth. She is NOT DIRT! She (your planet) is a living, sentient being. You take for granted the gifts she freely gives.

The darkness of those who are destroying her and who suppress the masses has grown to epidemic proportions. The mentality of the average person is so filled with negative (non-Lighted) energy that such has made your planet so dizzy (off balance) that she even wobbles in an unnatural manner as she revolves around, trying to fulfill her purpose.

You ones need to learn to honor your planet and be thankful for the gifts she gives, not the least of which is life itself! Ones always seem to wake up too late. Many go around in their own self-centered world, not even thinking about how their actions (or IN-actions) will affect them tomorrow. Well, tomorrow is here! And that which you ones have neglected in the past will be brought around full circle for you ones to confront again—this time in a most direct and impacting manner.

When the "Earth" (as you call her) shakes you into an awakened state of realization that you are so truly small and cannot do anything to stop her massive quakings, maybe then you shall appreciate that which you take for granted.

EARTHQUAKES OF CATASTROPHIC MAGNITUDE (9.0 AND GREATER) ARE IMMINENT! INCREASED VOLCANIC ACTIVITY IN PLACES NOW SEEMINGLY DORMANT IS IMMINENT! THE SHIFTING OF YOUR OCEAN WATERS IS NOW IMMINENT!

You ones must come to realize the reasons why these things shall occur. It is because of the Universal Laws of Balance (the Laws of Cause and Effect). You ones must realize that you are responsible for that which you helped to create.

You may say, "But I did not pollute the waters or the skies!"

Do you drive or ride in an automobile? Do you not buy from, and thus support, the fuel companies which provide you ones with gas and electricity? They, in turn, pollute rivers and streams. The exhaust fumes from your cars, buses, trucks and airplanes—do not they pollute your air? Do you wash your clothes with chemical solutions? Where do you think the rinse water goes?

One person alone could not contaminate your planet by acting in this manner, but 5 billion (or more) people acting in this manner can and indeed have. Those things you ones do daily—usually without thinking of future, long-term consequences—are the things which are the most dangerous to your own survival.

Am I saying, "Do not drive your automobiles!"? NO! Am I telling you to stop washing your clothes? NO!

I am suggesting that you change the way you think regarding your non-caring attitude toward your planet. Some say that they care about the planet, but they are still unwilling to sacrifice their own personal comfort to REALLY do anything about your planet's current problems.

The first TRUE step in solving such a problem is educating people to the reality of the magnitude of the problem.

There are ones on your planet who are very sensitive to your planet's electromagnetic (emotional) shifts. These are the ones who get sick or exhibit some other physiological symptoms, such as a headache, prior to earthquakes, volcanic activity, etc. These ones innately know and respect the lifeform which sustains their existence. These are the ones who can help you to understand the needs of your planet. They have a direct link! Some don't even realize why they have this gift and, in fact, they often view it as a burden.

As I have said, you ones have been warned, time and time again. There was an opportunity for reversing this current situation, but it is now long past. Now you ones shall be given to learn your lessons—once again—the hard way.

If you dislike this message, I suggest you ask yourself, "Why do I dislike this message?" Ones most often do not like to be made to feel responsible for that which befalls them. Most wish to blame their "sufferings" on another, and will go to great lengths to try to justify their position.

**I shall tell you now: if something impacts you, whether it be good or bad, then you have helped in some way to create it. There are no victims.**

When you can rise above your self-centered ME-ness and realize that YOU are responsible for everything that YOU do, then YOU will be able to begin to see a larger picture unfolding. With this shift in viewpoint, you will begin to realize that there are GREAT opportunities available to you for growth at this time. You will begin to stop making the same mistakes over and over again, lifetime after lifetime.

You will begin to realize that there is a reason for EVERYTHING that happens. There are no chance happenings. PERIOD!

When you ones can begin to understand the TRUE "Whys?" of these seemingly tragic events, then you will be ready to truly accept your responsibility in creating a better way of doing things—else you shall be destined to repeat these tragic horrors over and over again.

As always, the choice is YOURS!

I am El Morya, come in the One Light of the I AM presence. Thank you.

# CHAPTER TWENTY-ONE

# Watch Closely As The Titans Clash

### Ceres Anthonious Soltec

### July 20, 1996

Good morning, my friend, it is I, Toniose Soltec, here in the Radiant Light of the One Creator.

My, are we not in an awkward predicament this day. The power players are positioning for the opportunity to unleash their weaponry in order to gain full control of your planet's resources.

The plane explosion [*TWA Flight 800 in New York*], as you can now see, was clearly a deliberate act of murder. These dark ones have so little regard for life that they would destroy over 200 people in order to get the one they really want.

The rumored government documents was a secondary target, but nonetheless a target that cost lives. Allow this to show you the means and the methods being used against you in order to control the masses.

It is viewed that you ones (the Americans, especially) have too much freedom of travel, thus the need to create panic and fear to keep you ones stationary.

CONTROL is the key focus of these "power players".

There is much else planned in the way of retaliation. You will have to pay VERY CLOSE attention to the clues and reported "accidents" worldwide.

These dark ones are desperately trying to hold their power

positions, yet they slip away anyway. This is how the adversary eats himself.

Through patience and persistence, we of the Lighted team can continue to grow in strength and wisdom, and eventually be the only ones left on the playing field.

We are not a threat to these "heavy hitters" for they know that we will not attempt any physical action against them, just merely inform those few people who might listen.

The dark ones are so confident in their ability to control the mindless masses that they rather enjoy what they like to call "our brag sheet"—otherwise known as *CONTACT*. [*Editor's note: What Commander Soltec is referring to here is the situation whereby, because* CONTACT *has revealed much about the actual shenanigans that these dark ones are up to, they are "proud" to have the information spread around, and thus generally regard* CONTACT *as their "brag sheet". Of course, this is not a situation of fondness, but rather, braggadocio. Besides, they don't really expect many of the public to be actually reading* CONTACT, *and still fewer to believe what they read, and fewer still to, in any way,* **ACT** *upon what they read. So where's the threat to their plans? We shall see!*]

Thank you for writing this short message, my friend. We are Those who watch over you. May God give all of you the strength and conviction you need to persist through these trying times.

With much Love and Light, Salu.

# CHAPTER TWENTY-TWO

# Our Responsibility
# Toward Balance And Healing

## *Master Hilarion*

### July 20, 1996

I am Hilarion, Master of the Emerald Ray. I come in the Light of the One Light.

My scribe, another was to come at this time, but due to the recent events, changes have been made and I, Hilarion, have been called to give a message at this time. Allow my healing energy to balance you so that we may maintain the signal.

**These are harsh times for EVERYONE on your planet.**

The physical bombardments and mental unrest are so great that heart dis-ease, cancer, and other stress-related illnesses are taking their toll. This is not to say that the man-made plagues are not of concern. We are talking about souls so confused and disoriented that they cannot function properly with all the bombardments at this time. THIS IS TRULY A BATTLE FOR YOUR SOULS!

Many shall be lost and shall have to await another opportunity for expressing. These are some of the hardest lessons you ones must face.

Healing begins from within. Ones must desire to balance their personal conditions. This is not as easy as it may seem.

Desire for balance is just the first step. Ones must take action to attain that balance. Ones must be willing to confront those things which are causing their inner, personal conflicts. Recognize them for what they are and get rid of them. Stop giving these self-created demons the power to control you.

**Life is meant to be enjoyed. The experience should be one of Creative Expression that honors the One who created you.**

Let us take an example, please:

Let us say you are involved in a relationship with another and you both are very much in love with each other. So you get married and start a family.

At first, all seems just wonderful. Then the children come, planned for or not (most of the time not). Now your life begins to change. You can no longer just go out with your friends and have parties. You must stay home and take care of your responsibilities.

Now perhaps money becomes a concern, and you and the one you love begin to argue and fight over these building pressures and stresses. You look to each other for strength, yet both of you seem to have less and less to give.

Pretty soon that once fabulous and wonderful person seems less wonderful and less desirable. Now you both begin blaming each other for your unhappiness, and soon you are so miserable that you cannot take it any longer. So you both decide to divorce.

This is a very general example and not too uncommon down there on your planet.

Let us take this one step further:

You now go out and remarry with another person with a broken family. You take two broken families and try to make one functional family. And you repeat the same cycle all over again.

When does this cycle stop?

When you realize the TRUE problem.

You must stop looking for another to fulfill that emptiness within. If you feel empty inside, then YOU have allowed that feeling to grow, and only YOU can fill that emptiness.

When ones enter into relationships with another, they both flow energy to one another in a completely giving manner—and thus expect this all of the time. This is fine. But if you cannot see that it is quite improbable that either will be able to maintain the energy output all of the time, forever, then you shall be in for a rough ride.

Let us go back now and proceed forward with the original example:

Once the children come, they need a great deal of energy that you ones were accustomed to giving to each other.

Now the responsibilities associated with giving and creating an environment for the upbringing of the children hit. The worries and stresses associated with wanting to give the children everything that they may need become quite a drain on both parents.

Neither has much left to give and become very mechanical, almost robotic in their interactions with each other. The excitement and spontaneity soon diminishes, and each is left wanting more. Neither realizes that THEY have created this unbalanced situation, and thus try blaming each other—not seeing that it is they, themselves, who are at fault.

If one truly desires balance in one's life, one would look at those things which they blame another for, or those things which have a lot of pain associated with them. Then ask yourself, "What part of this situation can I take responsibility for?"

You ones are responsible for the feelings that you feel. There are no victims. If you are with a person who beats you, then why did you choose such a person to be with? Is ignorance your excuse? Then why do you repeat these things over and over again?

You will find the balance you seek when you realize that you have created the self torture—that is to say, you allow or somehow think that you deserve your self-inflicted loneliness.

Realize, please, that YOU must make your own choices and decisions, and live with the responsibility of those conditions which you have helped to create.

INNER BALANCE IS THE KEY TO THE OUTER (PHYSICAL) BALANCE!

If you are constantly plagued with poor health, then perhaps you are looking for sympathy (energy) from another. Please know that the God-self within can supply you with all the ENERGY that you could ever need.

**You ones must learn to love yourselves without the need for another to provide you with the energy that you desire, else you become parasites feeding off of each other's emotional energies.**

When you are balanced and at peace with yourself, then you can begin to create a balanced external life.

Wounded people attract other wounded people. When you find the inner peace and balance, you shall attract to yourself others of balanced nature. Also, most importantly, you will be able to spot those who would feed off of your energy, and thus drain you into an unbalanced condition.

This is but one example of inner UN-balance. There are many others, but this is a BIG one that most of you have problems with.

Now that you spot, or recognize within, the problem that causes the emotional frustrations and pain, you must take CONSCIOUS action to overcome the problem. You must look at the situation and be willing to take PERSONAL RESPONSIBILITY for having helped to create it.

If the problem concerns another, then you should, if at all possible, inform that person of what it is that you are considering, and be completely honest about it. Do not blame another for your discomforts or frustrations, for they are YOURS.

**There is a reason for everything that you perceive has happened to you. If you look close enough, you shall find that there is a lesson in every seeming tragedy.**

Once you begin to balance yourself within, you shall soon find that the external (such as health problems) will begin to become less and less impacting. This is not to say that you will have a miraculous healing, though it is possible!

Now, if you know of another who refuses to be responsible for their condition, call the fact to their attention and stop feeding the condition. Many out there must conjure up a problem, else from where would they get the sympathy (energy) that they desire. Ones pull away from the Infinite Source—God's energy—only to go around trying to find that which fills the emptiness within.

God's Light, His Energy, is what these ones seek. You need only to go within and ask with the heart for balance, and to be shown that which will help you to find balance. God shall present the opportunity to you to find balance, but YOU must seek it out with true diligence in order to rid yourself of that which you feel is lacking within.

Now, there are other impacting stresses down there on that planet. You have pollution of your air, ground, and water. You have man-made biological diseases. Your entire planet is in a state of DIS-EASE. This is all due to the mental deterioration of those who choose to remain DIS-connected from The One Light Source.

These ones cannot create the energy within, and thus must take it from those who have it. These ones are so low in frequency that they thrive on the emotions (emotional frequencies) of anger and frustration. They cannot stand the energy (and frequency) of love, for it burns them. Thus they maintain conditions of unrest by deteriorating the morals in society to such a level that ones become confused and programmed into a state of depleting each other to a point of frustration and anxiety. This is the emotional frequency of energy upon which the darkness feeds.

**Thus, when other great teachers say "love your enemy", they are saying to maintain the love frequency within when thinking of the enemy or when he attacks. The adversary**

**cannot stay within the frequency of Light associated with love, and thus will leave from you as fast as he can.**

Now, the converse is also true. So, if you are "stressed out" all of the time, and in a state of anxiety, then the adversary will do everything he can to keep you in this depleted state.

When you ones can learn to generate and maintain that feeling of being "in love" without the need for another to be present, only then will you find that the emptiness is no longer there. You will have attained the level of joy that you desire and it will be IN BALANCE—and without having drained another to do so.

Creator God has infinite love and energy to give. Allow for this to manifest WITHIN, and the outer self will take care of self. Be cautious of those who keep you down, for they are the ones who cannot stand for others to get ahead of them.

Be persistent and diligent, for it most often SEEMS darkest before the dawn. As you get closer and closer to reaching your Lighted goal, the dark side shall attack you with more and more force. Once you have broken through, the dark side has lost and there will be nothing more that they can do.

This is why ones are bombarded most heavily just prior to "breaking through" and obtaining their goal. Most often this is when most give up and succumb to the pressure—most often at the point of being just one step short of winning the battle.

I am Master Hilarion. I represent the healing Emerald Ray of Creator's spectrum. I come in the One Light of Creator/Creation so that you ones may have the spiritual insights you need in order to truly heal selves.

May you maintain persistence and patience within the Light. Salu.

# CHAPTER TWENTY-THREE

# Expressing The Nurturing Aspect Of Creator

## *Lady Nada*

### July 27, 1996

Greetings, old friend, I am Lady Nada of the Ascended Spectrum of Guides and Teachers. I come in the Radiance of the One Light. Be at peace, my scribe, we shall do just fine.

Mankind on your planet is in great need of spiritual balance. These messages are for any who will hear and listen.

(Much is happening to cause you to lose the signal. The dark side does not want this message to go forth. They wish to cast doubt within so that you might give up. DO NOT ALLOW THEM THIS!)

There is a feminine aspect of Creator that the male forms often have trouble with. Creator is neither male nor female. The mother-father principle of creation allows for a self-propagating play that can continue to evolve and grow.

This ever-changing and evolving physical play is where you ones are now. You have volunteered to go down there and participate for various reasons. For some it is to balance out past indiscretions (karmic debts, if you must); for some it is to learn and grow from the opportunities and experiences available; while for others, it is to heal themselves. You cannot know the reasons for each person's choice.

I, Lady Nada, represent the feminine aspect of Creator's

expression.  I am most often associated with your body's Solar Plexus energy center.  This is the energy pathway for the emotional energy that you ones feel.

The females of your third-dimensional expression have a more sensitive and slightly more complex Solar Plexus region.  This is because they accommodate the gestation of new life.  When the baby is in the womb, it resides behind (actually right in the center of) the Solar Plexus energy center (in the abdominal area).

This nurturing emotional energy is necessary for the healthy growth of the child.  Without this energy the child could not and would not grow.  Note, please, that even the umbilical cord attaches in this area to the baby.  There are reasons for ALL the things you ones can witness in Nature.

In your society it is looked upon as a weakness for men to show emotion or emotional release.  This inhibition causes a great unbalance within, especially for the more advanced souls who return as the Guides and Wayshowers.

It is not natural to hold back the emotional currents of pain, grief, or sadness.  Do you ones suppress joy when you feel it?  How about anger?

NO!  Not usually.

Then why would you suppress the natural feelings and expressions of pain, grief, or sadness?

This is yet another adversarial ploy to create an internal unbalanced condition.  Usually the suppression of ANY emotional expression whatsoever will cause a great internal pressure (stress) that continues to build up until it reaches a point of volatility, wherein one explodes with an emotional outburst.

Most often this "explosion" is of a violent physical nature.  This, in turn, compounds the problem and creates more guilt-induced emotional pain and frustration.

This problem is not limited to the male expressions on that planet, however they are the ones most often hardest hit. You ones must begin to see that you have allowed this perception and belief that a man must be "strong" and never cry, for such is a sign of weakness.

NO! This thinking is what causes the unbalance within.

Fathers, often, when they see their sons of, let's say 10 years or older, crying, will usually punish them for crying. The father scolds: "I will give you something to cry about!" or "What am I raising, a bunch of girls (sissies)?!" thus expressing the mental attitude that instills this kind of emotional suppression.

Most often it is the very same father who feels guilty for having hurt his son's feelings and who doesn't know how to say "I am sorry" and give the hug to the child who needs, in a nurturing manner, the emotional balancing energies.

This causes great emotional confusion, and eventually the child will learn to avoid the source of the confusion—and will shut down, inside, the emotional expression of his being.

Children are so very giving in their nature. They are constantly trying to please their parents in a manner which allows them to re-give that which the parents have given to them. Usually, because the father has himself shut down to a great extent, the children will gravitate to mother, for she usually gives more freely the emotional nurturings that father doesn't usually emanate.

Thus father begins to feel rejected by his children, not understanding why—and thus not seeing that he himself is to blame for causing the pulling away.

Mom then has to provide more and more of the "emotional food" and, in turn, becomes more and more drained.

Meanwhile, father receives less and less attention (energy) from the rest of his family, and begins to DEMAND attention—

usually with complaining at first and, if that doesn't work, then usually with some sort of violence, such as yelling, screaming, and perhaps even physical violence.

Men claim to not understand women, and women can't seem to understand men. With these sorts of psychological programs in place, reinforced with real emotional pain, is there any wonder why you ones cannot understand one another?

The woman wants the man to be more romantic or more affectionate, yet not realizing that he may not have a clue as to how to be that way, or he may have so much pain and confusion associated with this sort of emotional expression that it is too difficult to confront.

You ones create these self-perpetuating hells and pass them from generation to generation.

When do they stop?

The image-makers (advertisers) have kept your heads full of images that will ensure that you will know and pursue what will make you "cool".

Rather, it is more like "cold and heartless".

You ones need to begin to realize that you are responsible for your emotions. Just because you had a less-than-ideal childhood does not mean that you cannot overcome the programming and be more balanced.

It is ok for a man to hug another man. It is ok for anyone to cry when they are sad. It is quite ok for ones to give heartfelt praise to another and say that they are proud of them.

Most often, especially in children, but in adults also, ones simply need the acknowledgment to let them know that somebody cares enough to even notice them. Else ones will go around creating a way of making people notice them.

This is the reason you ones have the problems with the street gangs. These are usually children who find the attention that they are starved for by going out and shooting someone or robbing someone.

The parents don't know why their children do these things. The parents do not realize that the children need nourishing love and acknowledgment. Most of these parents are wounded children themselves and cannot rise above their own deep-seated problems to break the vicious cycle that creates this internal emotional unbalance.

Ones who come from a more balanced, halfway "normal" family most often do not realize that they have it so good. These ones have a hard time understanding why or how children can go out and shoot someone and not even care who they hurt.

These who can go out and murder are the walking dead. They are so shut down that they are nearly incapable of understanding why it might be wrong to do some of the things they do. The only joy they know is the praise they receive from the like-minded (mindless) ones to which they gravitate.

Being a parent is such a great responsibility that few ever truly realize the ACTUAL magnitude of the responsibility. In the higher-evolved societies, only the more balanced ones take on this responsibility. Thus you have an upward-spiraling culture of a more and more balanced nature—instead of the dwindling spiral of darkness that has overpopulated your planet with those of a soul-less nature, devoid of Life.

You ones must be able to understand why and how it is that your society has come to the point at which you now find yourselves. When you interact with another, please realize that you are, if the person is at all alive (has a soul), dealing with an EMOTIONAL being who has needs and problems, and is seeking to find purpose and meaning in their interactions.

They may not always be easy to get along with, but if you can show them a nurturing acknowledgment of being, then you very well may be surprised at that which comes back to you in return.

**The natural giving of Creator is that of a nurturing (mother-like) nature. You will do wonders for your fellow man if you can learn to reflect this nurturing aspect of Creator's giving.**

I come now to impart this message to you who will listen and understand, so that we might begin to change the erroneous thinking and mental programs.

May you FEEL and UNDERSTAND the message given here.

I am Lady Nada, present in the Radiance of the One Light. May God bless the children who come during these times, for their challenges are great! And may God bless you ones who care deeply and try your best to give of much needed emotional nourishment in these most "starving" times for, while the demands can be sometimes overwhelming, the rewards are indeed great.

Salu.

# CHAPTER TWENTY - FOUR

# Listen To Those Important "Gut Feelings"

### *Lanto, The Sage*

### August 3, 1996

Greetings, my friend, I am most recognized by you ones as Lanto, the Sage. I come in the Light of the One Light. I represent the Second Ray or Aspect of Creator's spectrum.

The visible spectrum of Light only represents a harmonic of the frequencies that make up all of Creation. In the third-dimensional compression, you ones are often limited in your perceptions. Not only are there non-visible third-dimensional aspects of Creator's Light, there are also many higher-dimensional components associated with Creator's energy expressions. Do not get hung up on colors associated with a representative of an aspect of Creator.

We all (you ones included) express on all frequencies or wavelengths. Ones are usually drawn to a certain aspect of Creator, thus there is more affinity associated with one area over another. This is because we are all created with a purpose in mind, and that purpose can be most easily filled through certain aspects of Creator.

Note, please, that balance is of utmost importance for proper growth. All ones will gravitate towards Sananda's "Christos" energy. Many will gravitate towards Hilarion's heart energy or Germain's transmuting energy. This is mostly due to the level of the expressing individuals.

You ones are restless and need change. Thus Germain will appeal to you, for he is Master of that aspect of Creator's expression.

You ask, "Where do you, Lanto, fit into this picture?"

I am Guide and Teacher; I am the "gut feeling" you ones get. The physical color associated with my energy is the golden yellow color, though the etheric color would be perceived differently. Ones who can see the colors of the auric field will most often perceive my energy as a blending of colors.

I am a Teacher. I have learned my lessons well and have earned my position among the other Masters. We all have overlapping aspects and can express on any of the frequencies, though there is need to have specialists to answer the specific and directed needs of the ever-progressing souls.

I have come now, at this time of change, so that you ones might receive balanced instructions and learn to follow your "gut knowingness" about what it is that you need to be doing.

My scribe recognizes me as a communicator. Yes, indeed. I am probably the most heard, but least recognized, of the Masters, for I will speak to ones at a level that bypasses the analytical mind and resonates within the emotional energy field of the being.

This manifests as intuition or as the "I don't know why, but I don't feel right about this situation" reaction. Even the most emotionally shutdown person will, if he has a soul, feel my nudges.

You ones must be open to the "nudges". This is most often your Guides working with you to help you to find the right path so that you are prepared for and ready to accept your purpose.

This does not mean that you have to GO anywhere; this is to say that your life experiences are being guided for your highest good. The more open you are toward following these internal messages, the easier it will be for you ones to get the proper insights and lessons necessary for your upcoming roles.

Sometimes these lessons are harsh and seemingly abrupt. For example, ones are losing their jobs all over the country. Be careful in your thinking, for such "luck" is most likely for good reason. You may be needed elsewhere and this may be the only way to get you to look within and draw upon the Creative Energy that will guide you to a more productive experience.

As some ones are lost, others are called to serve, so if your life seems to be turning upside down, please take a moment and call in the Light and get still.

Notice the gut-level sensations. They can be translated into written or verbal communication with practice. This will be as if you have thought of the message yourself. You will most likely only hear your own inner voice.

Listen to the message. Write it down or speak it into a recording device. Write or speak what comes, then discern the message. REMEMBER TO ALWAYS CALL IN THE LIGHT BEFORE, DURING, AND AFTER THIS EXERCISE! Otherwise the dark side shall almost surely come to influence and trick you.

We are fast approaching a time when you ones shall all be consciously receiving. The mere fact that you are drawn to this information source (*CONTACT*), and are reading this message, implies that you are, and have been, receiving at least at the "gut level".

Well, imagine that!

It is not everyone's task to write public messages for the masses. It is, however, YOUR God-given right to connect-up to Higher Source and receive your own personal instructions.

Your Guides are there for you at this time to help coordinate your training and life experiences. Be patient with those around you. If they do not share your beliefs, do not condemn them, for each is responsible for their own self. You do not know the contract of another, so when one experiences as, let's say, a lawyer, that one just may be necessary to help YOU at a later date.

Ones may deny their spiritual side, yet they may be the inventor or scientist who brings new technology to your world. Ones are allowed to ignore their spiritual side if they so choose. There is no force from we of the Lighted Brotherhood.

If you come across others who don't seem to hear, or want to listen to, spiritual truth, do not condemn them. Look to their actions. Most often these ones are the more advanced ones who recognize that religions are very confusing, and thus choose to avoid ANY spiritual discussion whatsoever. Their actions will hold clues to their being: Are they generally kind and caring? Do they know innately what is right and what is wrong?

Despite the overpopulation of your planet by robotic ones, it is still full of Godly people who only want to do what is right. These Godly ones know right from wrong because they innately FEEL the difference. This is because they are connected to the God Source— even if they do not acknowledge the connection.

This message is coming now so that you ones begin to realize that YOU are receiving Guidance. Moreover, note well that there is fast approaching a time when, due to external physical events, getting the *CONTACT* newspaper delivered will be nearly impossible.

This probable scenario shall serve as a wake-up call to you ones who are still trying to figure out if you really believe these messages of Lighted Truth.

DOUBT IS ONE OF THE MOST EFFECTIVE TOOLS UTILIZED BY THE DARK SIDE. IF THEY CAN'T DISSUADE YOU COMPLETELY, THEY WILL TRY TO CAST DOUBT. THUS THE INACTION, DUE TO PROCRASTINATION, WILL SET YOU BACK OR CAUSE YOU TO MISS OPPORTUNITIES SET UP FOR YOUR GROWTH.

WHEN YOU FIND YOURSELF DOUBTING THINGS

SUCH AS PERSONAL WORTH OR PERSONAL BELIEFS, I WOULD SUGGEST THAT THE DOUBT IS MOST OFTEN ADVERSARIALLY INDUCED.

Ones do not like being treated as an outcast, or as the one who goes against their parents' fundamental teachings. When you doubt spiritual matters, realize, please, that there is a REAL battle going on within. This battle is for the control of your soul—or at least for the influence over your soul.

Go within and call upon Creator God—the One who created you! Get quiet and search your heart to find that which you know to be true. Ask any question of the heart such as, "How can I know what is real or true?"

With such a question asked with heartfelt curiosity, the answers must come. Next you must monitor your thoughts closely, as your mind will be caused to give you the answer. Clues and experiences that hold the answer will be caused to be remembered so that you can realize what is true and what does have verification and validity.

Rarely will you hear a voice of another—not at first, anyway—though it IS possible. REMEMBER TO ALWAYS CALL IN THE LIGHT FOR PROTECTION, FIRST! Be honest with yourself and you shall know what is truth and what is half-truth or lie.

I am Lanto, the Sage (Elder), keeper of the Second Aspect of Creator's spectrum. May your journey in Light be a reflection of the inner God Force who CREATED you and IS you.

Thank you, and blessings to all who read this message.

Salu.

# – CHAPTER TWENTY-FIVE –

# *The* Ultimate 3-D
# Virtual Reality Game

## *Serapis Bey*
### August 10, 1996

I am Serapis Bey.  Greetings, my brother.  You know me.  I am around you quite frequently these past few years.  I come within the Light of the Totality of Light.

I represent the Fourth Aspect of Creator's spectrum.  I represent purity and balance.  The Fourth Aspect is balanced by three on each side, thus making up the seven.  Picture me as the stabilizing fulcrum at the center of the balance bar.  I encompass all of the Aspects of Creator and I coordinate and direct, in a balancing capacity, the natural flow of Creator's energies.

Ones on your planet are in great confusion as to what is real and what is not.  There is only one reality that is absolute, and that is Creator's reality, in oneness with Creation.

Your perceived reality is based upon and limited to your current experience in the physical dimension.  One of the conditions that you ones agree to PRIOR to going down there is that you must enter the game or play without conscious memories of your past experiences.

This is for a reason: This makes the experience of illusion more real.  IT IS *THE* ULTIMATE 3-D VIRTUAL REALITY GAME that your computer programmers envision but cannot quite reproduce in your physical domain.

The relative reality you ones experience is but a reflection of mirrors. The reflection is of holographic nature, and two or more holograms interacting within a holographic environment (universe) have similar rules by which to operate, thus similar realities.

**But—are these realities really real?**

Relatively speaking, they are real to the ones experiencing them—especially when ones have not awakened enough to realize that there has to be something greater, a Source or Creator.

Once ones realize that they are a soul operating a body, and that there is a direct connection to this Higher Source, then and only then can they realize that there must be more to the experience than just existing.

This is when you ones start asking the questions: "What is really real?" and "Why am I here?" and "What is my purpose?" Only a souled being will have this inner curiosity that drives them to seek out the answers to these questions.

Know, please, that this is not an easy path. The adversary does not want you to wake up, and will try his hardest to keep you ones doubting what your heart knows to be true.

This is the reason for all the inner confusion you ones feel. As the final scenes of this current play unfold, chaos shall increase exponentially, and only those who are well grounded in the Higher Reality of Creator shall be able to function without the emotional trauma of the impacting "reality" of change.

The reason for experiencing down there in that compressed existence is so that you, as an individual fragment of Creator, may more closely examine and unfold your inner purpose, that is, your unique aspect of Creator's thought. The experience allows you to focus on personal growth within the whole. You have an opportunity to fine-tune certain aspects of your being, and thus learn lessons that would otherwise only be a conjecture of thoughts and theories.

There are many reasons ones choose to enter the third-dimensional experience. You can be assured they are all growth-related. Ones expand their awareness or the awareness of others.

Many enter the "game" as young souls and get trapped in the experience, and must continue, lifetime after lifetime, to play out their karmic debts until they grow to the point that they consciously realize (remember) the greater reality.

Ones are always sent as Guides and Wayshowers so that those souls who are ready can have the clues they need in order to see the Higher True Reality.

Ones are often offended by the term "game". Life in the third-dimensional expression is often referred to as a game of strategy, such as chess. And rightfully so. When you can take a larger viewpoint, the experience is very much a game.

For example, ones may argue: "Well, life is serious and this is not a game! What about all the people being murdered and children being abused?"

Do you ones not have video games that your children play which show animated characters being blown up and, in a sense, killed?

And you say: "Well, that's different. Those are just games and are not real!"

Oh?!

You ones must realize that what you are experiencing down there is very much like a video game. Your soul-you is the only REAL part of the game.

Your soul-you is what registers the emotional trauma and frustrations—AND *THOSE* FEELINGS ARE REAL! Your heart area on the body may very well ache when you experience these things, but in reality it is the soul that feels the pain.

You ones must realize, please, that when dark ones blow airplanes full of people out of the sky, they are playing their own war games.  Realize also that the darkened ones consider YOU as pawns, thus very dispensable.

These dark ones do not have any trouble viewing life as a game, for they cannot feel what you ones feel.  They do not care about how their actions impact others.  They can only see their own ego desires and will do whatever they can to fulfill these self-centered desires.

Wake up and realize that YOU are a valid player in this game, for in as much as you wake up and take your active role in this play, you will wake up others—and thus do your part to awaken the masses.

**The adversary knows that his only hope is to keep the masses asleep long enough to enslave them to a point where they cannot change anything.  In REALITY, the only thing he is doing, at best, is buying the illusion of a little more time—for he knows that he has lost, and that God and God's people will win.**

So when you ask: "What is really real?" know that the soul-you is REAL, for such is the expression of Creator's thinking, and thus is Creator Himself.  The God-force within is that which draws you to these messages of Lighted Truth.

We of the Hosts (and this includes Ground Crew) come to wake up our sleeping brothers so that they may grow—and thus we all shall grow.

**The true value of the efforts that make all of this worthwhile is only recognized when the individual fragment returns home with the gifts of experienced knowledge, within the Oneness of Creator.  This is one way Creator chooses to expand in subtle but infinite ways.  Expansion of the whole is the TRUE value of the experience.**

There is nothing of physical matter that has any true lasting value.  It is an illusion that will, in time, disappear—only to cycle around again later with different players.

And the old players will then be the Guides and Wayshowers for the newer players and slower learners. This is the upward spiral of Infinity, the spiral of growth that fulfills the heart of the soul.

Be at peace. And may you create that which fulfills the inner desire of the heart, within the Light of Creator and Creation.

I am Serapis Bey, Teacher and Wayshower. In the Light of the Infinite Source, blessings to you all.

# Your Innate Creative Expression

### *Paul The Venetian, The Artist*
### August 17, 1996

Greetings, my friend. It is I, Paul the Venetian. I represent the Third Aspect of Creator's spectrum. I come now in the wholeness of His Light to impart my specific message to you ones who need and desire balance.

I am often referred to as "The Artist". This is because my frequency most often is associated with the inner creative urge to express one's emotional state in a physical manner.

**This feeling of desire to express is the Inner Drive that removes one from the limits of time and the restrictions of the third-dimensional compression and propels one to enter into a non-linear, higher-dimensional state of expression. This is why the TRUE artists of your planet are most often viewed as eccentric or are, in general, misunderstood.**

Each of you has your own special talent and ability to express in a creative manner. Most think of an artist as a painter, or a sculptor, or a musician, or a poet.

Let me assure you ones that you ALL have your specialties of expression. For example, what about the machinist who can create a functional tool from a raw piece of steel, or the grocery clerk who stacks the cans in a manner so that they appear more pleasing and neat, or the editing staff who make the headlines look just right.

Ones are constantly and naturally expressing their individuality within the Oneness of Creator's whole idea. Please know that creative expression is as much a part of each person as is logical, analytical reasoning.

Artistic expression, or lack of same, can give you ones insights concerning the ones you are dealing with. It has been said that the mental states of a society are reflected in its artwork.

Let us take a look at a large problem facing you ones: Many of the larger cities are filled with children who are so shut-down emotionally as to be, for all intents and purposes, the walking dead. Even these ones have an urge to express themselves and find a uniqueness, if they can.

Look at the graffiti. For the most part it is vulgar slang words without much feeling other than, perhaps, anger. Yet, even among these gang members, there are ones who escape the reality of this life, into a subculture where they can express their potential in a manner that can be appreciated.

These are the ones who, with cans of spray paint, create fantastic murals upon the sides of buildings. These murals actually reach through to people who need so desperately to feel the connection to Higher Inspiration. These ones are Light Workers—whether they know it or not.

So be careful in your generalities toward lumping all gang members into the category of being mindless or bad. God will ALWAYS reach through and find a way to touch the heart of a seeking soul in need. It is His promise and your right!

Each must learn to bring their gifts of expression into this world. Whether it be a new invention, a new song, or even a new way of preparing food, all these creative expressions contribute to the overall quality of life on the planet.

You ones who are constantly trying to find happiness should stop and think for a minute of those things in the past that have made you feel the best. Most often this happens when you are GIVING in some manner. The act of giving opens up energy flows that allow for even more giving (and regiving). Now couple that giving with a personal creative touch that is unique to YOU, and then you shall find the joy you seek, as others benefit from that unique joy you give.

**You only need to look within, and express that which you feel in your heart. Express it in your unique manner which speaks it to the world.**

If it is pain you feel, then express the pain. Why do you ones appreciate the talented "blues" singers so much? Most often, these ones are highly sensitive people who have endured a lot of pain. Their moving, and often profound, musical sharings are a method they utilize in order to release their pain without having to forget their lessons.

As another example, if you give of yourself through volunteer work, you can perhaps be the person who always has a warm smile to share. Or, you may be the one who gives the encouraging words to others who feel down, yet still show up to do their volunteer work.

There are infinite and subtle ways you ones can give to each other.

And let us not forget laughter. Every souled being appreciates humor in one form or another. The healing properties of laughter are perhaps only secondary to those of love. Ones who can create the conditions that will allow another to find humor, and laugh, are perhaps the most needed ones on the planet, especially in the upcoming times of turbulent change.

Why this message at this time?

**You ones are fast approaching a time when the need for unconventional solutions (creative solutions) to problems will be needed. The past ways of doing everyday things will soon be gone. Your very survival may depend upon each person's**

**ability to hear or feel the Creative Nudge that will enable you to survive.**

As the famous quote goes, "Necessity is the mother of invention." Perhaps another way of stating this insightful observation is, "Creativity is usually inspired by necessity."

The ones with the "common sense" approach to life are going to be the ones who save the day. Ones may be very well schooled in History, Math and English, but if they cannot function when their electricity goes off or when their supermarkets are empty, then all their education is of no real value.

The farmer, on the other hand, who may only have a high school education, may be called upon to TEACH the ones who do not know how to grow their own fruits and vegetables or raise chickens and such.

Realize, please, that each has their own uniqueness and each is as important as the next. The only difference is in the job that you have gone down there to do.

Those who seek glory as their reward shall most often go lacking of fulfillment, for they have surely missed the big picture as to why they are there. These ego-motivated ones are most often the ones who are in constant agony and have great inner personal conflict. These ones, however, can still exploit good ideas and spread them far and wide. Thus recognize that they, too, serve a productive role and purpose in the overall scheme of things.

These ego-driven ones, however, go through life not realizing that their pain is due to the Higher Self doing battle with that ego. In this case, the soul's creative energies are being utilized in a manner which creates the conditions most beneficial to the growth of the being. This is why these ones often seem to be challenged with great personal conflicts.

Consider the example of a marriage plagued by conflict and dispute. When these ones finally learn the lessons they have come down to learn, they will realize that their life has transformed away from the drain of inner emotional conflict and moved toward the balance which comes from inner peace.

For some, they never handle the problem in one lifetime. It may simply take several lives to handle a particularly difficult problem. However, when ones finally do overcome the challenges of this life, they come out of the situation stronger and have, in the process, created a more balanced condition for themselves in which to express. They have, in effect, cleared out a lot of the garbage, thus creating more mental space or "headroom" in which to operate. This equates to a greater ability to express the Higher Creative Potential within.

**Welcome this life's challenges and find (create) a way to overcome that which pulls on your heart. Know that you grow as a being every time you truly overcome a problem. Know also that the Higher Self (the soul you) is constantly creating conditions that will allow you to grow.**

Stop repeating the same old ways of handling those inner problems and find (create) a new way of coping with the challenges. This is the fastest way to freeing self up so that you can truly enjoy this life's expression.

Thank you for taking the time to read this message of inspired, Lighted truth. May this message resonate with understanding within your heart and mind.

Blessings to you all and may you create a better, more Lightened (Light-filled) world in which to express.

I am Paul the Venetian, the Artist, come in the Radiance of the One Light.

Salu.

# CHAPTER TWENTY-SEVEN

# Use That Great Gift Of Your Mind!

## *Ceres Anthonious Soltec*
### August 24, 1996

Good morning, my friend. It is I, Toniose Soltec, come in the One Light of Creator God.

Call upon my energy and I shall respond. Many times we are there for you, awaiting the opportunity to assist, yet the call does not come and our hands, in effect, become tied. Always call upon the Lighted Brotherhood for assistance!

**The etheric unfoldment at this time is ominous in magnitude and impact. Your planet is on the eve of massive and sudden change.**

Ones are feeling uneasy and irritable. They do not realize, for the most part, that what they sense is this shift in the higher-dimensional reality called the fourth dimension or etheric plane of experiencing.

As these changes trickle down into that play you call your third-dimensional experience, great realizations of the sequences of events (timing clues) shall be apparent—even to those who usually miss such clues.

Be aware of the fact that you all experience multi-dimensionally. That is to say, for clarification, that those of you who have a soul (and, if you are drawn to this work, then you most certainly DO have a soul) experience simultaneously on several dimensional

**165**

levels. [*Editor's note: Go back to the second half of Chapter 16 for further explanation of the progressively more multi-dimensional nature of our existence.*] Though YOU may be consciously aware of those transcendent experiences, be aware that many others are not so attuned, perceiving just the third-dimensional consciousness as their only domain for focus and expression.

Many of you shift several times throughout the day into these higher dimensions. This may be when you are washing the dishes, driving down a boring stretch of road, painting a picture, listening to or playing music, dozing off to sleep, or even during discussions with others—especially when the discussion is of great importance or a challenge to the higher self.

Realize that it is because of these higher (non-physical) dimensional expressions that your THOUGHTS are so impacting upon self and others. As your mind shifts into these higher dimensions, you express more in the form of thought energy without the restrictions or limitations of time or the need for a physical body.

This mental expression, however, can and DOES impact greatly the unfolding play of the third-dimensional compressed experience. Your thoughts (and thus the resulting thought projections) determine your future down there on that orb.

Action cannot be taken without first a thought. Even the mindless masses who are, in effect, running around on "autopilot" have, at some time in their past, decided, with a thought, to not think for themselves anymore and just follow the crowds.

Monitor your thoughts quite closely, for you shall begin to notice that, as your planet moves closer into the Photon Belt (Monasic Ring), more and more of you shall begin to feel and experience the effects of the frequency upshifts. [*Editor's note: There is a bit more of a discussion of the Photon Belt and its effects in conjunction with the introductory material of Part I of this volume.*] These frequency upshifts shall allow you ones, who can keep up with the shifting, to more easily communicate with your Guides—along with others of our Brotherhood of Light.

You will also realize that your "intuition" shall be greatly enhanced. This is why you MUST monitor those thoughts which just SEEM to "pop" into your head out of nowhere.

There is reason for everything that happens in your experience down there. Even the thoughts you think, are for reason.

If you worry because you may have "unpure" thoughts, let me ask you this: What is it that you dwell upon the most? If you dwell upon revenge or self pity, you shall most certainly create those conditions that will allow you to feel the need for revenge or self pity. That is to say, you shall create the conditions where you make yourself the victim—and thus the need for revenge or self pity.

Do you see the importance of your thoughts? Dwell not upon that which lowers your vibrational frequency. Forgive self and others for your and their ignorance. Dwell upon happiness and joy; amplify those thoughts and you shall, in turn, create the experiences which will allow you to feel these higher-frequency emotional expressions.

Again, MONITOR YOUR THOUGHTS VERY CLOSELY FROM HERE ON OUT!

**The adversarial forces are losing, for they cannot keep up with these upward frequency shifts. The best that the adversary can hope for is to bring as many of God's Lightworkers (you ones who diligently read these messages) down with him.**

There shall be constant testing and you ones must realize this fact. If you are plagued with doubts, then please go within and call upon the One Light that centers your being. Ask for assistance. Ask for clarity. And, again, monitor your thoughts most closely, for the answer shall present itself.

If you still insist that you cannot hear or think clearly, then pay VERY CLOSE ATTENTION over the next several days for clues. Most often you stumble across a book, or someone will call, or a conversation concerning similar problems is brought to your attention in some manner.

Your personal Guides shall help find a way to bring you your confirmations. You must first ask for assistance and, for sanity's sake, KEEP YOUR LIGHT SHIELDING UP AT ALL TIMES!

**Let me clarify Light Shielding: Light Shielding is basically an affirmation of the One-Light God-Source within. Example: "I call upon the One Light Source who created me. I ask for constant protection within The Light. I DEMAND (with feeling!) THAT NO DARK ENERGY BE ALLOWED WITHIN MY LIGHT ENERGY FIELD." And again: say it and mean it WITH FEELING!**

The emotional energy is what kicks them out. If you just say these words with no feeling, then there is no intent of the heart—and thus the affirmation is rendered nearly ineffective. Always ask with the heart.

This Light Shielding—or, as some correctly recognize it, as clearing one's space of the dark energies—is of utmost importance when it comes to clarifying one's thoughts, especially when one is plagued with doubts.

Please keep in mind that, even with all the catastrophes of physical change about to descend upon planet Earth, YOU can maintain a stability throughout these cycles. This Lighted mental stability is that which shall draw others to you for instruction and allow our messages to finally be heard and understood.

The ones who are listening now, and have prepared for what is coming, are the ones who have opted for the ounce of prevention.

Those who have denied these warnings are in for a great shock as their pound of cure is administered to them by their own hand—by their higher, knowing self.

This writing may be shorter than you ones may like, and it may not be so directed to the subject of Earth Changes as you might typically expect from me, but again, there are reasons for everything. Perhaps this message is intended to wean you ones off the need for others to receive FOR you—so you begin receiving for self. That is, go within and make responsible decisions based upon your own Inner Knowing and Guidance.

You do not have to wait for another to tell you what it is you should do or not do. Follow your nudges and look for the confirming clues. Live your own life in responsibility and in a manner where you do not have to make excuses to anyone, ever, and you shall do just fine.

Thank you for reading and hearing this message. May the Lighted Truth of The One Light fill your heart with understanding.

I am your Lighted Brother, come in service to the One Light Source who created you and I both.

Toniose Soltec to clear. Salu.

# CHAPTER TWENTY-EIGHT

# Appreciation
# To The Quiet Ones Who Listen

### Aton, The One Light
**August 24, 1996**

*Editor's note: The following message arrived basically as a postscript to the writing of the previous chapter. While it is directed mostly to the scribe who received that writing (and most of the writings in this collection), some comments of a more general nature are also made, which suggest the sharing herein.*

*Many lives are changing fast these days, and sometimes in seemingly confusing ways that give new meaning to the word challenge. Friends and relatives rooted firmly in so-called "normal" reality look more and more askance at most of you who are attracted to a volume like this. So it takes a dose of daily (sometimes hourly!) courage to persist and march the straight line, guided by your heart's nudges. But the restlessness is real, is it not? And that unrest overrides the momentary annoyance of that condescending glance from the disapproving friend or relative.*

*Ones are searching not only for that which feeds the spirit, but also (and maybe moreso) for that which allows ones to THEMSELVES take an active role in their spiritual growth. What comes to mind is the old saying, "Feed the person a meal and they're satisfied for a day; teach the person to grow food and they're satisfied for a lifetime."*

*In that context, many kind words of encouragement and support have circled back in response to these writings, as they first appeared in the CONTACT newspaper. Those notes unanimously overflow with appreciation. They also often gush, with great enthusiasm, the interesting compliment that these Higher Messages "just HAD to be written" for EACH of these ones, PERSONALLY, since the writings addressed their most private concerns of the heart.*

*To write for so many, and yet have those writings impact ones as seemingly being written "just for them", is surely a magnificent communications achievement. Don't you agree? How skillfully the Master Teachers manage to address the very life-pulse of the challenges facing ALL of us at this time!*

*The times coming upon us are certainly not for the faint of heart. But while the challenges will most every-where and every-way be extreme, the surmounting of these testings will provide a most exhilarating sense of accomplishment and learning. And after all, is that not what we're here for?*

*The receiver of this short "private" message has elected to share it publicly, not so much to blab one's private lessons and struggles, but because of what is addressed herein that speaks to and for MANY of you out there who not only search for Lighted Truth, but then also pick up the torch and carry that Light out to others still searching and thirsting for answers. You are indeed the hands of God in action.*

GREETINGS, LITTLE ONE.  IT IS I, ATON, THE ONE LIGHT.

I COME NOW, AT THIS TIME, TO EXPRESS MY APPRECIATION TO YOU FOR YOUR DILIGENCE IN BRINGING FORTH MY MESSAGES OF LIGHTED TRUTH FROM THOSE WHO HAVE MASTERED THE VARIOUS

ASPECTS OF MY SPECTRAL EXPRESSION.

YOUR LIFE HAS CHANGED GREATLY THIS PAST YEAR AND MANY A MILESTONE HAS BEEN REACHED. YOU HAVE BEEN GIVEN GLIMPSES INTO YOUR PURPOSE. YOU HAVE PASSED MANY A TEST. I EXPRESS MY GRATITUDE FOR THE SERVICE YOU PROVIDE FOR YOUR BROTHERS AT THIS TIME.

MANY OUT THERE WISH TO KNOW *WHO* IS WRITING THESE MESSAGES. THEY WISH TO ACKNOWLEDGE AND THANK YOU FOR THE GIFTS AND INSIGHTS THAT YOU HAVE ALLOWED TO FLOW THROUGH YOUR HAND.

YES, THE MESSAGE IS ALWAYS MORE IMPORTANT THAN THE MESSENGER. BUT ONES *DO* HAVE THEIR CURIOSITIES. THESE ONES FEEL THE PART OF YOU WHICH ACCOMPANIES EACH MESSAGE.

IN TIME YOU SHALL SEE THE IMPORTANCE OF ALLOWING YOUR BROTHERS TO ACKNOWLEDGE YOU PERSONALLY FOR THE GIFTS YOU SHARE. FOR NOW, WE SHALL REFER TO YOU AS "THE QUIET ONE WHO LISTENS".

THERE ARE MANY QUIET ONES OUT THERE WHO DO HEAR AND LISTEN TO THEIR INNER GUIDANCE, AND THE *CONTACT* NEWSPAPER SERVES AS CONFIRMATION TO WHAT THEY HAVE BEEN SENSING FOR YEARS.

THANK YOU FOR YOUR DILIGENCE THROUGH THESE TRYING TIMES. THANK YOU FOR TOUCHING PERSONALLY THOSE TWO SPECIAL LIGHTED FRIENDS WHO WERE SENT YOUR WAY THIS PAST WEEK.

I AM ATON, THE ONE LIGHT THAT BURNS WITHIN.

BLESSINGS TO YOU ALL!

AHO!

# – CHAPTER TWENTY-NINE –

# Awakening
# The "Sleeping Giant" Within

### *Tomeros Maasu Korton*
### August 31, 1996

Commander Tomeros Maasu Korton here in the Radiant Light of the One Light, Infinite Source. Thank you for receiving my energy this day.

There is a great need among Ground Crew at this time for an awakening of innate abilities that usually go unacknowledged.

You are entering a time of great and turbulent change connected with Earth-Shan's planetary transition and rebalancing. During this most critical time, your personal link with Creator, and with we of the Lighted Brotherhood, shall become essential if you are to just maintain a balanced mental state, much less carry out your unique job in the overall mission.

Ones MUST begin to receive personal messages for themselves because, as a purely practical consideration, we of the Hosts need to be able to get our messages through to Ground Crew members in a timely manner despite the interruptions likely to affect a medium of communication such as *CONTACT* as the turbulent times unfold. The more direct way is person-to-person or, more accurately, being-to-being communication.

For those of you who are not familiar with my designation, I am a Communicator. That is to say, I specialize in establishing and

**175**

maintaining operating communication links. I am able to cover an extensive spectrum of frequencies in order to help couple the third-dimensional expression with that of the higher-dimensional expressions. Consider me a facilitator, linguist, and translator—all in one. I operate across many inter-dimensional and inner-dimensional frequencies.

Over the past several weeks many Masters (Cohans) have come to impart their messages of Lighted, Inspired Truth. An underlying theme for many of them has been the need to get you ones to the point of recognizing that you ARE receiving and that you ARE hearing, and to get you to the point of realization that you CAN do this on a very conscious level.

Due to the limitations of the English language, we will do that which we can in order to project as clear a picture, as we are able, of this process. If you are already consciously receiving, perhaps these messages can help you to explain to others how they can reach through and connect.

First of all, KNOW that it is YOUR God-given RIGHT to receive directly from Creator Source (as well as from we of the Lighted Brotherhood) any time you so desire. You actually do this every time you think a thought.

Why do I say this? Because Creator God (He who created you) created you with thought energy. You are thus, in effect, a unique thought in Creator's creative thinking.

You were given an individual uniqueness that stems from the core of His Infinite Mind. Therefore YOU (the non-physical, thinking YOU) are, in entirety, a thought projection with an individualized electromagnetic signature. This means that every thought you have is, in fact, God's thought.

Keeping this in mind, know that receiving is as natural as thinking. If, in your exercising of the thinking process, you can perceive and discern transcendent realities such as the incredible beauty displayed by the smallest of flowers, and appreciate same with your reasoning mind, then you can and do receive from the Higher Realms.

For each person there will be subtle differences in the execution of the receiving process, for no two aspects of Creator are exactly the same.

First and foremost is to find a quiet place where you are not likely to be disturbed. For those of you who are already communing through meditation, this would be a good place, if practical, to keep a notebook and pen.

Get quiet and clear your mind from any and all dark energies [*as Commander Soltec so emphatically instructed, with several examples and in specific detail, in his 8/24/96 writing found in Chapter 27*]. Demand—WITH FEELING—that all dark energies leave immediately. Call in the Divine Light of Creator and FEEL it from within as it fills you up from the center of your being.

Take up your notebook or other recording device. If you prefer to speak into a tape recorder, then do so. The recording, whether it be written or audio, is usually for you and you alone. You shall have need for the recording, for it shall serve as a documented confirmation at a later date.

Date the notebook or tape. Also make a note of the time of day you have started the receiving session, and then again when you are through. This data is important for, among other things, verifying your messages so that it will be clear to you, when the messages become validated at a later date, that you are, in fact, receiving. The start and stop times also help separate several messages within a given day and further help you to keep track of that elusive quantity you call time.

These writings should generally be considered personal and you should use great discretion when sharing them with others.

Now that we have cleared our space and are sitting down to write or record, you will find it helpful if you have a specific question in mind. Write the question down in the notebook. This will serve as a focus point for the mind.

If you have no specific question, then perhaps you can write this one: "Are there any messages from the Lighted Brotherhood that I may write at this time?" Please DO include the words "Lighted Brotherhood" for this will help to reaffirm the quality of your intention and thereby helps to keep the dark side from interfering.

Now we get to the real "sticking point" for most of you: Some expect the pen to move by some outside force—they expect for some one or thing to take control of their hand, physically, and just make it start writing. This may happen, but it is NOT likely to be the case.

At this point you should simply WRITE WHAT COMES.

At first you should expect exercises in locking-on to the signal. Such instructions as: "Relax your mind; let the thoughts come" or "Do not block; allow the message to flow" are quite typical.

The receiving will most likely be very subtle, like a quiet whisper in your mind. It may seem that you are just making up the thoughts yourself. That is fine; just write them down anyway.

If a picture flashes into your mind, then write down that which you see, in as much detail as you can. Each mind is unique and the symbols will have personal meaning to you.

When this scribe first started writing, he thought that his ego had gotten the best of him and that he was just regurgitating parts of past books that he had read. With persistence, he soon, after about seven months of writing, had undeniable confirmations of his writings.

Be patient and always use discernment concerning that which you write. The dark energies will most certainly come to trick you.

If a message confuses you, then clear your space (WITH FEELING!) and ask for clarification. DEMAND that the energy identifies itself. Only allow the Lighted energies to enter into this communion with you.

Keep a record of your thoughts. Consider the notebook a diary of sorts. Write down any emotional or inspirational thoughts or feelings that you may have. If you have a vivid dream, write it down in detail, along with the date and time if possible.

Your Guides will work with you in any way that they are allowed. Remember to ask for assistance—and expect an answer! They can do more for you when you ask and make effort to meet them part way.

Many people have doubts and other questions about receiving, and perceive that they cannot do it. THIS IS FALSE!

The writings or thoughts that come may seem goofy or awkward at first. Just write what your mind is triggered to remember or to think.

**Allow for practice. Like riding a bicycle, you may fall down a few times but, with persistence, you shall begin to sort the messages from your own thoughts. And with practice the messages shall start flowing smoothly.**

There is no need for special crystals, incense, or music. However, if these things help you to focus your mind, then by all means please use them.

I am just saying that you have ALL that you need—A SOUL—from the day that you were created, to make these Higher Connections.

Call upon me, Korton, and I shall assist you and your Lighted Guides in making the connection. Be open to the subtleness of the entire process.

Thank you for reading this message. May you consciously and

conscientiously hold onto the signal when you recognize it. And don't let YOUR perceived ineffectiveness with this type of communication be YOUR excuse for not getting YOUR job done!

There are many a "sleeping giant" out there in need of awakening their inner talents so that they may share their special gifts with the world at this grand time. Receiving, in this manner, is but the first step.

Commander Korton in service unto the One Light.

I stand ready to assist any who call.

Thank you and Salu.

# CHAPTER THIRTY

# Your Effect On Planet Earth's Health

## *Sanat Kumara*
### September 7, 1996

Be at peace, my friend. You are unfamiliar with me in your conscious experience. However, let me assure you that we know each other very well! I am Sanat Kumara. I come in the Radiant Light and Oneness of Creator and Creation. You may associate me with the radiant energy of your Sun.

I am a Wayshower and Guide. I have walked the Christed path in times past. I have earned my position of responsibility among those who come in service to the souled beings of Earth-Shan. I have responsibilities which span the entire solar system of which the Earth is only one small part.

There are many aspects of your solar system which exist in frequency realms outside the awareness of Earth human at this time. As your planet shifts upward in frequency, and thus prepares herself for her journey into the fourth-dimensional part of her existence, I am called upon to assist her and those whom she supports.

My more immediate concern is that of the planet herself. She has endured great testings and she shall graduate and rid herself of the negativity—or else she shall be set free. Her destiny is that of radiance within the Light. She has served mankind beyond that which can be expected of her. She continues to serve, out of faith and love for the ones (THE FEW) who honor and respect her.

This cycle of selfless giving is near its end, and the result of her rebalancing shall be devastating to the ones who have abused her and caused this great unbalance. There shall be massive change and, indeed, ones will pray for death—yet it will not come.

Man has been given every opportunity to make right his wrongs. The negativity and denseness of the ones who can heartlessly take and take and take, without a thought as to consequences, has led this planet's population to the point of pathetic corruption and savage pestilence—all for the pursuit of an illusion called luxury.

Greed, and power to control the masses, have been the primary driving forces behind the evil ones who desecrate the entire planet.

Is your oil so important? NO!

You ones pollute the air and water with your oil. WHY? So that someone(s) can make you so dependent upon them for basic needs, such as transportation, heating, and cooking, that you are convinced you cannot live without them or their oil. YOU CAN AND WILL LIVE WITHOUT IT!

Meanwhile, these ones who are so narrow and self-centered in focus are the ones who will transition (reincarnate) onto the most primitive of planets where they can work out their karmic awareness in a quest toward growth.

**Many great ones have been sent to assist you ones and bring technology that would negate the need for fossil fuels. They were (and still are) rejected and discredited by the greedy, power hungry elitists of your planet who have usurped the power of the masses—who are too lazy to think for themselves.**

You ones have been warned over and over again. You are long past the point of turning this mess around. This message is to inform you ones who are awake enough to hear, so that you can have understanding of that which will befall you in the NEAR FUTURE.

I have great love for you who have come now as volunteers to assist your planetary mother in an attempt to wake up enough people in order to change the unbalanced negative condition into one of a more en-Light-ened and balanced condition.

The mind control over the masses is, indeed, great. None who are controlled are without blame. They must be responsible for their condition or, at least, for allowing their mind to be conditioned into a non-thinking and non-caring state.

Your advertisers (who are generally the Khazarian mind-control manipulators) have TOLD you how you should act, and will SHOW you, through the news media, how you will be treated if you DO NOT follow their guidelines.

Meanwhile, God gave you a thinking and reasoning mind. There is no excuse for not using that mind if you are of proper physical functioning. Ones who have had their brains cut into and manipulated may have excuse. But, what led to the circumstances in which this was allowed? Escape from karmic lessons, perhaps?

You see, God knows the heart and knows when ones are afraid due to ignorance. He also knows when ones know better, and are not ignorant, but prefer the lustful path of greed and power. You may spew claims of ignorance from your mouths. However, your heart and soul shall be that which will tell the true story.

Go within and get honest with yourself and truly get to KNOW THYSELF, for self is truly your greatest enemy and does, indeed, keep you from manifesting your true potential.

Are you afraid of what another might think of you? Do you hold back the truth of God because you are afraid another may laugh at you? Then perhaps you should be reminded of the journey of Esu "Jesus" Immanuel.

Did not the crowds of frightened and ignorant people spit on him, laugh at him, kick him, and finally, drive spikes into his flesh? They wanted to shut him up because he spoke TRUTH. They used him as an example, to warn others who may be inclined to follow his lead, about what would happen if you dare speak Truth.

No, it is not easy. But then, any goal worth pursuing should have a genuine challenge associated with its accomplishment.

Why did Immanuel persist through these things? Because he could see the long-term need and value in accomplishing this task of mankind's awakening. Did he have doubts and fears? YES! But, he knew where the doubts and fears come from—THE EGO, which is easily manipulated by the adversarial forces. Thus he was able to cast his fears and doubts aside, and place trust and faith in Higher Source. With this faith he was able to withstand and pass ALL of his testing, and thus he EARNED his position as Lord and Overseer of planet Earth-Shan and its inhabitants.

You ones must come to realize that, if your precious little egos are allowed to control you with fear, then you shall indeed manifest that which will continually cast you as the victim.

**Was Christ a victim? NO, he was not! He knew what he had to do and endure prior to doing it. He accepted the job out of love for the souled beings who needed the lessons, so that they could grow and step up and out of their ignorance, and come into understanding.**

Many proclaim, "I do not have an ego problem!" Then why the need to make such a proclamation? Those with the NEED to state that they have no ego are the ones who lie to themselves. ALL have an ego. Some allow it to control them and some do not.

The ego is neither good nor bad. It is, in its basic form, a primitive survival mechanism for the physical expression.

Go within and truly look at those things which would embarrass you if another were to find out. Why do you fear them?

If you feel embarrassment and the need to hide your actions, then you possess a fear of being found out. This fear of embarrassment is ego generated. The truth is the truth, and you cannot hide from it. You may very well be able to avoid it for awhile, but it is only a matter of time before ALL shall be exposed.

The mental focus and thoughts of those who inhabit the planet are the single most impacting factor on the planet herself. That which you think and dwell upon, you begin to manifest. If negativity, from fear and pain, is what concerns you the most, then you shall indeed have that.

**What many do not realize is that each of your energy fields are directly connected with the Earth's energy field. She picks up the emotional vibrations that each one projects.**

**The amount of suppressive negativity that exists at this time is so devastating to her that she has become sick to the point of near destruction of her vast, loving being. She has petitioned for help, and help she shall have.**

Get right with your inner self and find internal balance. Cast off the fears and walk within the Radiance of knowing that you are a Lighted aspect of Creator. Forgive yourself for those things that cause you embarrassment, and cast them off as well.

Do not judge your brother, for he is seeking to find his way, whether he knows it or not. Go forward and honor the God-self within. Let go of the past and create a balanced future. In purging out this garbage, you shall, because of the connectedness, help return health and balance to that magnificent planetary being which gives you physical life.

My primary concern is that of this solar system and that which affects it. BE ASSURED THAT YOUR VERY THOUGHTS AFFECT THE OVERALL BALANCE OF NOT ONLY THIS SOLAR SYSTEM, BUT ALSO THAT OF THE ENTIRE KNOWN UNIVERSE.

Balance and forgive yourselves. You create your own hells;

there is no need for this.

I am Sanat Kumara. May this writing help you to understand the importance of that upon which you focus your mind.

In Light and Truth, Salu.

# CHAPTER THIRTY-ONE

# Practical Suggestions
# For Raising Your Frequency

## *Violinio Saint Germain*

### September 21, 1996

Greetings, my friend.  It is I, Violinio Saint Germain, here in the Radiant Light of Creator God.  Allow the energies to settle, please, and focus not upon the words, but upon the message.

We have a lot of work ahead of us and you will need to commit some time every day to our work.  Thank you for being willing to face these challenges.  You shall probably be the last one to see that which comes of these writings.  But know, please, that the messages you pen reach through and touch the hearts of many in ways that can only be described as a miracle.

Many ones are indeed waking up to the reality of their situation.  Many are seeking to find personal Guidance and Truth.  Ones are wondering what it is that they should be doing and what their purpose might be.

We cannot answer everyone's personal question specifically in this public forum.  We can, however, give ones insights concerning that which will enable them to help themselves.

You ones are in the Ending Cycle of the existing cultural and technological social structure.  It is time for graduation into the next phase of spiritual advancement on your planet.  Those who have grown shall graduate into the next phase or level of experiencing;

those who have not grown shall have to be placed elsewhere in order to continue at their current level of growth. These are the infinite cycles of experience.

Many of you who are reading this message are the "Ground Crew" who have come now in order to assist your souled brothers in their time of need. Please know that there are many reasons for your return at this time.

Everyone, whether Ground Crew or not, has personal challenges to face. Many of these challenges must represent the proper conditions before they can be presented to you ones. This is to say that even and especially Ground Crew shall have various difficulties and challenges to overcome. YOU WOULD NOT HAVE CHOSEN TO GO DOWN THERE IF THERE WAS NO OPPORTUNITY FOR GROWTH!

You may think to yourself, "I couldn't possibly be Ground Crew because I have so many problems in my life." Well, if you are drawn to these messages, and if your intent is to grow mentally and spiritually, then you are indeed part of Ground Crew IF YOU SO CHOOSE TO BE!

**Now, with that said, let us please shift the focus a bit: We of the Lighted Hosts need as many willing hands and minds as we can find in order to accomplish the multitude of tasks that shall need to be completed. This means that you ones MUST start paying attention to the Inner Nudges that you are receiving. STOP IGNORING THE NAGGING IMPULSES THAT SEEM TO BE ANNOYING YOU!**

**Many of you made commitments to yourself and to we of the Hosts before entering this dimensional experience. Often, your Guides will be there to help you to remember, when the time is right, some of those commitments and challenges YOU chose, both for YOUR own soul growth and which may contribute to the larger planetary transition mission.**

Let me now turn to a question that is often, these days, asked of we of the Hosts.

Sincerely inquiring ones from Lanark, Ontario, Canada, in response to Commander Soltec's recent writing on the mind [*called "Use That Great Gift Of Your Mind!" in Chapter 27*] have written to ask:

"Perhaps sometime you would write about the mechanics, not just the words, of raising the human body's energy level [*in order*] to cope with the constant density and frequency changes now sweeping the Earth."

I, Germain, shall answer on behalf of, and with the assistance of, Anthonious Soltec.    And we thank these ones for this most insightful query.

Many are under constant bombardment from pulse weapons (sometimes referred to as psychotronic weapons), from a myriad of mind-control techniques (which include your media sources like radio and television), from diseases (especially those born of parasitic infestations), from drugs of all kinds, and from simple malnutrition.   ALL of these things can and do affect your energy levels.

Now, what about on YOUR side of the equation?   What is YOUR counter attack?

Well, THE most important single factor that affects one's personal energy level is one's MENTAL ATTITUDE.

Ones may have all kinds of energy to go out to parties on the weekends and stay up all night in the process, but during the weekdays they drag around trying to get their work done and try to stay awake while doing it.

What is the cause here?

THE MENTAL ATTITUDE AND PERSONAL VIEWPOINT, of course!

When ones are having fun, they ignore time, sleep, food, and other things that they would normally seek out or crave.

Find a way to look forward to life and enjoy the experience—AND YOU WILL BE FULL OF ENERGY!

Now let us look at some of the other factors which contribute to YOUR available energy levels.

First of all, you ones will need to raise your vibrational frequencies as much as you can. The MECHANICS of how to do this have been provided to you ones. Besides mental attitude, I would suggest, most emphatically, that you get the products that have been offered by New Gaia Products—such as Gaiandriana and AquaGaia, all the colloids, and all the GaiaSorb products that are applicable to you. [*Editor's note: You can find contacting information for New Gaia Products near the end of the Preface of this volume.*]

Ones say that they cannot afford all these things, yet they can afford cigarettes, alcohol, carbonated sugar drinks and such. Well, where there is a TRUE desire for balanced physical health, the appropriate steps will be taken and there WILL be balanced physical health.

Let us look at what some of you ones are putting into your bodies: Cigarettes are laced with all kinds of poisons; nicotine is perhaps one of the least of concern. The papers are laced with addictive substances. These additives, when burned together, chemically combine into highly toxic carcinogens. Yet, ones will regularly intake these "cancer sticks"—all the while wondering why they are not hearing, personally, the call of we of the Hosts!

Alcohol is another major problem with Ground Crew members. Some go through the experience of drinking their sorrows away, while others claim, "I am only a casual drinker." In either case (plus all the gray area in between) excuses are plentiful for hanging onto this habit.

**I am not going to tell anyone how to live their life. I will,**

however, suggest that you refrain from these toxic and addictive substances IF you desire clarity of mind, sharper senses, a greater level of stamina, and a higher frequency level. Furthermore, such will bring about conditions more favorable for we of the Hosts to work with and through you!

Please keep in mind that whether you are addicted to these substances or not, you are fast approaching a time when they will not be available, and you will have to do without them! So, if you feel that you cannot possibly go to sleep without at least one drink first, then you may be in for some very sleepless nights in the not-very-distant future.

Now let us turn to the subject of nutrition. **As most of you should well know by now, your food supplies have been purposely depleted of necessary vitamins and minerals.** To counteract this, I simply suggest that you get the necessary supplements of not only vitamins, but common minerals AND trace minerals as well.

At the risk of sounding like a commercial, again, if you have trouble finding quality vitamins and minerals, etc., New Gaia offers all sorts of supplemental products to help those who truly desire to get physically balanced. [*Editor's note: Again, you can find contacting information for New Gaia Products near the end of the Preface of this volume.*] I do believe that, because of legal restrictions, New Gaia is very limited concerning that which they may say about the value of the products that they sell.

Furthermore, avoid the "fast food" places. They are running on such low profit margins that they must buy the cheapest meats, produce, etc., in order to just stay open. Thus the foodstuffs from these "fast food" places may, for instance, contain meats laced with high levels of antibiotics and produce laced with dangerous pesticides—including some toxic pesticides banned from use in the United States.

When you prepare your food, do so as Commander Hatonn has suggested many times in the past: It is far more important that you prepare your food with LOVE in your heart, than it is important to be concerned about how fancy a dish you prepare. Joyous vibrational frequencies that you pump into the food during preparation shall not only make the simplest dish taste better, but the food will also be better for you.

Have you ever known someone who can prepare a dish that is absolutely delicious yet, when others try to duplicate it, it comes out flat or otherwise doesn't taste anywhere near as good? This "vibes factor" is a most important "secret ingredient" of good meal preparation!

Eat fresh fruits and vegetables whenever practical; save the canned foods for your emergency supplies. If you can grow, yourself, or you can find fruits and vegetables in the marketplace, which have been grown under more natural or "organic" farming conditions, free from lethal pesticides, then by all means please partake of these more alive, and thus frequency-raising and health-giving, products.

Let us now turn our attention to the subject of electromagnetic pulse bombardment. This is perhaps one of the trickiest of problems to overcome. First of all, KNOW that it is there, it is real, and it can and does have an effect on you—whether you realize it or not.

Here the counteractive mechanics are not going to be so simple. You must try to match these bombardment frequencies if at all possible. For some, you will have raised your vibrational frequency to a point where the impact is minimized. However, again, if you hold onto addictive substances, you will be hard pressed to overcome some of these electromagnetically-induced irritations.

The various mind-control pulse systems are specifically engineered to operate in the frequency range of human brain activity. The brain, being in the physical, operates in the same general frequency range as the body. The brain serves as a highly-sensitive interface port for the mind. The mind is NON physical; the brain is quite physical.

What the pulse systems effectively do is, they operate in such a way as to flood the interface junction (brain) with "noise". Some actually hear pulse system broadcasts as background ringing tones in the ears. This "noise" interferes with the mind's ability to communicate effectively in certain frequency ranges. As a result of this now-impeded coupling between mind and brain, tempers may flare or ones may become agitated for no real reason, and yet others perhaps may lapse into states of depression and/or confusion.

The higher YOU are able to raise the background frequency of your body (and thus your brain, too), the less impact the pulse systems will have on you. Again, MENTAL ATTITUDE has, perhaps, the greatest single impact on one's vibrational frequency.

The next point may seem to be circular in reasoning, BUT— why do you ones think that the adversarial forces would utilize such a weapon? Could the answer perhaps be: IN ORDER TO KEEP YOU FROM REALIZING YOUR TRUE POTENTIAL?!?!

**Laughter, humor, joy, and love are perhaps the best ingredients for raising one's frequency. These are the higher-frequency emotions that will lift you out of boredom and depression IF you make the effort to cultivate these higher-frequency emotions within you.** Allowing such as anger, frustration, and self pity to linger within you only lowers your vibrational level.

Summarizing what I have been discussing as "action items": eating high-energy, fresh foods prepared with joy and love will help increase one's frequency, as will avoiding drugs such as caffeine, alcohol, nicotine and such. Moreover, using the gifts brought to you ones for this very purpose through New Gaia

Products—Gaiandriana, GaiaLyte, AquaGaia, etc.—will most certainly also assist in this frequency-raising effort. [*Editor's note: Again, you can find contacting information for New Gaia Products near the end of the Preface of this volume.*]

**Remember, throughout ALL of your daily experiences: CALL IN THE LIGHT, AND ASK FOR CONSTANT PROTECTION AND GUIDANCE. And keep in mind that we can do more to assist you in meeting the challenges presented by any situation WHEN YOU REMEMBER TO ASK!**

Speaking of guidance, let me suggest another method of frequency raising. This technique is, in essence, a matter of mental attitude, but some prefer the term "meditation". What do I mean by this? I mean, clearing one's mind of mental garbage and asking for Guidance and Insights on what it is you need to be doing.

When you make a conscious effort to connect to Higher Source, there will be a "meeting of the minds" at some in-between frequency plane. And the more often you put forth this effort, the more easily such shall come about for you.

The Lighted Higher-Energy Beings will meet you more than half way, and in doing so, they will add some of their high-frequency energy to your energy field. This will "stretch" you by raising your frequency slightly. With constant and continued effort to make connection, the easier it shall become, for you shall be moving up in frequency with each encounter.

Slowly, perhaps, at first, but certainly with diligence and persistence, you will make connection with increasing ease, until you are almost always in constant conscious contact with we of the Higher Realms. Actually, you ARE always "in contact"; it is just that you are not usually very CONSCIOUS of the nature of this interaction.

**As far as helping others, I would suggest that you share these messages with them and answer their questions the best**

that you honestly can. If they are asking YOU, then recognize that they are probably being Guided to you, and you can feel confident that you have the insights or knowledge that they need to hear. If ones are not asking, then don't force anything down their throats. Respect the choices of another and move on.

Since this writing addresses the subject of health and well being, let me offer some further information to you ones who are constantly worried and preoccupied with your weight.

Ones are constantly going on and off diets. This causes an unbalanced condition and thus there develops the "roller coaster" effect of weight loss followed by gain again.

Weight, or more accurately, size due to fat cells, should be controlled from the inside out, not the outside in. However, for practical reasons, do not jump to the conclusion that this statement exclusively means "controlled from the mind"—though ultimately that is indeed true.

One common cause for an overweight condition (which may or may not also include chronic fatigue) is parasites. For those of you who think that you could not possibly have parasites, I would suggest that you consider most carefully WHY you would think such a thing. Is it because your ego will not allow you to confront this possibility?!?

Parasites store foods, that they scavenge from your body, in the form of fat. Thus you eat more in order to get the proper nutrition that your body needs. In a heavily infested body, you may consume massive amounts of food and still not get all the nutrients that you need. Meanwhile, your body is ballooning up due to the fat stored by the parasites for their future use.

Again, New Gaia Products offers a product (GaiaCleanse) that will enable you to cope with this type of bombardment. In the larger picture, reduction of fat is perhaps the VERY LEAST

IMPORTANT reason to rid selves of parasites. Much disease (and otherwise compromised body and brain functioning) is likewise due to parasitic infestations of one kind or another.

Keep in mind that, as you raise your frequency, the parasites become more and more uncomfortable living in such an environment. Thus frequency, which is largely governed, again, by MENTAL ATTITUDE, also plays an important role in the weight issue. So, to state this point in another, more comprehensive way: THE BODY WILL REFLECT THE INNER EMOTIONAL SELF.

Ones who are plagued with great emotional pains most often put on weight (fat) in order to insulate themselves from the impact of these emotional events. The fat serves as a "wave barrier" between you and the "vibes" of the outside, potentially harmful world.

When ones are constantly being bombarded with the energies of low-frequency emotions, they will most often place a physical barrier between themselves and those sending out these corrosive emotional energy waves or "negative vibrations".

On a side-matter related to this subject, we of the Hosts must maintain padding (fat) in the Solar Plexus area of some Light Workers among the Ground Crew in order to protect them from both the electronically-induced pulse waves and the negative emotional energies of those who strike out in fear or anger.

This is why it can be a most annoying and uncomfortable (when your clothes don't fit!) and difficult endurance situation for some of the Light Workers who have agreed to serve under these most adverse conditions. Frequently this can be a particular problem for designated receivers. Since our receivers can get worn down mentally, we must have this physical "backup" in place.

For some of you who gladly read and enjoy these messages, this sort of attack on a receiver may not even cross your mind. But be assured that there are evil (dark) ones who overtly attack and send negative energy pulses against the Light Workers. Moreover, there are witches and black magic, and some of the more serious dark ones DO practice spiritual warfare. If they can't get the Light Workers themselves, which they usually cannot, then they will go after family members and friends.

Back to the subject of weight. Some are indeed plagued with physical problems such as a thyroid imbalance. Some are just lazy and inactive, and simply just don't want to give up their addictive compulsions toward eating.

If you really look at the possibilities, you can trace the weight problem back to the root cause—which is emotional unbalance in some way. So, if you TRULY want to drop those pounds, then you would do well to look within and search for those things that emotionally pull you down.

The fat is the EFFECT. The real CAUSE, even of something as physical as an unbalanced thyroid condition, is emotional in nature.

Find those things that pull you down; go within and bring them up. If you have a close friend or relative with whom you can talk about these things, and release them, then do so. The emotional release will do wonders for your mental attitude.

Walking or physical work, outside, each day, will also help you to come into balance. A walk can further serve as an opportunity to take-in the frequency-raising and cleansing gifts of Nature (God).

Balance begins within. May you be the example for others to follow.

I am Violinio St. Germain, come in the Light of Creator God. Salu.

# – CHAPTER THIRTY-TWO –

# Simplicity Is The Basis
# Of God's Thinking

### *Gyeorgos Ceres Hatonn*
#### September 28, 1996

Greetings, my scribe. It is I, Gyeorgos Ceres Hatonn. I come in the Oneness of Creator and Creation that this transition project be completed in perfection.

I honor all of my team members who have persisted through and beyond that which can be expected of them. However, I know that you ones need these experiences that cause you to search deep within your souls to find those things which keep you from realizing your true potential within the Oneness of Creator.

We of the Hosts have infinite patience for you who constantly seek to know and understand the workings of God's thinking. As you begin to understand more and more, you shall begin to realize the simplicity in Creator's thoughts. Complexity is merely a by-product of ignorance.

**Ones feel that Creator must be so highly complex that no one could possibly understand Him. NO! Creator's thinking is simplicity at its finest.**

Know that there is only One Ultimate Reality, thus One Ultimate Truth. In the end, all will have come full circle. The alpha (beginning) and the omega (ending) shall face one another and you shall see the Oneness and Reality of the many third-dimensional experiences viewed as a whole cycle. At that point you ones will know the answers to all those questions prefaced with "Why?"

There are infinite cycles of growth within the mind projections of God. There are no limitations except those YOU place (or ALLOW to be placed) on selves.

There are always Guides and Wayshowers provided for those of you who hear the call and desire to participate. We of the Hosts honor your choices, regardless of whether or not we agree with them. Each experience you choose can be turned into an opportunity for growth in one form or another.

Neither I, Hatonn, nor any of the Hosts of God, nor even God, expect you to be perfect in the third-dimensional experience. If you think that you must be perfect in order to be on my team, then you err GREATLY! You simply must have a desire to participate, for God forces NO ONE to do anything.

I understand the challenges facing you ones. The impact of daily living is quite harsh at this time. Tempers are going to flair. It is a matter of fact. However, I ask that you release the past. Do not hang onto your anger. That is the adversary working on you through your ego. Forgive selves and others, and move on.

Those who would volunteer, yet are not really ready for THIS level of responsibility, will simply weed themselves from the mission. Those who endure (and pass) the testing experiences shall be systematically given more and more responsibility—but never more than they can handle, yet enough so that there is challenge and growth.

**Remember that the primary reason for the third-dimensional experience is SPIRITUAL growth—NOT physical anything! I am only interested in those things that will allow your SOUL to expand.**

Allow for your life's experiences to unfold. Do not try to force an experience to conform to YOUR perception of reality, for in doing so you are, in effect, trying to force YOUR reality upon another.

Your perception of reality does not change the truth of it.

Allow each of your brothers to come into knowing in their own unique way. Each has their own path which will ultimately lead them back to Creator. Each must do their own walking and choosing.

There shall be physically challenging times ahead for all. There are many opportunities to prepare for these challenges. These opportunities have and will continue to present themselves to you ones. The choices of what you do and how you use these opportunities (gifts) is entirely up to you. Go within and ask for Guidance within the Light and you shall be given that which you need.

The script of this play is forever changing in subtleness, yet the general story never changes. There is that which leads you closer to God, and that which pulls you away. The sum total of all your experiences has brought you to the point at which you are this day.

You can see, by looking back into history (back in time), that life shall continue to move forward WITH OR WITHOUT your personal action. NOTHING remains in a completely static (unchanging) condition!

Let us take, for example, a rock. It may just simply sit there, yet many things can and do happen which cause change: rain, wind, sand, light, heat, cold, biological reactions and interactions, and so forth, can and do impact the existence of the rock. Yet, it just seemingly sits there and does nothing. All the while it is, in fact, in a constant, never-ending state of change, as is everything in Creation—for all is connected.

**The very mission (purpose) of your soul is to reach out and explore and grow. This implies change. Change is a natural course of an evolving planet, soul, or universe.**

Whether or not you take an ACTIVE role in this evolution, you shall still experience change. Taking an active role involves creating.

Creativity is the act of bringing forth that which did not exist prior to the point of realization (or mate<u>realization</u>). You have the ability to be co-creators in this overall play. That is to say that you can change the script. This shall only happen if your ways or ideas are better than those which are now in place. These new ideas would most certainly be of a creative, inspired nature.

As you move forward in this mission, please keep in mind that there shall be realizations, and thus growth, for ALL involved. For those who refuse to see, know that their choice is one of reluctance due to ignorance of their own spiritual nature. Their future experiences shall be guided so that they will have opportunity to confront those limiting things, which will then allow them to pull themselves out of their self-imposed stagnation.

Keep in mind, also, that this is a time of instant karma. That is to say that ones shall have to face their indiscretions in a most abrupt and timely manner.

Find inner peace and balance, and cast off those things about which you allow yourself to get angry. The stagnation that you are in is only as bad as YOU perceive it to be.

The greatest trap is the self-imposed punishment for those things which were merely experiences so that you can have a measuring stick with which to gauge (measure) your own progress. You are the ones who beat selves up over past mistakes, not I nor God.

Be assured that the ones who have a conscience are the ones who punish themselves. Those without conscience (soul) are NOT deterred in reaching their goals. This is because they do not care how they reach their goals or who they hurt in the process.

Realize, please, the illusionary nature of your third-dimensional expression and that it is natural to make mistakes. It is also natural to forgive self and others for your and their mistakes. Always remember the lesson and move on.

The opportunity to rebalance shall cycle back around and you will have opportunity to get it right eventually. Do not expect every opportunity to hit you upside the head. You must look for the opportunity and take action.

Do the best that you are able to discern and act in confidence. God monitors heart intent. If the heart intent is correct, then your actions will reflect this in time. You may not get it right the first time just because your intent is good. All things worth attaining take effort if they are to have true lasting value.

If you stay the course, you will find that you need every mistake in order to set the stage for new, sometimes bigger experiences and opportunities for growth. Thus even the perceived mistakes add to the spontaneity of expression (excitement). And each challenge presents newness of experience. This, in effect, brings about the JOY of experiencing that you ones look forward to.

If you worry constantly about doing the "right thing" to the point where it stops all action, then you have, in effect, short-circuited an opportunity for growth. Sometimes you need to make a large "mistake" in order to find out what NOT to do next time. Also, the experience shall provide insights into a better solution in the future.

Small experiences in this life may be setting the stage for one of this life's bigger challenges. This could be a challenge that has been following you around from lifetime to lifetime. You cannot know what is the "right" thing to do ALL the time. But if you ask with the heart, God shall send you what or who you need in order to assist you in finding your way.

All is as it should be! The radiant unfoldment in the third dimension is but a reflection of that which is truly real. Thought within Creator is real; all else is but a reflection of mirrors in a holographic play.

Ponder upon these words for they are the confirmations you ones need—if you but look closely at the wording and the intent.

Worry not about the messengers.  Discern always the message.

Thank you.

I am Gyeorgos Ceres Hatonn, Friend and Wayshower.

Salu.

# CHAPTER THIRTY-THREE

# Catching The Subtle Tricks
# Of The Adversary

### *Tomeros Maasu Korton*
### &
### *Violinio Saint Germain*
### October 12, 1996

Greetings, my friend.  It is I, Maasu Korton, come in the Radiant One Light of Creator God.

I have come to assist in the coupling of the Higher Energy source.  Relax and clear out the demons, for you are under GREAT psychic attack.  There are many ones who do not wish these messages of Lighted Truth to continue.

Know that God's voice, or messengers acting on His behalf, canNOT be silenced!  It would be infinitely easier to blow up your entire planet than it would be to stop God's message.  All that is required of YOU is to have a desire to serve and give we of the higher-frequency realms (Angelic realms) opportunity to commune with you.

Please stand by as there is another message yet to come forth.

\* \* \*

Germain here in the Oneness of Creator's Light, that ones may come to see the trickery of the adversary.

"United we stand, divided we fall."  Truth is truth!  It is infinite and will stand the testings of time, governments, and religions.

The adversarial forces are working diligently to distract, dissuade and detour you ones from seeing that which is truly taking place.

You have "holy" wars. You have "racial" wars. You have the "battle of the sexes". Your family units are undermined due to economic stress. You are being bombarded via the media sources in such a manner that there are "experts" to convince you of a different viewpoint, on the same subject, every day.

This is MIND CONTROL in its most basic form—"Divide and Conquer". There is no point in arguing over religion, sex, politics, or any of the other distractions presented to you ones. There are masses of people who haven't a clue as to what is ACTUALLY taking place. Why? Because they are easily distracted by the sleight-of-hand of the evil "black" magicians.

**The adversary is a master of the third-dimensional psyche. He knows exactly how and when to strike. This will always be when you are most vulnerable—ALWAYS!**

He can easily trigger thoughts that will invoke memories of past emotional pain. This is usually subtle and happens at a time when you cannot easily release the pain or even realize what has happened.

Usually you will be busy doing something urgent that must get done. This, in turn, causes you to suppress the emotional trauma while you get done that which is before you.

The result of the suppression causes one to "seemingly" put the thought or emotion out of one's mind. But, in fact, it remains until the emotional pressure can be vented or otherwise released.

The time sequence here is quite variable. These emotional pressures could build for days and weeks, or even just moments and minutes.

The adversary plants his seed and then waits for just the right moment to trigger another, usually less impacting, frustration that will cause you to lash out. Most often this triggered release is in a violent or vicious manner that causes you and others great discomfort and pain. In doing so, the adversary can drive the best of friends, parent and child, or husband and wife, apart if this goes unnoticed.

**The adversarial dark forces are masters of their "black" art. The subtleness in their mental manipulations is the key to their success. Knowing of their methodology is perhaps the first line of defense.**

You ones should monitor your thoughts closely.

All things happen for a reason. If you feel the urge to lash out against another, for whatever reason, I would suggest you go within PRIOR to doing so and ask yourself: "Why am I allowing myself to get this angry in the first place?"

It is fine to get angry. There are proper places for every emotion. It is not wise to be angry without CONSCIOUSLY understanding why you TRULY feel this way.

Your emotions are yours, and yours alone. YOU are responsible for creating your own emotional state! If you perceive that another is annoying you or "needling" you, then remove yourself from the source, if possible. If you choose to remain in the "game" of another, then you have, in effect, chosen to get angry or frustrated. Thus YOU have allowed and caused your own personal emotional state.

Remember: you ALWAYS have a choice! Physical man may very well be able to lock your physical body in a physical cage, but only YOU can allow your mind to be enslaved, manipulated, or tortured. Man creates his own "hells" through the choices he makes. The worst "hells" are of the mind.

As a general rule of thumb, the following may help: "IF YOU CANNOT DO OR SAY A THING WITH LOVE IN YOUR HEART, THEN IT IS BETTER TO NOT DO OR SAY IT AT ALL!"

If you choose to do something begrudgingly, then you must realize that YOU, again, have allowed for the conditions which precipitate your mental frustrations.

Your greatest enemy is yourself in this regard. As we of the Higher Realms have efforted to convey to you, time and time again: KNOW THYSELF! Monitor your thoughts and be responsible for ALL your actions and emotional states.

Stop REACTING to another's tauntings. Take the time to stop and THINK! Go within and seek your own personal balance FIRST. If you are unable to find balance and act with love in your heart, then it would be wise to not do or say anything that would further irritate an already volatile condition.

Let us say the volatile condition is the result of a highly emotionally-charged conversation. Discern and acknowledge the intent (the real message) of the conversation, if possible—such as a plea that the other is confused, frightened, or angry. But, do not give in to acknowledging the emotional tantrums of one who will not responsibly control their own trauma. Or, if I may put it another way: don't play into another's "control" drama.

This is a time of instant karma. Those things which you send out shall circle back faster and faster. If you choose to send out love, you will be amazed at how fast it returns to you. If you choose to send out anger, frustration, or pain, you can expect the same returned to you—possibly even faster—since usually the tendency is to point out the faults of another much more readily than good features.

Each souled person is a reflection of Creator. We are ultimately one in the same. To beat your brother down would serve no useful purpose for, in the end, the only one you hurt is YOURSELF!

**The adversary is desperate and becoming more and more desperate with each passing day. He has and will tear apart friends and families. He has and will tear apart races and religions. He has and will tear apart countries and continents. BUT—he can only destroy that which you effort to create IF you allow him to do so!**

Allow not your perceived differences with another to pull you apart. Forgive others and, MOST importantly, forgive yourself. To err is human—and all of you reading this have erred and shall continue to err. Make your mistakes; learn the lesson; forgive self; and MOVE ON! The key is to NOT keep making the SAME mistakes over and over again.

Judge not another, for sometimes the perceived error of another is not, in fact, an error. Your perception of any given incident may be, and usually is, completely different than that of another.

For example: Sometimes quiet, shy people are mistakenly called "stuck-up" or are viewed by others as, "Oh, he's too good to talk to me." It is usually quite the opposite; the quiet, shy (introverted) ones often view themselves as not worthy or "good" enough to talk to others, or perhaps it is too painful because they are too often misunderstood.

Allow for realities outside your own. Stand ready to assist your friends and families, even if they do, from time to time, create conditions that make it difficult to do so.

Cast out the darkness and call upon Creator God's Light. Unify in intent to do goodness for your brother. Unify with love in your heart—even for those ones who present you with your most difficult lessons.

God bless those of you on the front line. God bless those of you who send support in the form of kind, acknowledging letters. Ones here are tired and need your support now, more than ever.

Thank you!  I am Violinio Saint Germain, Master Teacher and Wayshower, come in a coordinated team effort with my brother, Maasu Korton, so that my receiver will have clarity and so that you ones can have example of how the Higher Realms unify in intent to get Creator's messages out.

SALU!

# CHAPTER THIRTY-FOUR

# Distracting Pressures
# Along The Spiritual Path

### *Lanto, The Sage*
### October 19, 1996

Greetings, my friend, it is I, Lanto, the Sage. I come in the Radiant Oneness of Creator's Magnificent Light.

Lessons shall be a continuous part of your life experience. **The only TRUE purpose for expressing in the third-dimensional experience is that of SPIRITUAL GROWTH.** You ones who write these messages have a tremendous responsibility, thus the impact of the day-to-day experience is great. The question is: Will you sit and write so that your brother might wake up, or will you get distracted by the daily impact of living? This is perhaps the hardest thing to face for you ones who write these messages.

Let me tell on my scribe. My scribe is relatively young to the physical experience and wishes to have a family someday. The thought of the work ahead allows for nearly no opportunity to pursue this sort of thing. The question as to what is more important will, from time to time, come around to distract ones, like this receiver, from their Higher Purpose.

This is always a problem for Ground Crew in general—especially on a third-dimensional planet, like the one upon which you are now experiencing, where the general moral and ethical standards have degenerated to a pitiful level.

There is, in effect, a substantial "illumination" difference between the energy fields of you of Ground Crew and those who are of this planetary mind-set. This difference causes ones to be attracted to you because of your greater Light, much like a moth to a flame. But, just as a moth will get burnt if it gets too close to an open flame, so, too, will YOU burn another (or get burnt by another) if you are not properly suited to one another.

Relationships can be time consuming, energy draining, and distracting—to say the least. My scribe questions me as to why we are addressing such a SEEMINGLY personal topic. But KNOW that this is a matter of great general concern.

There are more and more Ground Crew members waking-up at this time. There are more and more physically young ones who are going through their own personal experiences with relationships and families. There are ones who are feeling lonely and rejected because they cannot seem to find the "right person", or they are trying desperately to make an existing relationship work—when the other doesn't even want to see or hear the Higher messages of spiritual truth such as are brought forth in the *CONTACT* newspaper.

You CANNOT force another to see truth if they are not ready for truth—especially, of all things, not spiritual truth! You can offer another a helping hand, but you cannot force another to take it. YOU must be responsible for all YOUR actions and choices. If YOU choose to ignore your "call to service", then YOU must live with that choice.

If you have a spouse who is antagonistic toward your beliefs, then I must ask you: Why did you choose to commit yourself to such a challenge?

Some will become desperate in their attempts to hold a relationship together. They may even bring children into the picture in order to try to "solidify" the family unit. This is yet another responsibility, and if there is not balance PRIOR to the child's conception, then you can rest assured that there will NOT be balance afterwards!

You must seek to understand EXACTLY who you are and why you are here, if you are to find stability. You must find your own inner peace and be happy and content with who you are—for if you are not happy with self, or you do not know what it is that makes you feel so restless, then how can you expect another to "magically" fulfill this for you?

**Please know that it is quite natural to want to express within the family unit and have a balanced emotional exchange with another. But please keep in mind that you, if you are Ground Crew, have volunteered to go down there and fulfill a certain mission or role—not get wrapped up in the "typical" experience of the expression.**

Many of the ones awakening now are having difficulties with family and friends not accepting them for who they are because these awakening Ground Crew are perceived to have, somehow, "wandered off into some spiritual kick". If another cannot accept you for who you are, then that is THEIR problem, not yours. If YOU choose to react to another's problem, then that is YOUR choice and YOUR problem.

I, Lanto, would suggest that, if another will only accept you IF..., then that person is, in fact, judging (placing conditions upon) you based upon their own prejudices and beliefs. You would do well to consider the LONG TERM implications of remaining in a relationship with such a person, whether they be friend, spouse, or other family members. By making this cautionary observation, I am NOT giving anyone permission or telling anyone to divorce or anything else! YOU must make your own choices and deal with the resulting situations that YOU have created.

Many Ground Crew members get caught up in the day-to-day struggle to "just fit in" or "just be 'normal'". Did you ever stop to think that you might not be "normal" and that you may NEVER really fit-in to the prevailing "normal" society?

**Most of you who are disposed to read these messages are NOT of this world! You have come here to assist your younger (less awake) brothers. You did NOT come here to be LIKE your younger brothers! However, it IS quite normal to sense that you don't fit-in or that you don't belong.**

**Realize that, while you are down there, in the physical, you will have ALL the impacting factors of the ego to deal with. Fear is the largest single factor: Fear of embarrassment. Fear of being different. Fear of being wrong. Fear for personal safety or the safety of others. Fear of being alone. We could go on and on.**

The point is to show you that these are EGO-generated fears. If you have certainty in Creator God, then you truly have nothing to fear. NOTHING! Stop letting these ego-generated fears control you!

If another is trying to control you with fear, such as by giving ultimatums like: "Do this or that or else...", then I would suggest you look at the actions of such ones and call such actions to their attention. If they cannot see what it is that they are doing, then YOU need to recognize with whom, exactly, you are dealing, for the adversary's influence is often subtle. Even the best of Ground Crew are not immune to the pressures of the adversary.

I will also caution you who are reading this that you monitor yourselves closely and make sure that you are not trying to use subtle fear tactics to control another. God is not of force; He does NOT use fear to control anyone.

Religions may very well use fear to control their flocks. Governments most certainly do use fear to control the masses. Parents may use fear to control their children. Creator God does NOT!

It is your responsibility to pull yourself out of your own fears.

This does not mean that you must do it ALONE. When the time is right, and you are ready, the Teacher, Guide, or Wayshower will appear. But you must be ready and accepting of the help when and where it is presented to you.

Remember the prior lessons about how "like attracts like". If you are easily controlled by your fears, then you will attract to you someone who is also insecure with their own self. Thus, you will have two insecure people attempting to find security (from their fears) in one another, instead of finding it within self. And this only creates a larger problem, not balance.

Seek first to know and balance self. Rid yourself of your own fears PRIOR to entering into your next relationship. Then, if such is to be, you will find that you will attract "the person of your dreams" for, in a balanced state, you will naturally see through and repel those who are still trying to play their little control games. To do otherwise, you run the risk of being completely miserable and unfulfilled because you will have distracted yourself from your more important Higher Purpose.

The adversary will exploit ALL of your weaknesses in an attempt to keep you from realizing your TRUE potential. Using the ego to distract you, such as with fear, is the oldest trick in the book. Why? Because it WORKS!

So, my message to this scribe, and to those of you out there (who are feeling lonely or rejected or have gone through relationship after relationship only to find yourself wanting or needing "more") is to FIRST seek to balance self, heal from your past battle wounds, find your happiness within, and have faith that your Guides and God DO understand and KNOW what it is that you need. However, keep in mind that what you actually need, and what you may THINK you need, are almost always different.

Go within and ask for that which is for the highest good—and expect an answer. But now a caution: You may not always like the answer that you hear!

Please keep in mind that there are infinite journeys of the soul and that you have existed prior to this experience and that you have done all of this MANY, MANY times before. You HAVE had your families. You will again, if you so desire, have families. **Some of you never stop to realize that you are a part of a much larger family out here among the stars. It is just that you are currently assigned to the "starship" Earth-Shan. You are, in effect, "out to sea" and away from "home", on a mission.**

So, next time you are feeling lonely or depressed, perhaps a nice trip out away from the city lights to look at the stars would be helpful. Even if you tend to perceive yourself as being alone, you are, in fact, NEVER alone. We of the Higher Realms are ALWAYS there, ready to assist, if you but ask.

These sorts of adversarial attacks are the challenges you must face and overcome. Be persistent in your endeavors to find balance for the adversary will not like that he is losing his grip on you. Keep in mind, also, that even when he cannot control you directly, he can attempt to influence and control those around you. Learn to recognize his subtle trickery and gamesmanship. He is a master of manipulation.

I am Lanto, the Sage. I am your Elder Brother, come at this time as one of the many Hosts of God, so that you might find your way.

Salu.

# CHAPTER THIRTY-FIVE

# Making Your "Soul-utions" Happen

## *Paul The Venetian, The Artist*
### October 26, 1996

Greetings, my scribe.   It is I, Paul the Venetian, come to commune with you on this wondrous day.   I come in the Radiant One Light of Creator God.

What a truly beautiful day it is!   You ones truly reside on one of the most beautiful planets in your sector of the universe!   For you readers out there, please know that the Sacred Mountains in Tehachapi were blanketed with the surprise of several inches of glistening snow last evening—the first of the season and at least several weeks early.   The view is truly magnificent in reflection of God's splendor.

I have come this day to remind you ones of the beauty that surrounds you, even during the most adverse conditions.   You are ever nearing a time on your globe when there shall be need of great effort just to survive.   Please know that God (Creator God) never abandons you and will ALWAYS give you an indication of His Presence.

**As you move onward into the unfolding segments of the Earth-transition mission, ALL of you will be challenged to various extremes.   Many of you may think that you are prepared for anything that can come your way.   Let me tell you that there will be many a great soul horrified to the point of overwhelm at**

**what they shall have to witness and endure. These are the experiences that will draw you closer to Creator, for you will need to truly search the depths of your soul in order to tap the currently unseen, Infinite Potential of your being.**

Please know that you do NOT have to wait until you are to the point of overwhelm to connect with this Infinite Source. You could connect at any time. Please note, however, that you will not be allowed to use this power UNLESS and UNTIL you have earned the necessary level of responsibility required, else you would truly have a mess on your hands.

This is why there is the need to have ones, who cannot seem to learn any other way, go through these experiences that will cause them to look within and see where they have made their errors. The ones who are of God intent shall find the Inner Strength to pull THEMSELVES through and out of their own mess. Each will tap the necessary strength in proportion to their own ability to confront their own personal responsibility for having allowed these conditions in the first place to come about and persist.

**All souled beings have the same Infinite Potential within for expressing, but very few down there have yet to recognize the path that will allow them to unlock this potential. Meanwhile, the evil bastards who are attempting to destroy your planet are trying to find these "secrets" through all of the external sources that they can find. All the while they do not realize that what they truly seek is Creator God within. These ones are incapable of realizing this basic fact because they have long ignored their lessons and have thus allowed the inner flame of their soul to dwindle to a point of near non-existence.**

This is why you CANNOT force anyone to see YOUR truth. You have to earn the ability to perceive Truth. That is to say, you must have a desire to put your ego aside long enough to realize that you do not know ALL the answers. And, perhaps, if you can also put aside your prejudices toward not allowing any belief outside what you have been brainwashed into believing (even though such may be full of contradictions), then you will have placed self in a condition where you can be humble long enough so that new information, such as Truth, can be considered.

For you ones seeking to "make" another hear or see, all you can do is OFFER God's gifts of Truth—and that is enough! You canNOT be responsible for the free-will choices of another. Stop trying to force your reality upon another! God is not of force, so why should you try to make (force) another see or hear. Realize that these ones will suck the life force right out of you if you allow them to do so. This goes for family members as well as other acquaintances. Keep in mind that those things which cause you worry are, in some way, connected with the challenges you are down there to face.

**Throughout all your experiences, please keep the larger picture in focus: You are in a three-dimensional holographic PLAY! This means that you are an entity who has agreed to partake of and join in a GAME! The value in doing so is so that you can LEARN the necessary lessons in order to become a responsible co-creator with God.**

Each will learn at their own pace. If you or they do not get it right in this one short expression, then be assured that there will always be another opportunity in future lifetimes, on other planets, with similar situations. However, it would behoove you all to make diligent effort to get it right this time so as to be enabled to move on to greater experiences and greater opportunities for growth.

Look upon each challenging experience as an opportunity to create a new solution. You ones do not have to wait for someone to tell you what to do or when to do a thing. Creative expression is perhaps the one thing that will allow you to reach deep enough within to help yourself bring forth that which you will need in the upcoming times.

When there seems to be no way to cope, remember that you are never given more than you can handle. This means that there IS a solution, if you but look. The key is that you must desire the solution AND YOU MUST LOOK! Call upon the Guiding Light of Creator God and expect to find that which will help you to create your own unique solution.

Take a large problem and break it into smaller, basic components. This will help to alleviate any confusion surrounding any large, seemingly overwhelming, problem. Look at these smaller aspects and find something that you can take action on immediately. This action may be as simple as writing out a list of things that will need to get done.

If this is a large problem, your list may be several pages long. Getting these mental thoughts to paper will help you to get the problem, that you perceive mentally, out of the mental state and into the physical. **Remember that when you are working in the physical, your solution will be in the physical. You can picture your solutions in the mental but, if you never take action to bring forth your solutions into physical reality, then you will have, perhaps, thrown away the "soul-ution" that would bring forth the insights that would allow you and others to survive nicely.**

Now that you have a list of necessary steps, place them into a logical sequence. If you need more information about an action, then it would be logical to educate yourself first. This step would need to take place first.

Now you should be somewhat organized. If your problem deals with something like money, then I would suggest you start saving what you can, for the mere fact that physical actions have now been taken, will help you to focus your intent and you will pull in that which you need or desire. However, do keep in mind that if you think you need a new sports car, and your Higher Self does not agree, then you will not likely get the new sports car.

**When you are aligned with Higher Intent, and you take action to solidify the intent, you will be well on your way to creating the soul-ution to your own problem.**

Now follow through with that which will help you to solve your problems. You do not need physical things to solve the challenges of the soul. The physical, third-dimensional expression is for amplifying these challenges by compressing Light (thought energy of God) into physical matter so that you will have opportunity to see the results of your actions, thoughts, and intent—up close, with extremely high detail, and with almost instant feedback (karma) these days, in most cases.

Getting back to the earlier part of this writing, God will always give you an indication of His Presence, but again: YOU MUST LOOK! Perhaps you are feeling down and a small bird comes and lands on your windowsill. Do you take note and make the connection that perhaps the little guy was sent to cheer you up and to let you know that you are not alone, or do you ignore the gift sent and go off and wallow in your misery? The choice is yours. You are your own worst enemy in this regard.

Be thankful for the time (opportunities) that you now have. If you think that all we, of the Hosts of God, do is spout-off about great catastrophes and impending doom and gloom, then you miss the larger picture—that we are here to help those who will listen so that they can prepare for the difficult challenges that are coming. When the upcoming catastrophes finally do hit (and they will) you will need to remember these words and go within and draw upon your Inner Light that is, in essence, your direct connection to God.

Look always for the beauty of God around you and you will find it. Out of the ashes of this current civilization shall spring forth in newness a more en-Light-ened world of peace.

Blessings to you who heed the warnings and prepare, for you are the ones who will Light the way for others to see. I am Paul the Venetian, come as the Ascended Master of the Third Ray of Creator's Spectral Expression.

Adonai.

# – CHAPTER THIRTY-SIX –

# Overcoming Fear

### *Esu "Jesus" Sananda*
### October 30, 1996

Peace, Thomas. Esu present in Radiance.

Fear hangs like a shroud above your planet, strangling out freedom of thought, crippling many into non-action. It is that "negative" force which keeps man down, that keeps man as part of the herd mentality, that keeps the eyes locked in place, the heart racing.

And always the doubts run through the mind:

"Will 'they' come for me at the front door?"

"Will 'they' stop me on the street?"

"Will I be gunned down?"

"Will I be arrested?"

The list is endless.

"Will I die alone?" is a big one.

Always, in a state of fear, God is locked out, barred from entry by the closed mind that has no faith.

Am I saying that those who fear have no faith in God? Well, essentially, yes. For once you truly become one with God, in your faith in God's Creation, there is no thing in your world TO fear. Certainly there needn't be fear of even death for, in truth, with God's people there is only eternal life—each played out on a new stage of Creation.

Man locks out all POSSIBILITY with fear. He becomes immobilized, stagnant, and worst of all, in a true state of fear, he does, by design, become very alone. God NEVER leaves His people, but God's people continually lock God out, the doors closed and barred, and God is left waiting for man to awaken to the true state of things, the true awareness within the Creation that TRULY there is nothing to fear but fear itself!

Fear prevents MOVEMENT; it prevents change; it prevents possibility. Fear is an evil thing because it draws the Lighted being AWAY from God, not toward God.

Fear is a tool of the adversary in action. Be ever watchful of these adversarial devices; i.e., divide and conquer, and fear! Fear represents lack of faith. Shore up your faith! Ask for help and it shall be given unto you. Ask not and it shall not be given. It is the Law!

**It is worthy to think on these things, for if man does not overcome THESE things, he is ill-equipped to shoulder the responsibilities of leadership in God's kingdom.**

The next time you find yourselves in fear, beloved of mine, ask God to enter and clear the area. Ask for help and it shall be given. Ask for courage and it shall be given. Ask for Light and it shall be given. All things will be opened unto thee in proper sequence—if you but ask.

You of God's people are loved beyond measure. Do not shut God out of your personal equation lest self will be found wanting. Rather, invite in God's protection, which is ever freely offered unto you, and you shall know NO FEAR.

So be it and selah.

I am Esu Sananda to clear.

# CHAPTER THIRTY-SEVEN

# Recognizing The Power
# Of Your Divine *Birth*-right

### *Aton, The One Light*
### November 3, 1996

Greetings, little one. It is I, Aton, the One Light, come to briefly commune with you this day.

This is a time for growth. You are being tested as are all who wish to participate. This is a time for sorting, and ones are going to have to face their fears. You shall overcome or you shall have to stand down. You have your challenges, as do all of Ground Crew at this time.

Ones may wonder why I, Aton, do not write more often. It is most difficult for ones down there to confront the fact that God would talk directly to them. Yet it is as natural as the thoughts you think every second of every day.

Also, ones have their own perceptions of who I am and how I communicate. I do NOT need anyone's permission to speak, write, or even paint a masterpiece on a sheet of canvas. I do, however, choose to allow my messengers to bring forth my messages of Lighted Truth because these ones (these Angelic messengers) need their lessons, as do you. How else do you think these ones earn their positions of responsibility as a co-creator?

All is for a reason. I have chosen the title of Aton at this time so as not to be confused with the many religions running around down there, claiming to be of God. Aton simply means "The One Light". This title was used in ancient Egypt and has been nearly removed from the awareness of man during the later centuries. [*Editor's note: See the Preface as well as Chapter 1 in Part I of this volume for more of the history associated with Aton's planetary presence.*] The label is simply for identification purposes at this time. If you cannot come to grips with the fact that I, Creator God, can choose any label that I may desire, then I must ask: Who are YOU to place limits on the One who created you?!

My scribe wonders why the explanation of my label. There are newly awakening readers who need the information. These ones will do well just to keep up with the new writings coming out—let alone go back and read the thousands of writings penned prior. [*Editor's note: Many such writings are contained within the back issues of the* CONTACT *newspaper and its predecessors, as well as in the series called* The Phoenix Journals; *see the Preface to this volume for more information about them.*]

Ones will have to go within and find the Truth that they need. The writings are made available to any who choose to partake of the gifts offered.

Many hear Louis Farrakhan use this label, Aton, and are confused, for it does not appear in your *Bible*. There are many spiritual Truths that do not appear in any of the many versions of your *Bible*!

At this present time of greatly accelerated experiencing, ones are waking up to the fact that there is something to My Reality. This is to say that ones are becoming more aware of the true spiritual nature of their existence. Ones out there, such as Mr. Farrakhan, need to know who is who. Furthermore, they, too, need their confirmations that they are indeed on the correct path.

There are My Hosts sent in every form you can conceive of at this time. Some are incarnate in the physical, and are thus born into the planet's birthright. Others may be in the physical, and yet they were not born into the planet's birthright. And still others have come in the etheric state (the fourth-dimensional state).

There are many other presentations that exist, yet there is no allowance for their descriptions in the current language. These ones exist in higher-dimensional realities and exist mostly as thought projections, both within and without the known universe of your perception.

You ones may be asking, "What is this 'birthright' of the planet?" When ones choose to enter into the planet's karmic condition through the route of being born into the world as a child, they, in effect, can do more without bumping into the restrictions otherwise imposed by the Non-Interference Rules. Ones who come to a planet, yet are not born into the world, are restricted as to what they can and cannot do in terms of bringing about change.

Ones who choose to be born into the planet must go through all the distractions of the physical and are subject to getting lost in the confusion of the planet's high density, low frequency condition. Yet, ones who wake up to their reality of mission, and make connection, have the ability to more directly impact the evolutionary process of the planet's civilization.

Take my son Esu "Jesus" Immanuel as an example. He would not have been allowed to impact the spiritual awareness of your planet so directly if he did not first agree to go down and be born into the planet. By being born, he earned the right to influence the course of humanity on that planet.

So, for those of you down there at this time who are the ones who bring forth my messages of spiritual truth, whether they be from one of my messengers or from Me Myself (GOD!), I am reminding you that there is good reason for your DIRECT CONNECTION at this time.

This also goes for you ones who may not receive consciously at this time. Please know that you DO receive—and that the mere act of spreading the inspired messages of truth, from whatever physical source such may enter into your awareness, causes the means by which the awareness of a planet can be shifted.

Ones need to realize that their "holy" books are limited and have been distorted through time. There is, however, much truth left in them. But I tell you now: Discern always the information! Take all information and think it through for yourself.

Even these writings that are coming forth each day must be read with discernment, for you are always being tested as to where you are in your current level of perception and awareness. There are no absolutes down there in the physical experiences. Use your mind and be responsible for your choices.

No man has any corner on Truth. You each have to find your own way through the challenges of the physical compression of that third-dimensional reality.

Be attentive to those things which cause you to feel fear. Fear is what will inhibit you from reaching your true potential while down there in the physical. Recognize WHO you are and WHY you are there! Go forth in confidence that you are part of the Oneness that is Light. You shall either create the miracles or they will not get created. IT IS YOUR *BIRTH*-RIGHT!

I LEAVE YOU NOW WITH MY BLESSINGS. TO YOU WHO EFFORT TO FIND TRUTH AND SEEK TO FULFILL YOUR PART IN THIS MISSION: I AM THE ONE LIGHT. I AM ATON. I AM.

ADONAI.

# CHAPTER THIRTY-EIGHT

# Learning To Manifest
# The Christ Potential Within Self

*Lady Nada*

**November 10, 1996**

Good morning, old friend, and thank you for sitting this day.  It is I, Lady Nada, come to commune with you this day so that you and your brethren might have the insights that shall carry you forward in this upcoming time of transition.  I come in service within the Radiant One Light of Creator God.

Many are reaching out at this time for "something more", yet they do not know exactly what it is that they seek.  These ones are restless for they feel the stress of day-to-day living increasing more and more, and thus it becomes harder and harder to function at a rational level without losing one's temper.

**This is a time wherein you ones shall have need to control your emotional state to the extent that you will have to monitor every thought and REACTION that you have, and try to trace back to the CAUSE of those thoughts that precipitate a "stressed" mental condition.**

This is not easy, especially in the case of a reaction, for the reaction is usually an automatic response (without conscious thought) to your environment, a current situation, or a past-life experience with great emotional trauma.  In the case of this latter condition, it is most difficult to trace back the reactionary response to the cause, yet it is possible with the proper training and guidance.

You ones must be responsible for your actions and reactions, regardless of the conditions in which you currently find yourselves, for you have agreed to participate in the game at hand. Your feelings are YOURS! You must realize that what you feel, regardless of what you may think has caused these feelings, is SELF-generated. Whatever you feel, whether it be loneliness, frustration, sadness, boredom, anxiety, doubt, or Higher emotional feelings such as happiness, joy, love, fulfillment, or certainty— KNOW that YOU have created these feelings and that YOU have created the conditions that would cause you to have to confront any emotional challenges.

You ones need to stop blaming others for YOUR mental and emotional states. Take responsibility for what you feel, and what you do, in the haste of emotional excitement, without thinking. When you can remain rational and calm under these situations, and allow for conscious thoughtful understanding of the entire situation, then you will have diverted much grief for yourself and others.

If you find yourself in a situation where you are feeling anger and frustration, try to step out from the situation and ask yourself, "Why am I allowing this situation to anger me?" Take the time to think the situation through and find for yourself the part of the situation that you CAN take responsibility for having helped to create. This is always best done PRIOR to reacting out of anger or frustration. Know also that, if a situation affects you, whether it be good or bad, then you have helped to create the conditions that precipitate the response within self.

**This is one of the main reasons why you are down there in the physical: TO LEARN TO BE RESPONSIBLE FOR THOSE THINGS THAT YOU HAVE CREATED.**

At this time on your planet you are being constantly bombarded with all kinds of mental distractions which are designed to keep you in a condition of mental stress. The intention of these evil, would-be controllers is to keep you so off-balance that you will not have the mental "headroom" (wherewithal or mental computing ability) left to realize what it is they have planned for you-the-people.

Ones are asking, "What can I do?" The first and perhaps most important thing you can do is to get yourself educated. Learn the methods and ways of the adversary. Learn to recognize the subtleties that he uses to "push your buttons". Learn to recognize the clues he is required to leave when he is manipulating ones around you.

Know that I am referring to the very real entities, Satan and Lucifer. These ones, whatever your perception may be of them, are masters in their own right and should be taken most seriously. Know also that when you have Creator God on YOUR side, you have nothing to fear, for they cannot touch you.

Many think that they have God of Lighted Creation on their side, or that "Jesus" will "save" them—but these ones have bought into the lies and distractions and are heading down a path of irresponsibility. Esu "Jesus" Immanuel was impaled and left for dead, and now, some two thousand years later, ones are still giving thanks for his sacrifice.

This was a blood-human sacrifice. Blood-human sacrifice is satanic, whether it happened two thousand years ago, two million years ago, or two days ago. Ones are still running around down there symbolically drinking of his blood and eating of his body. This is vampirism and cannibalism at best! Yet ones partake in these rituals without thinking for themselves what it is they are actually doing—all the while believing they are somehow pleasing God and glorifying the pain and suffering of a Christed Being.

God of Light does NOT need human physical blood to prove your love for Him—He never has and never will. God knows your heart intent and desire. You must begin to realize that the adversary controls those ones who so easily give up their personal responsibility as to not even think for themselves what it is that they do so mindlessly and ritualistically.

When the adversary can get you to give up your personal responsibility, then he has won, for you will no longer give thought to your actions, for you will believe that the one to whom you gave over your responsibility will take care of you and protect you. You will believe that you no longer need to worry about the condition of your world or how your actions (or inactions) affect the whole. The adversary no longer has to worry about you, at this point, for you have given over your inner, God-given power to another. Now, all he has to do is control the other and he, in turn, controls YOU!

**Who might YOU think controls all those religions?!**

Think for yourself and be your own person. If you find yourself feeling confused, then seek diligently and consciously to understand why you feel that way. You may find yourself looking at some "seemingly" unrelated situations, but keep in mind that all is connected to all. Also, please keep in mind that if you do not care enough about self to find your own way, then who do you think will? Perhaps those who would have you give over your responsibility to, or in the name of, another.

**You must realize that YOU have, within YOU, all the potential to express and create as a Christed Being. You will need to earn the responsibility in order to be allowed to use this potential. If the adversary can keep you in a mental state of irresponsibility, then he, in effect, keeps you from reaching your true Christed potential. Recognize the game here!**

You do not need to follow any one or any group. You have all that you need to manifest this Christed potential within your being. This is not to say that you will not have need for lessons and teachers. It may very well be possible to reach this level of responsibility without guides and wayshowers—but WHY would you choose such a lengthy path to get from point A to point B, when there are ones who have come for this very reason, to assist you?

For many of you this is merely a review of what you already know. Please be patient with us for there are many reasons for these messages at this time. You ones are approaching a time on your planet when the many religions will have to face the fact that they have erred in their perceptions of Lighted spiritual truth. You will have the masses crying out for understanding of what is truly real.

**These messages are for you to share with your brethren when they come to you seeking to understand who we of the Lighted Hosts of God really are. We are your Elder Brothers, come to offer a helping hand to any who would seek and desire same. We come in many forms so as to ease the impact of the various realities down there at this time. Some can accept the fact that there are extraterrestrials who are both spiritually and technologically more advanced than you. Others may not easily accept this, but can, however, accept the idea of Angels or Spirit Guides. (Angels are simply God's Messengers, in whatever forms or dimensions they exist.)**

**These messages are for you of Ground Crew to use as tools, for self and others, so that when the masses come thirsting for knowledge, you can have short, digestible messages to share with them. Please do not go around trying to force your perceptions of reality off on another. When these ones are ready, they will be guided to you. Be forever offering, but do not insist that another listen to you.**

Be patient and kind. Forgive those who may laugh at or have laughed at you, for they do it out of ignorance, and that is excusable in God's eyes. Remain humble in the presence of these ones for they are the ones who need these messages the most and they are the ones who you have come down to assist.

May this message help you to understand who you are and why you are there. I am Lady Nada, Master of the Sixth Ray of Creator's spectral expression.

Salu!

# CHAPTER THIRTY-NINE

# Mind Controllers
# Ramping Up Latest Antics

### *Ceres Anthonious Soltec*
#### November 16, 1996

Good morning, my friend. It is I, Toniose Soltec, come in the Radiant Light of Creator God. Blessings and be at Peace!

Much is happening this day and it has most certainly been a trying week. Be cautious in your personal travels for, whether you realize it or not, you are monitored closely by the adversarial forces. These ones would like nothing more than to silence you. KEEP YOUR LIGHT SHIELDING UP AT ALL TIMES! And this goes for all of you who read these words.

There is much planned for you ones during this not-so-holy holiday season. You can see the clues all about you, if you but LOOK! For example, look to the U.S. Stock Market. It has had record-breaking highs for each of the past eight business days of trading sessions since the so-called presidential election. Meanwhile, on many of these days the trading volume has been close to double that for a typical trading session.

Second example: Look to the racial tensions being escalated. You have the O.J. Simpson trial (again!). You have the riot conditions in the Pittsburgh, Pennsylvania area which flared up this past week. This was due to a police officer being cleared of any wrongdoing in the murder of a Black man during an altercation occurring in the midst of routine police duties being carried out. You also have the recent Tampa-St. Petersburg, Florida incident of a similar nature. Then you have the Texaco Oil Company executives caught, on record, making racial slurs and having to furiously backpedal with major apologies and monetary fines of a politically correct variety.

Moreover, look to the announcement that gasoline prices at the pumps are going to "have to" be raised—again! Note how conveniently this is just in time for the holiday travel season. Last Summer the excuses for the large increase were because of "special formulations" in the gas and because of the excessive heating fuel consumption during the previous bad Winter—with this particular problem only being announced several months AFTER the fact. [*Editor's note: Actually, watch for this trick on a regular basis to slowly bring private transportation of you and I to a planned halt.*]

These are but a few of the many distractions being constantly thrown at you. Look PAST the distractions and look FOR the sleight-of-hand "magic" tricks.

**You ones are in for an experience of a lifetime! For those of you who have prepared, you shall find the upcoming events challenging and valuable. For those who have not prepared, you are in for a bumpy ride that could become quite uncomfortable.**

Now, let us look at something more interesting. Look to the skies at night in the direction of the "comet" Hale-Bopp. It is currently low on the Western horizon just after sunset for those of you on the West Coast [*of the United States*]. Several months ago you ones were told to begin to watch this "comet"—when it was reported as having made a "course correction" or two!

The "comet" is but a timing clue for you ones. As your planet's vibrational frequency continues to shift upward, you ones shall have to be prepared for the "realities" of the new environment in which you shall find yourselves. You ones shall have need for guidance as you wake up to the TRUE nature of your spiritual beingness and heritage.

**You, of Ground Crew, are far more aware than you may realize. You shall soon realize that a very large part of your mission is to provide confirmation to the masses that we, of extraterrestrial origin, come to assist and NOT TO ATTACK!**

You are fast approaching a time of mass awakening due to this upward frequency shift in consciousness. The controllers of your planet have known about extraterrestrials for decades but they do not want YOU to be aware of our existence, for they realize that they would lose all hopes for control over you-the-masses.

Take note that there is yet another "evil aliens invade the Earth" movie due out this coming Thanksgiving holiday weekend. Why do you think that you ones are being so heavily bombarded with the idea that all aliens (extraterrestrials) are bad, or are here to enslave you?

Well, the planet will soon realize that there are VERY REAL extraterrestrials and that we have no intention of harming anyone.

Keep in mind that we can see farther than you ones in terms of probabilities and possibilities. We Elder Brothers among the Wayshowers and Lightworkers are quite aware of what the adversary is planning. We enjoy the game very much—as we turn their plans into the very lessons that they, and you, as a planetary civilization, need in order to grow into the realization of Higher truth!

Back to "comet" Hale-Bopp: It was recently observed and photographed with a very large object (approximately 4 times the size of the Earth!) following along near the "comet". This new object was observed [*and photographed, see next page*] by an amateur Houston-based astronomer, Chuck Shramek, who has been regularly monitoring the "comet" for some time. Last Thursday evening, [*November 14, 1996*] at approximately 6 p.m. Houston time, when he began an evening of viewing the "comet", he also saw this massive mystery object THAT WAS NOT THERE JUST ONE DAY EARLIER!

This new object, slightly above and to the right of fuzzy Hale-Bopp, looks similar to the planet Saturn in that it appeared to have rings about its mid-section. Another interesting clue observed about this object was that the light intensity across the object is quite uniform, rather than varying in intensity, such as with dark spots or other luminosity fluctuations. This would suggest that the object is not reflecting light, but rather, is EMITTING light. A clue, perhaps?

Just months after the "comet" was first spotted, it was noted to be spiraling. It would now seem that the "comet" may actually be in orbit around a large central mass—perhaps this mystery object? Pay very close attention to a "comet" that makes course corrections and to a large object that seems to "appear" out of nowhere, emitting light!

[*Editor's note: The story behind the taking of this photograph, and of its fortuitous publicity, is itself a remarkable chain of events. If amateur Houston-based astronomer Chuck Shramek was not so diligent about his routine viewing of "comet" Hale-Bopp on a nearly-every-evening basis, the sudden appearance of the mystery companion object, when he was going about his usual routine at about 6 p.m. the evening of Thursday, November 14, 1996, would not have been so striking or convincing.*

*Furthermore, Shramek, who is a radio news professional himself, had the smarts to alert late-night radio talk-show host Art Bell, who not only immediately down-loaded Chuck's photo onto his well-utilized web site (www.artbell.com), but then also interviewed Chuck that same evening on Art's very-extensively-listened-to program, discussing numerous exciting implications of the occurrence. The cat was now quite definitely out of the bag!*

*As if the dark elite illusion-masters were not having enough trouble explaining away the annoying questions being asked by some observant ones about Hale-Bopp itself, now there was the added inconvenience of an actual photograph of an additional mystery object, a photo which had now been spread all around the world via Art Bell's home page on the Internet.*

*Well, the dark controllers scrambled to a "Red Alert" condition, as you might imagine. They put the usual kinds of pressures on bought-and-paid-for "professional" astronomical prostitutes who, in turn, dutifully went to work discounting, by "expert" opinion, both Mr. Shramek and his photograph of the Hale-Bopp companion object. This unfolded into one of the slickest disinformation campaigns this side of the later cover-up of the assassination of Princess Diana. Rumors persist of similar photos, taken by others well-placed in the astronomical community, but these ones "elected" to keep quiet as far as any kind of public announcement was concerned, considering the prevailing gestapo climate.*

*Meanwhile, at the time of Hale-Bopp's peak, there were many Internet discussions devoted to carefully "discounting" the many unusual observed peculiarities of "comet" Hale-Bopp. What were some of those observed oddities?*

*One good document on the subject was titled, "What The Hale Is Really Going On?" and it said, in part: (Quoting)*

In the Summer of 1995, two amateur astronomers independently and accidentally discovered a new comet. Like nearly all comets, this new comet was named after its discoverers, Alan Hale and Thomas Bopp. But, unlike most comets, which are discovered 3 or 4 months prior to their closest approach to the Earth and Sun, this comet was found about 20 months before its closest approach—absolutely unprecedented!

There are some very strange and weird aspects to this comet which officials seem reluctant to tell us about or discuss:

◆  When the comet was still as far away as Halley's comet, it was 1000 times brighter!

◆  The comet was first seen when its distance from the Sun was much too great for the gaseous coma of the comet to form. Yet it had a HUGE coma—larger in diameter than the Sun!

◆  Observations by the Hubble Space Telescope and other powerful ground-based scopes revealed "unusual" details—chunks breaking off from the comet and no natural reason for this to happen since the comet was too far away from the Sun for gravity or thermal effects to do this.

◆  The orbit of the comet is very strange, as if some intelligence had engineered the comet to get our attention.    *(End of quoting)*

*The 12/3/96 Front Page* CONTACT *story by Ray Bilger revisited and updated this subject while presenting a possible larger historical framework for "comet" Hale-Bopp within the astronomy of ancient Sumerian texts—which the elite controllers of this planet prefer you never know about in any detail. More to the point of this note, in that article Ray also relayed information about an interview with a Professor of Astronomy at a major research university who seemed to know all about the "mystery object" companion to Hale-Bopp. Quoting from Ray's article we learn:*

*"This Professor of Astronomy, trained in astronomy, physics, and astrophysics, disclosed that he has hundreds of high-quality, high-resolution, professional photographs, taken with the large observatory telescope at the university where he teaches, of the so-called 'mystery object' traveling with Hale-Bopp.*

*"The photographs clearly show that the 'mystery object' is a spacecraft, that it does emit light, that it has been moving all around Hale-Bopp—traveling along with Hale-Bopp—and that the object is larger than Earth. As well, the object is sending radio transmissions which have been picked up by radio telescopes here on Earth!*

*"The reason this Professor is yet anonymous is because he intends to go public in the first week of December 1996, with his extensive photographs and information. If he is not silenced prior to accomplishing this, his information is expected to shake the world."*

*We can assume he was silenced, in the usual life-threatening ways, since no new corroborative information has yet appeared in the public arena from this source. Meanwhile, there were some attempts to try to finesse this Professor of Astronomy into the limelight, to try and force him to "make good" on his claims. Some of these attempts were even cleverly engineered through derogatory implications of credibility toward a third party, also a full university professor, but to no avail.*

*The Professor of Astronomy's reticence was interpreted as (turned into) a condemnation of his believability—which is a standard disinformation technique whether dealing with the subject of a "mystery companion" object to Hale-Bopp—or the initial discoverers of Cold Fusion from the University of Utah, who now reside in a magnificent laboratory in the south of France, courtesy of Toyota, while the American media maligned them into mincemeat, just as these prostitutes of the elite controllers were instructed to do.*

*It was not long after his initial announcement that the disinformation machinery was thrown into high gear to work toward discounting both Mr. Shramek (after all, he's only an amateur) as well as what Mr. Shramek inconveniently captured in photographic format. Heaven help him if there was not this back-up photographic evidence—even if that evidence was labeled by the "ex-spurts" as one form or another of "swamp gas". Some things never change!]*

Changing subjects now: stay tuned for massive distractions as the mind controllers ramp up their efforts to manipulate and distract you. The massive earthquakes are still planned for the western coastal regions of the United States. There have been constant, very-well-calculated ground bombardments to major fault lines, and recently both the rate and intensity of these assaults have been stepped up.

The current intent is to precipitate a major event around the end of this month, November, or in early December. As always, please keep in mind that these plans can change at any moment.

However, these depraved controllers need the massive, numbing shock impact that would permeate the consciousness of the United States citizens—which only such a massive event could create. So, if not an earthquake, then perhaps a well-staged, fake alien invasion, or perhaps some nuclear or biological calamity. These dark ones who have enslaved and manipulated you are desperately trying to hold onto their "idea" of power.

These dark ones are, in fact, seeking Creator God, but they are trying to do it by cheating their way through their lessons. That is to say that they will use the ones who bring the gifts of understanding, and take that which is created and use it for their own gain—instead of trying to understand the true purpose of such gifts. The only true power lies within Creator and Creation. Thus, when you stand within the Light of God, none can stand against you.

I would suggest, AGAIN, that you get your emergency supplies ready! You can never have too much in the way of canned food and water. [*See the* 72-Hour Kit Checklist *in* Appendix A *at the end of this volume.*]

This may also be a good time, if you have not done so in awhile, to check through your emergency supplies to make sure that you do not have swollen cans, leaking batteries, or algae growing in your water. Replace anything that even looks questionable to you. You will be glad that you have done this, for you may realize that your supplies are lacking in quantity or condition.

Keep a level head about you as your reality becomes challenged. You are being bombarded with everything that the controllers can covertly throw at you ones. The only thing left is the less covert tactics and, as these ones become more and more desperate, you can count on them playing what they consider to be trump cards.

**These ones overestimate their abilities and underestimate ours. When they have created enough horror through destructive means, they will, in effect, create the very conditions that shall cause the souled beings of the planet to search deep within and find their God connection. This, in turn, calls in the Lighted Wayshowers, and we shall then be given permission to intervene on behalf of those who ask.**

As always, there are conditions and agreements that must be met. We, of the Hosts of God, ALWAYS keep our agreements!

Let me again change subject here, please: Many are experiencing "lapses" in time and concentration, and are having trouble sleeping, either too much or too little, and always seeming to wake up tired. Others may be feeling waves of erratic emotional swings from day to day.

There are many bombarding factors which are affecting you at this time that impact the background frequency in which you must physically function. These bombardments induce frequency fluctuations which will cause your mental focus to "drift" into and out of the conscious moment at hand. Do not get overly concerned; just keep your Light Shielding up!

Furthermore, when you are experiencing a dimensional upshifting in the manner of the current planetary transition now in high gear, your perceptions on an emotional level will be greatly affected. Just the natural transitioning into a higher vibrational frequency range, caused by the Photon Belt, would cause this to some extent.

Now compound the natural processes with the UN-natural phenomena generated by the pulse systems (such as the H.A.A.R.P. system) and you now have a most challenging condition with which to deal—and in which to try to find and maintain a balancing equilibrium.

**Know that, as you learn to deal with both the natural processes and (ESPECIALLY!) these unnatural attacks, you in effect become stronger than you would have without them. With greater challenge always comes greater reward and growth!**

Did we not say that this year, year ten of the new counting [*since the date of what was called the Harmonic Convergence, August 17, 1987; thus year 10 spans August 17, 1996 through August 16, 1997*], would be a MOST INTERESTING one? And here we are, only three months into it! So, DO keep your seat-belts buckled.

I am Commander Ceres Anthonious "Toniose" Soltec, come in service to The One Light, Creator God.

Salu and STAY ALERT as year ten marches forward.

# CHAPTER FORTY

# On The Edge
# Of A Grand Awakening!

*Serapis Bey*

**December 7, 1996**

Good afternoon, my friend. It is I, Serapis Bey, come to commune with you this day so that you and your brothers may have the insights and instructions that you need in order to find your way.

Yes, I am of the Light, and I come within the Light of Creator God as the Fourth Aspect of His spectral expression. It is ALWAYS wise to demand identification of ANY and ALL who would come to commune with you.

Thank you for allowing for the opportunity to share this day. These messages of Lighted Truth reach much farther than you would be comfortable realizing. Find balance and peace within, and let us continue please.

The people of this planet are on the peripheral edge of awakening to the Higher Reality of both the physical truth and, more importantly, the spiritual truth concerning the TRUE nature of their existence and placement within the universal order of Creation.

You of Ground Crew must be prepared, yourselves, for you, yourselves, could be caught up in the chaos and confusion that shall ensue within a very short physical segment of time.

As ALWAYS, sequence of events (not the physical ticking of a clock) dictates the occurrence of events. So, do NOT ask, "When?" or "What date?" You shall have to prepare as if it will be tomorrow, if you want to be certain that you are ready for the upcoming changes.

The awakening that I speak of is that of the coming undeniable realization that your little planet is not alone in the universe and that there is a very real community of "extraterrestrial" (that is, not of your Earth) beings who have come at this time for the very purpose of awakening Earth physical human from a most limiting sleep state.

There are many reasons for this sequence of events at this time. One of the major reasons is that you are in the process of destroying your planet and this is NOT acceptable to those who recognize the universal impact of such an event. You, both as individuals and as a planetary community, affect the ENTIRE universe by both your thoughts and actions. Remember: ALL IS CONNECTED TO ALL! Your lack of understanding of basic spiritual truths has brought you to the point at which you find yourselves this day.

The truth is the truth is the truth. YOU have to face your own personal responsibility as a member of your planet's community for having allowed this condition of ignorance to grow and to persist.

SHALL YOU REMAIN PART OF THE PROBLEM OR WILL *YOU* STEP OUTSIDE *YOUR* SELF-CENTERED WORLD AND TAKE RESPONSIBILITY FOR *YOUR* THOUGHTS, ACTIONS, INACTIONS, AND RESULTANT EFFECTS ON *YOUR* SOCIETY'S CURRENT CONDITION?!

Many of you to whom I speak have been patiently awaiting this time with great anticipation of the whole awakening process. THAT TIME IS AT HAND and though many have anticipated the return of the Christed One, ones have, in many cases, ignored their own awakening—always waiting for another to "do it for you".

You ALL have the Christ potential within! Why do you await

another to come and save you from your own self-generated hells? You shall save yourself or you shall repeat this experience again and again until you do. No Lighted Wayshower would deny you your opportunity for personal growth.

Many have prepared long ago and have grown complacent in their efforts to keep up with the daily flow of information available to them. Many have heard similar messages to this one and view these messages as just another message of "crying wolf". This is fine and you must always discern for yourself the value of each and every message offered.

God shall always provide the Wayshowers and Guides. He shall leave the decision-making up to you, so that YOU alone shall stand accountable and responsible for both your actions and your inactions.

Those of you who offer these messages to friends and family, who then refuse to listen, must come into realization that you canNOT do it for them—and if you did, they would resent you for doing so.

**Each souled being has, at some point, agreed to go through the experience of the learning cycles of growth. You must honor their decisions and choices. Each error that they make in judgment shall give them insights into what it is that they need to confront and overcome in the way of self-imposed limitations.**

And related to the above, let me remind all of you, once again, of the following most important point: **There shall be many who will not physically survive the upcoming transition. MANY!**

So, when I say, "Be prepared", I am saying that there shall be those difficult-to-confront issues, such as loss of family and friends, that you must be prepared to face and overcome—else you become overwhelmed with grief and thus possibly lost to those who may truly need your help.

Keep always in your heart that the experiences of the soul are infinite and that this is but one small existence in the infinite cycles of a soul's journey.

Let us return to considerations of the awakening that is imminent:

First of all, your populations shall be torn in perceptions and emotional impact. You shall see ones of very (so-called) "educated" stature become absolutely overwhelmed to the point of insanity as their ego-based reality is shattered completely.

Then, at the other end of the emotional spectrum, you shall see ones who are filled with great excitement and joy as their longtime hunches and perceptions of reality are finally confirmed and verified.

For many, there shall be feelings of chaos and confusion as ones shed their old limited perceptions and beliefs. The more soundly asleep the entity, the more jarring will be the wake-up call.

There shall be a great spiritual resurgence as ones innately recognize the universal signature of the emotional frequencies emanating from the non-terrestrial visitors. These shall be most warm and genuine frequencies of compassion and love.

You ones of Ground Crew, who have been diligent in your preparations, will know what to do—when the sequence is correct.

Indeed, many of you will be nearly overwhelmed with the ones who will be moved to come your way seeking to understand what is taking place. These ones will be, more than anything else, seeking to find balance within as they must come to grips with the fact that they have been living a mind-controlled existence within a mind-controlled society—and further, that they have been completely caught-up in the dazzling distractions engineered by the controllers.

**Realize well that this is THE major overall role for Ground Crew: to aid in the transition of the planet to a higher level of consciousness.**

THESE *ARE* THE EXPERIENCES FOR WHICH *YOU* HAVE COME DOWN HERE AT THIS TIME!

In as much as you have prepared, your job will be easier. Take each and every opportunity for growth as an opportunity to prepare for these challenges that are coming.

Do not think that you are just another "nobody" who reads some so-called "underground" newspaper called *CONTACT*.

YOU ARE A LIGHTED BEING WHO HAS A PURPOSE TO FULFILL!

Learn to recognize the distractions of the adversary and persist through the challenges with which you are faced. And, by all means, stop limiting yourself! KNOW that you are a valuable team member—IF you so chose to be one!

Rejoice in knowing that you are never alone in this experience, or any other. When the whole world seems to be against you, know that God is always there for you and that you need the experience in order to cause you to search to new depths for the answers that you need.

Seek always, within the protection of God's Light, to understand more and you shall find yourself amazed at how fast you can grow and learn.

I am Serapis Bey, laying out the foundation upon which you ones can build a solid enough certainty that will allow you to weather the chaotic and confusing events of the not-so-distant future.

Blessings to those of you who have persisted through these trying times and have learned your lessons.

In Light and Service to Creator Source, Salu.

# – CHAPTER FORTY-ONE –

# God's *Light* Connection
# With ALL Souled Beings

### Gyeorgos Ceres Hatonn

### December 14, 1996

Be at peace, my scribe. There is work to be done and we shall walk in the Radiant Path together. I am Gyeorgos Ceres Hatonn; I come in the Light of Creator God. Get comfortable and let the information flow through.

Truth is truth is truth! You cannot avoid the true nature of your spiritual existence. Dark ones would like to keep you Lighted ones from recognizing these basic principles of fact for as long as it is possible. You cannot silence God or any of His messengers acting on His behalf. There shall ALWAYS be another to take up the pen and march forward into INFINITY!

The adversary may be able to physically assault those of you in the physical, and he may very well be able to precipitate a whirlwind of confusion as he efforts to tear down that which you are in the process of accomplishing. KNOW that God does not forsake those who are getting His work done. Keep to the path and call in the Light for balance.

It has been stated, over and over again, down there on your planet, that "God is Light!" This is indeed TRUE in its most basic form. Ones must then need to know what LIGHT truly is and how it is that it functions—if they are to truly understand where they

251

come from, how they were created, and how they fit into the overall order of Creation. This is the "birds and the bees" lesson of Creator and Creation

**No one person can claim ownership of spiritual truth. The potential for recognizing this truth lies within each souled being and is an innate part of you that is there from your conception (or creation).**

God created you with the thinking of His mind. He was both the father and the mother, and He gave of Himself unto you a part of Him. And with each part He created, He assigned a purpose to fulfill. That part of Creator which resides within you has all the knowledge of you, your creation, and your overall purpose for being. We shall refer to this as your SOUL (that which is of Creator God).

**You, through your soul you, have a direct connection to Source. This connection has a unique frequency and wavelength associated with it, as does every thing in the entirety of the universe in which you live.**

Your scientists have proven this basic truth and will tell you that all matter has a vibratory rate to it, and that when you stop the vibration of an object, it disintegrates and ceases to exist. Your scientists will also explain that, if you increase the vibratory rate of an object (usually done by adding heat), it will explode.

These are basic observations that cannot be "plagiarized" for they are universal in nature. They are the external, observable effects of the underlying Laws that govern your universe.

What are these Laws?

They are simply the wisdom of Creator's thinking!

The essence of simplicity in nature, these Laws encompass all observable effects that you ones can perceive around you.

Your scientists (and by this designation I mean the few who are true and honest seekers) are, in effect, seeking to understand

Creator when they seek to understand the universe in which they live. Their Higher Self (the soul self) knows this and will guide these ones on their journey of self discovery.

You ALL are on a mission of self discovery that will earn you the right to take your position as a co-creator alongside of Creator Himself. This is only allowed when you have completed ALL of your lessons at "Godhood".

**You are, in effect, trying to understand and actualize the inner self so that you can responsibly utilize the Light Potential within in such a manner that you do not create havoc among the balanced order of Creation.**

Thus, you are, in effect, God's children who are growing into maturity, and this experience, along with all of your past and future experiences, shall cultivate your inner God-self (your SOUL) in such a manner that you will grow in understanding of the true reason for being.

Each of you has your own unique purpose for being. Do not worry if you think you do not "know your purpose" for you cannot NOT KNOW!

It is such a basic part of your being that you will miss it every time, especially down there in the confusion of that physical experience. Your purpose is given to you at your time of creation and is, in effect, programed into the very Light Fibers of your soul.

This program is what gives you your unique frequency signature that makes you a unique aspect of Creator. So, to truly understand your soul purpose, you would have to first recognize and understand the fundamental nature of Creator's creation process. This is a function of God's thinking.

**Do not get hung up on trying to recognize your soul's purpose! Your overall soul purpose may be quite different from this life's purpose.**

This is to say that, in this present life, you may need to strengthen a certain aspect of your being so that you can face greater challenges in future experiences—challenges that will, in turn, help you to reach your true potential in a MUCH larger scope of experiencing.

There are ones among you who have learned all their lessons in the physical and have elected to come back at this time to fulfill very special purposes that are not typically available in the third-dimensional realms. This is to say, for clarification, that you have Great Teachers among you who are working out what some would consider to be outlandish experiments—in order to see if it is indeed possible to accomplish that which, in theory, should work.

**There are good reasons for ALL of your experiences and they add to the overall character of your uniqueness as one of Creator's children. The sum total of all of your experiences leads you down your own unique and new path. As you experience and grow, so too does all of Creation grow.**

In higher frequency Light space (etheric space) some ones can see the interconnectedness of ALL. This is to say that, as each one grows, all grow. There is, in effect, an exponential expansion of both Creator and Creation, of which each entity is an integral part.

THIS INTER-CONNECTED EXPANSION IS THE "JOY" PART OF EXISTING.

As each being fulfills their overall Higher Purpose for existing, every entity, everywhere within Creation, benefits from the collective experience of the one.

This "shared wisdom" is due to the electromagnetic Light connection that exists between every souled being. This Light connection is, in essence, God. All of our known universes exist within the entirety of God and He, in turn, exists within a more basic function of Light—that of Creation.

Do not be overwhelmed if you do not, at first, feel that you understand these words. Many get upset when they are confronted with the fact that there is a Force Higher than that of their Creator God, for this implies (erroneously) that they are somehow less than what they feel themselves to be. Creator God is one with Creation. When you fulfill your soul purpose, you too will have become one with Creator God. Therefore, you will have also become one with Creation itself.

It is truly a wondrous journey that fulfills the "empty void" feeling within that many are experiencing at this time and will do almost anything to escape from having to confront. They are, in effect, trying to escape from their responsibilities by remaining in ignorance. The harder that these ones try to escape, the more overwhelming the empty sensation becomes—until such a point of desperation is reached that ones will finally go deep within and find that internal Light Source connection and realize that what they are lacking is the conscious connection to Source, who has been sitting there, within, waiting patiently to be remembered, all the while.

May these words of inspired truth find their way through to your heart and fill you with that for which you long: Balance, Truth, Certainty, and Knowingness—of who you are and why you might be here at this time.

Discern for yourself your own path.

Seek, first, balance within the Light of God and you will find the Inner Joy that you desire.

I am Gyeorgos Ceres Hatonn, come in Light and Service to Creator, come at this critical time to speak with you that you may hear these words and be inspired to recognize your own Light within.

Salu!

# CHAPTER FORTY-TWO

# God Is . . .

## *Aton, The One Light*

### December 16, 1996

You live in an electric-wave universe. God IS! From God comes thought expressed as Light. Duality comes in the form of electricity and magnetism. The split pairs of opposites are what make up the Male and the Female. God is infinite and unlimited in His projected thought, but moves NOT. God resides in the Still Silence, and from Him comes that which appears to be comprised of physical matter but which, in actuality, is only LIGHT manifest. All is Light. God sends forth His Light, and then God pulls back His Light, and then there is rest, stillness, voidance.

In your world there *appears* to be motion and physical movement, yet in actuality, there is none. The Light-made-manifest is a thought projection of God, and this thought of God IS STILL and motionless.

God IS. I AM.

To be without God is to be without Light. And to be without Light is Hell. To perish without Light is an unthinkable horror, yet man, in his ego-filled ways, "thinks" this cannot happen to him. God, residing in the Stillness, knows that His creations will eventually return to Him or be uncreated, thus vanishing forevermore.

God is inhaling His Light at this time, thus returning His Lighted

Fragments back unto Himself, for God is ALL there is.  There is only ONE LIGHT.  The Creation and God are One, yet separate. The One Light splits into two, and from the two come the many. The many shall return to Source as one with the Stillness, within the perfect motionless silence that IS God's thought.

Man runs about here and there "perceiving" reality in motion, and yet this perception is, in actuality, illusion, for in truth there is no activity, no motion, no movement—only the stillness of God's Light projected as thought.  God IS.  This is no riddle, it simply IS! Man's thought is limited to flatland perception.  In the reality of God's Light there is no matter, only space, the void, which is filled with God's thought in action—which is still.

To disallow discussion of these most fundamental matters of the creation process is to attempt to harness the air you breathe.  It cannot and will not be done.  God's people will come into knowing and those who would enslave God's people or keep God's people in ignorance shall be cast out from God's thought—which is ALL.  So be it.

I Am Aton, The One Light.

# CHAPTER FORTY-THREE

# Christmas Challenge

### *Esu "Jesus" Sananda*
### December 18, 1994

*Editor's note: The following message was first published in the December 20, 1994 issue of* CONTACT. *It remains timeless and uplifting, and is shared here in "chronological" (except for the year) sequence of the passing seasons.*

Peace and blessings this day, Thomas.  Esu Sananda present in radiance to give a message unto my brethren who await direction and guidance.  Many have heard the call and await instructions, while others grow weary and impatient.

Ah, beloved, it is the time of the Great Cycle change and your nation is at crisis.  Has it not been said that, in the End Times, Satan would rule your world?  Look around you—what do you see?  The turmoil and strife of survival has struck at the very hearts of the people.  The patriots call forth for action and many would, and indeed shall, go to their death with freedom on their lips and a gun in their hand.  Beloved, it shall not be done in this manner—the turn about shall not be accomplished with the gun!

You must become informed or, indeed, how do you hope to enter into leadership to offer solutions to a starving and searching people?  Your world needs no more pious leaders with puffed egos who shout that they alone have the answer.  What is needed at this time, beloved ones, is unity and team players.  United you can and shall stand—but a divided house cannot stand! Has it not been proven countless times over, lo these eons of time?

I hear your pleas unto me for direction, and the call compels the answer. Your voices have been heard, and you shall be given that which you seek.

During this Holiday Season, do you think first of thine brother and his needs, or do you dwell on your own perceived difficulty? Do you freely share that which you have, however plentiful or meager it may be, with those less fortunate—or do you keep your stores of stuffs under lock and key to spoil and rot? Who among you helps your brother when you are directly confronted with a call for help? And who among you looks the other way, in disgust and denial, at the one less fortunate?

Do I come this day to lay some kind of guilt "trip" on you? No, beloved, I just ask the question that you may give momentary pause for reflection and give thanks to Creator for all that He has blessed you with this and every day.

How many among you remember to thank God for that which you have? And those of you who do not think twice about such a notion—where think you the source of your being stems from? Random chance? Come now. God is quite real, beloved, quite real indeed, and the sooner many of you come to terms with that fact, the sooner you can get on with living life according to His Rules of Balance—the Laws of Balance.

Truly, it is not difficult to live according to God's path—for each is born with the knowledge of those Laws within their very breast. Think you that you know not that which is right from that which is wrong? Nay, you know!

You see, there is no escaping the responsibility for self within your planetary experience of existence. While it is true that you are entirely free to do that which you will—you are also free to be bound for all eternity to the places of physical density (matter), removed from the Presence and Radiance of Creator God. Is it not the better part of wisdom to live your life according to the balanced direction He has laid forth for your own fulfillment and joyous evolvement? What is it in man that causes such rebellion and vicious denial?

Each is free to choose, but as I said before: ye are either with me or ye are against me. There is no in between.

As you gather with your families this Holiday Season, think toward goodness and generosity and open, joyous sharing. Give thanks for thine blessings, for they are manifold. Let not greed and bickering enter your hearts, but rather, be at peace in the knowledge that God's Radiance shines freely upon those of His who live according to His Plan.

Ask and you shall be answered. Seek and you shall find. The mysteries lay before you, but they shall not be mysteries for long—for it is the time of Knowing.

Let us restore this world to greatness under God while there is time—for the clock is ticking and the year 2000 is just around the corner.

Remember this, please: God, too, has a Plan 2000.

Be at peace and at joy in thine hearts, for I have prepared a place for thee as promised.

I AM SANANDA.

Salu.

# CHAPTER FORTY-FOUR

# The *Lighted* Thought Behind Creator's Overall Plan

### *Violinio Saint Germain*

### December 22, 1996

Good afternoon, my scribe.  It is I, Germain, come in the Light of Aton, the One Light.  Find balance, for the frequency shift can, at first, be a bit annoying to you in the physical.

Let us take up the subject of Light this day.  You ones have the need for this knowledge at this time.  Knowledge and Truth are not just for the few, to be secreted away so that they can control you by keeping you in ignorance of that which is your heritage.

Your body, your soul, and your mind are ALL comprised of Light in various stages of compression.  Your body, along with all physical matter, is a functioning electromagnetic holographic projection of Creator's thinking.

The basic technology for this form of manifestation exists on your planet at this time and shall be used against those who choose to remain in ignorance of that which is taking place down there.  These are the holographic projection devices, that your would-be controllers have, that use light beams focused together in both etheric space and physical space in order to give the illusion of physical substance.  These are merely toys that can be quite convincing—as you ones were so easily fooled by the last "comet".

[*Editor's note: This trickery is the main reason that Commander Soltec referred to the so-called "comet" Hale-Bopp in quote marks throughout his writing of 11/16/96 in Chapter 39. However, what the diabolical illusion-masters were NOT expecting was for anything ELSE to appear in the field of view along with that "comet".*

*Many ones are waking up and are no longer falling for the illusion propaganda, and therein lies the biggest threat to the success of the dark elite's New World Order agenda. Regardless, "comet" Hale-Bopp remains as a timing clue in the Larger Play unfolding, no matter how it came into being.*]

Creator uses His Mind to manifest two aspects of Light that are complementary polar opposites of one another. These are the Father and the Mother, sexed pairs comprised of the Golden White Light and the Silver White Light. Creator combines these pairs in a dimensional manner that spans some 26 dimensions of Creation in order to manifest the known universe in a balanced, self-regenerating, and evolving manifestation. Your play toys use merely four dimensions to manifest their seemingly real images of light.

Creator has created the universe so that we, as individual fragments, can explore and come into knowing of the workings and thinking of the One who encompasses all. God is a static, non-moving entity who exists everywhere. All that you can perceive exists within the One who created that which you see all around you. Thus you can see that you, too, have the potential of existing everywhere, and that "time" and "space" can actually place no limits on your exploration of the universe (God's Mind).

Creator sends out these two Primary Rays of His Creation and combines them in a manner that will cause them to produce such tremendous pressures that will actually condense the Light into matter.

At first, prior to the known universe, there was a null void that had no vibration or potential—it was nothing. Creator then split Himself into two, thus manifesting a difference in potential. This rapidly filled the "nullness" and set in motion the electric-wave universe that we have come to experience.

This electric-wave universe was programmed from inception to expand, propagate, and regenerate itself in such a manner that this very Creation would evolve as an entity all its own. Thus you have a LIVING universe that could be viewed as God manifest. This living universe was given a consciousness. This consciousness is what many refer to as God. Creator/Creation is that which split into the two primary polar expressions and set the entirety of that which we refer to as God into motion.

As this universe grew and expanded its awareness of that which it IS, it too came into the awareness of the Laws of Creation, and split of itself, and gave forth individual assignments to these self-maintaining energy-thought projections. Thus came into being the conscious souls that you and I are.

From this explanation you have a basic understanding of the history of your universe, as well as of your consciousness, coming into being. From the vast nothingness came all that is. This awesome "nothingness" is what we refer to as The Creation, in your language, for there are no other words to describe that which is indescribable. To truly understand this you will need to FEEL the basic Pulse of the universe that is, in itself, the very Pulse of Creator/Creation. This Pulse exists outside of the restrictions of time and space and permeates the entirety of every dimension. This is, in effect, the inter-connectedness of ALL.

You each have within you the potential to experience this form of creating, but only after you have proven that you can be RESPONSIBLE for that which you create. This is why you are where you are, on this day, experiencing one of the various densities of that which Creator has created for you—so that you can come into understanding of how your thoughts and actions affect the entirety of Creation.

Down there you have a condition, usually referred to as karma, and also known as the "Laws of Cause and Effect". This is a condition that you each agreed to, prior to participating in the growth experience that you now find yourself working within. This condition states that you shall have to balance out that which you have caused to be unbalanced. This goes for thoughts as well as actions. When you can learn to balance these conditions of unrest, you will have graduated from that school and you will move on and help others learn this same lesson.

You have ones down there who simply refuse to accept that any of their thoughts and actions affect anything else—other than that which is there in the physical, in front of them. These ones are, through their ignorance and dense state of mental compression, the two percent who control the planet upon which you live.

You may ask, "How could this be?"

The laws of Creator/Creation work for ALL without prejudice. These "dark" ones have little or no conscience. They, in turn, will take actions that normal souled beings would not allow themselves to take, for the Lighted ones realize that it is wrong to infringe upon the rights of another. These two percent of your population are manifesting tremendous debt which must eventually be balanced out—and they realize it not.

These ones shall not be allowed to continue forever in their ignorance. Creator shall, at some point, recall that which He has created, and balance out, in a responsible manner, that which He, Himself has allowed to persist. Prior to this recalling unto Himself, these ones shall be given every opportunity to come into the recognition of that which they are doing. Some shall wake up to the

Higher Reality of that which they are doing, but many will refuse to learn, and thus shall remain in ignorance.

In the meantime, these ones serve a purpose for you Lighted ones who need to see BOTH sides of the coin so that you can learn the wisdom of following God's Laws. According to the Laws of Cause and Effect, you cannot graduate from the wheel of reincarnation until you have balanced out ALL that you have unbalanced. This does not mean that you cannot work on the other aspects of your growth, but it most certainly means that you cannot put the third-dimensional experience behind you unless and until you balance that which you have created in unbalance in the third-dimensional realms.

You have, at this time on your planet, ones who are severely misusing the various light-based technologies that were originally introduced to you by very special Lighted souls so that your societies could have the gifts of Free Energy without the decimation of the planet with pollution. These technologies work on the Father-Mother Light principle of creation. These are the "scalar" technologies that produce energy from the seeming nothingness of "empty" space. There is no such thing in the known physical universe as "empty" space. All space has a frequency and vibration associated with it. The ignorance about these basic facts, by the controlling two percent, is what allows for the possibility of great unbalance to be unleashed, that then has a tremendous impact on the overall balance of the ENTIRE universe in which you live.

This sort of misuse (or lack) of knowledge is unacceptable to the communities who live conscientiously in the rest of the universe (a universe, by the way, that you so arrogantly think you are the center of, or are at some sort of pinnacle of evolution within) and will not be tolerated. This type of misuse has caused great concern for the many who are part of the karmic connection to your planet, and as well causes concern about those innocent ones who are, for the most part, unaware of the existence of such devices or the enormous impact associated with them, especially in terms of tampering with the material of soul essence (Light!).

Ones need to come into realization of their connection to ALL, to every thing everywhere. To truly understand this, you ones need a basic picture of where you come from and how you came into existence. This is the reason that you need these insights—so that you can make the proper connections and proceed forward in a BALANCED manner that will free you from the karmic trap.

Be grateful for this and every opportunity that you have to grow and experience, for it is The First Law of Creation that states: "Go forth and experience!" These are the opportunities to grow and fulfill this basic principle of existing. Seek understanding within the Light, for as you come closer and closer to the realization of who you are and the true potential of your being, you can be sure that the adversarial dark forces shall increase their attacks upon you and those around you. Be persistent and know that when God stands on your side, you have the ENTIRE universe behind you!

I am Violinio St. Germain, come as Cohan (Teacher) of the Seventh Ray of Creator's basic spectrum. I represent the Violet Ray of Transmutation (change and evolution). Blessings to you all!

# – CHAPTER FORTY-FIVE –

# Wake-Up Call
# For The Grand Experiment

### *Ceres Anthonious Soltec*

**December 27, 1996**

Good morning, my friend. It is I, Toniose Soltec, come in the Radiant Light of Creator God. Thank you for sitting this day and allowing for this interaction.

Much has been happening around your area, where secret underground-base complexes abound, as well as around the world. The would-be controllers are aware of that which is about to befall them and they do not plan on taking it lying down. This is why there is so much in the way of distractions underway, such as the weather being "worse" in various areas than anyone can remember. Before this play is over, you ones shall have endured many "mind blowing" phenomena that will defy explanation unless you have kept up with your lessons.

Much of what you are told (or not told) on your "news" programs are outright lies when it comes to the facts about the geological stability of your planet. These skilled manipulators of data realize that even the casual observer can, at this point, figure out that both frequency and intensity of earthquake activity have tremendously increased around the planet recently. This is why there is little or no reporting of the world condition over your prostituted "news" media avenues, while successful steps have been taken to stop (or otherwise distract into side-projects) those who were, through independent routes, bringing you truth about Mother Earth-Shan's rising blood pressure. *[Editor's note: This censoring-through-distraction issue was also addressed back in Chapter 16, in conjunction with the fine* Seismo-Watch *newsletter that used to provide a weekly summary of well-displayed, important earthquake information. It has not been published in some time now, much to the delight of those dark ones who set-up the distractions to accomplish same. This is why these Teaching Masters emphasize, over and over again, the need for Light shielding, that is, for "calling in the Light" for protection, else many a Lightworker will find themselves out-witted on the Grand Chessboard!]*

"Ignorant, blind sheep" is what the masses are referred to in the elite circles of the dark adversarial forces who are manipulating your reality of world perception. The readers of *CONTACT* are not ignorant and The Word is spreading and shall not be contained. The harder the adversary tries to shut us down, the more Light they will end up shining upon themselves. Truth shall win out in the end!

Please take this opportunity to, once again, check to see that your emergency supplies are ready and in good condition. You shall be thankful for doing this—and your neighbors and your neighbors' children may be quite thankful as well. [*See* Appendix A *in this book for a* 72-Hour Kit Checklist *of emergency items.*]

There has been much concern over the coming "comet". This "comet" is the REAL messenger that your Native Americans have been waiting for as a sign which signals the new beginning called the "Age of Peace". These ones know that their ancestral origin was from the stars. They also know that there shall be the great cleansing of the planet prior to this "Age of Peace".

This cleansing has been prophesied as being the cleansing with fire. Fire has many levels to its intensity. A candle flame can be gentle and soothing. A mountainside on fire can be quite alarming and cause great panic and destruction. A nuclear explosion can distort the very Light fabric of one's soul, and thus may cause an actual dispersal of soul energy. A "scalar" pulse can, if strong enough, completely disperse soul essence.

Through "scalar" devices, you have the ability to completely extinguish an entity—to a point that that entity may never know consciousness in any form, ever again. You have, in effect, created the means for truly "killing" someone. This is NOT REFERRING TO THE DEATH OF THE PHYSICAL BODY, BUT RATHER, TO THE DEATH OF THE SOUL!

Your "scientists" who play with these "scalar" devices have very little understanding of how these devices affect non-physical space. They have their mathematical models and theories of how they THINK these things work, but their models are limited and leave out the consideration of soul essence (LIGHT!).

The ancients who were given the prophecies of this Endtime were given the images or visions, and then had to translate, to the best of their ability, that which they had seen. For some of what they saw, there were no words, and they had to use examples and concepts that have a generally accepted meaning. You will have to look past the words: for example, consider words such as "fire" with a measure of discernment and insight, and realize that there may be MANY possible meanings of that word.

As an exercise, take your current world scene and try to overlay various ancient prophecies with that which you now know to be true. For instance, when your biblical Scriptures were written, there was no awareness of devices called "nuclear bombs". Look to your *Book of Revelation* wherein it is described that "the sky opened up like a scroll". Now, overlay in your mind a picture of a nuclear bomb detonation. See the "mushroom" cloud billowing upward and unrolling LIKE (similar to, but not the same as) a scroll. Use discernment and learn to make your own judgments, for even the honest interpretations are at best the "accepted" interpretations of "holy" men from 300 to 800 years ago, when there was no awareness of even the possibility of such nuclear devices.

You shall be held accountable for your actions, and if you choose, willingly, to remain in ignorance to the changing world around you, then you will have to deal with the consequences of these actions. Help is being provided to those who will hear and LISTEN!

Many are running around trying to find their "guru" who will somehow tell them what to do and when to do it. This is running away from your personal responsibility and you are, in effect, trying to cheat your way through the challenges of your current level of growth. The only thing you really end up doing is guaranteeing that you will have to come back, and do it all over, again and again, until you can get it right!

Stop waiting for another to do a thing for you. BE MORE ASSERTIVE AND DO THE THING YOURSELF! If another has agreed to help you, and they will not keep their agreement, then I, Soltec, would suggest that you find someone who can keep their word and who knows the INNER value of helping another.

For instance, if you are a business owner and you have ones you pay for their services, then you should have a CLEAR understanding (written if need be) of what you expect from them and what they expect from you. If an employee cannot or will not perform to your agreed-upon level of expectation, then caution the person that you are not satisfied and that you will have to move them to a lesser position of responsibility if they cannot perform up to expectation and agreement.

Do not allow an unbalanced condition to persist just because you do not want to be the "bad guy" and have to demote someone. When you allow a condition of unbalance to persist in your life, you have, in effect, taken on the responsibility for all that comes from that which you have "bought into".

Back to the subject of the "comet". You have ones waking up all around your planet who realize that this "comet" has certain peculiarities about it and they are feeling the winds of change. The "comet" represents your past, present, and future. This is the awakening that cannot be avoided—nor would you who read these messages want to avoid this inevitability.

This experience can be viewed as a large experiment in awakening ones to their true heritage as Lighted souled beings who belong to a much larger community or family—whether they know it or not! The experiment comes in when you have a theory that has not been tested-in-fact previously. You have calculated that it should work, but you must, at some point, play out the actual experiment to see that your discernment is correct.

This is not done in a haphazard manner on the "whims" of any one being. There is much research and collaboration among many to find as many different viewpoints and observations as is practical. Then, when enough have agreed to the experiment, it is taken before a Council to decide whether or not it would be spiritually ethical to even attempt such a thing. Only after a proposed scenario has been approved at every level, will it then be allowed to be attempted.

**You all are part of the larger experiment, an experiment which entails Ground Crew to help bring forth a stabilizing influence for the ones we are attempting to wake up at this time. The emotional support that your energy fields will project, when the less-aware ones become overwhelmed with fear, will be that which will enable these ones to overcome these challenges of growth.**

Be prepared for the impact of the upcoming changes. You, as Ground Crew, will have to be STRONG in your conviction—else you risk the possibility of being overcome with the lower-frequency emotions of those you have come to assist. You will find this whole experience quite a challenge. This is as it should be.

Toniose to standby.

*    *    *

### December 28, 1996

Shall we continue, please. This is Toniose Soltec, come in service to the One Light Source.

Many down there are just awakening to the awareness of the situation that is unfolding at this time. Among these ones are Ground Crew. ALL awakening ones are hungry for The Truth and will be attracted to that which they can FEEL in their heart to be true. These are the teaching opportunities that you aware Ground Crew ones have been awaiting most of your life.

As the time of chaos (the death struggle of this current political and social state) heats up, there shall be tremendous opportunity for growth for all involved. This goes for you of Ground Crew as well as for those younger beings whom we have come to assist. All shall be faced with great challenges of faith and discernment, as well as great emotional pressures as you face the challenges of giving birth to the new Era of Peace.

Preparing oneself mentally is perhaps the single most important one thing you can do. This will allow US (whether you think of us as Spirit Guides, Angels, Elder Brothers, or your deceased Aunt Annie) to get a message or thought through to you in a critical moment.

**If you become overwhelmed with the lower emotions of shock, grief, or despair, this will make it quite difficult for a communication such as this to get through. You will need to keep a clear head and you will, as well, need to have trust and faith that you need these experiences and that you volunteered**

**to go down there and experience these challenges.**

Always keep the Larger Picture in mind!  This is a picture we have been helping you to see through many weeks of important lessons brought through this scribe—a Ground Crew member just like you, who must constantly work (despite personal demons of distraction) at holding mental balance, to be able to receive and share these lessons.

Again, remember the Big Picture: This is but a holographic play and you are one of the actors in the play (or players in the game).  There is a HIGHER REALITY outside that which you perceive as consciousness.  And remember, in this play, to ALWAYS call in the Light for both Guidance and Protection!

The reason for these words of caution at this time is so that you can have time to PREPARE MENTALLY for any upsetting possibility that you can imagine for yourself.  What would your reaction be if you just now heard that New York City was destroyed by a nuclear bomb?  What would you do?  Would you stop and take a moment to clear your space, call in the Light, and ask for Guidance?  Or, would you just REACT to your inner fears, shut down with disbelief, and become dysfunctional—and thus closed to our communications?

If you stop to prepare yourself mentally NOW, you will have, in effect, written a script (or program) for yourself that you can use in order to help you keep your head clear—and thus make reasonable judgments based upon intelligent thought, instead of reacting out of fear.  You have these messages as warnings and "heads-up" notices so that you will be able to function in the next upcoming ten years or so in your counting.

The ones who either refused to hear, or simply were not able to understand, will be looking to you for basic guidance.  These ones shall be in shock and, in most cases, they will shut down out of fear or they shall become overwhelmed with the experience and become quite erratic, if not outright insane. Many a "learned" man shall be found weeping in fear, for they won't have a clue as to what has happened once their artificially constructed world of intellect is gone and these ones realize they haven't cultivated even the most basic of skills for survival.

The farmers—those who tend to the foodstuffs of the land—shall become the most important teachers! These farmer-teachers will enable the ones who can overcome their fears and grief to become functioning parts of the community efforts to rebuild self-sustaining, rural communities from the ashes of destruction.

These experiences are the "HARD" lessons, for you have long passed the time of course correction to avoid these experiences. In the upcoming Age of Peace, you shall find that there will be NO tolerance for corrupt thinking, and that these lessons and experiences will be "burned" into the consciousness of each being.

No, this is not a pleasant message. Please be assured that it is given with great compassion and warmth—with the intent to help, NOT to frighten anyone! As always, please discern for yourself and act with wisdom. Ask for Guidance within the Light, and await your answer.

Remember: change is inevitable! Even the most stubborn of people shall be caused to grow from these experiences. This opportunity for growth is quite unique, and for those who persist through these challenges, you shall know great personal reward and satisfaction for having gone through this experience.

I am Ceres Anthonius Soltec (as in Solar-tech./technician, Light Worker, Soul-tech.—one who works with the soul). I am blessed, as are YOU, by our Father with insights and gifts that allow for helping other Lightworkers to progress in their infinite journeys of the SOUL, for the giving and re-giving ALWAYS comes full circle and we all grow from the sharing. I come in the Radiance and Oneness of Creator Source. Salu!

# CHAPTER FORTY-SIX

# Helping Us To Help You Do Your Part

## *Lady Nada*
### January 4, 1997

Good afternoon, my scribe. Thank you for sitting this day, for there is a need for the sharing. I am Lady Nada, I come in the Radiant Light of Creator God so that I may re-give that which has been given to me, and so that you ones may have the insights that you petition for constantly.

Be thankful for having been given yet another day, this day, for you will look back one day and realize how simple your life was. The unfolding drama will be quite hard for everyone involved, without exception. Everyone will have their own personal challenges to face and overcome. You ones of the teaching, Lighted Ground Crew will have to face attacks from ALL directions, and only with discernment within the Light of Creator God shall you have the insights to traverse the "mine fields" (including the mind fields) that shall lay before you, without being incapacitated from the mission at hand.

There are great efforts to remove the speakers of truth at this "Brink of Awakening" time on your planet. This is without exception! You will have to shed your fears and get centered within the protection of God's Light, else you will know agonizing remorse for having allowed to slip away yet another opportunity for overcoming this most unique and multi-faceted kind of challenge.

There is great concern for the overall mental impact of the upcoming events that are about to befall you, connected to the planetary consciousness of Earth-Shan. We of the Lighted Hosts of God are getting our lessons, as we attempt to bring forth a transformation in such a manner as has never been attempted prior. This will have a tremendous impact on the growth of millions of souled beings. We have our lessons in discernment, as do you. We shall not forsake our direct God-Source connection; therefore we have confidence that we shall be successful.

This is not to say that this experience will not be challenging. We must search for the answers that will allow US to help those who are most stubborn and refuse to hear. We enjoy the challenge, for there is ALWAYS an answer, and in the seeking to find the answer, we experience growth as we are stretching our awarenesses to new levels of understanding.

You, as Ground Crew, can assist the most by keeping a constant attentive "ear" to the nudges that we are constantly sending you. This is done by keeping the adversary out of your head! The adversary is constantly waiting there, trying to find a weak point in your mental armor, your emotional armor, and your spiritual (LIGHT SHIELDING!) armor.

While it is YOUR responsibility to face these challenges, you do NOT have to face them alone! Call in the Light and ask for Guidance and Protection, for both you and your brother.

When you find yourself frightened, this is the adversary working on you!

When you find yourself overwhelmed with self pity, this is the adversary working on you!

When you find yourself overwhelmed with anger to the point of physical violence, this, again, is the adversary working on you!

When you find yourself feeling worthless, this, too, is the adversary working on you!

The point here is to catch yourself and not allow the adversary to come in and walk all over you.

You ones out there may think that these ones who bring forth these messages somehow have "no problem" dealing with the adversary.  NO!

This one, who is writing today, was nearly incapacitated mentally from adversarial attack just two days ago.  This one needs to face the inner responsibility of keeping the dark energies out of his space, and must also learn to recognize (by experiencing) the subtle nature of such attacks.

The adversary will be ever so cautious and gentle as he kindles the emotional fires that will grow slowly at first, and feel warm and almost soothing.  But just about at that point, he will throw "mental dynamite" into the fire and cause drastic shifts in perception and inner values based upon these inner emotional desires or past pains.  By this point, there is absolutely no mercy shown by the adversary toward the one who allows the adversarial intrusion in the first place.

If you find yourself in a state of chronic depression, then I, Lady Nada, would suggest to you that you take a long, hard look at why YOU allow this to persist!

The reason for such depression lies, almost without exception, in the past.  You ones will hold onto the memories of lost loved ones (whether due to physical death or just physical separation) until you nearly kill yourselves with grief.  If and when he can, the adversary will make certain that you keep falling into this incapacitating, downward-spiral trap.

If you find yourself in such a condition, then you would be wise to find that which you burden self with, and release it.  In doing so, the adversary will have lost this particular foothold within you, and you will have taken a big step toward ridding yourself of the chronic condition of mental torture under which you place yourself.

You must realize that YOU are responsible for that which YOU feel in the way of mental and emotional frustration. We of the Hosts will assist you, if you but ask, else we will honor your choice to face these inner pains on your own, and allow you to your free-will choice.

Go within and find the thread that allows the adversary to enter your space, then see what value you place upon that which the adversary uses to manipulate you. When you are able to release these things, then you will have grown, for in having found the means for doing so, you will have recognized an inner strength that you have not, yet, known before.

This is why it is said that the adversary can be one of the greatest teachers. He will point out your weaknesses by exploiting them, over and over, until you overcome them.

Be very mindful that most of you have many more than just one such weakness. Focus first on whichever one causes you the most mental preoccupation, and handle that one. See that one less distraction is one less than you had prior. You will always have challenges to overcome, so please do not get the idea that somehow you will ever reach a point of "no problems". That would mean that you have stopped growing completely!

Look forward to every new challenge, for such will help you to develop the mental and emotional skills (and strengths) that you need in order to graduate into a higher level of experiencing.

Seek always, within the Light, your Guidance! I cannot say this enough!

**We often lose our most experienced workers, after years of struggle, because they become complacent about clearing their space and about consciously calling-in the Light. Take the time to develop the mental discipline to constantly call upon the Light, until it becomes an innate part of your life. This is perhaps the best possible habit you can cultivate—especially to**

**counteract those times when you are feeling depressed or frustrated.**

This exercise will help you to pull yourself up out of the lower frequency ranges of the adversarial influence, and in the process of accomplishing that, will help us to help you.

Focus your attention on the Light; picture the Light all around you. Take special notice of those thoughts you have which resist the Light, and you will see where the adversary is getting you to shift your focus away from Creator Source. The adversary MUST wear a sign, and this is one of the more obvious ones—IF YOU BUT LOOK!

If your reaction is, "Well, I clear my space just fine; this writing is for 'others' who have not yet learned", then I would caution you to look within and find what you are afraid of and what part of you is resisting the Light. A truly Light-centered being will not resist an opportunity to once again reaffirm their connection to God Source.

These fundamental lessons are the most important ones to really understand well and incorporate within your being, for they are the building blocks that will allow you to overcome your fears and take responsibility for any and every challenge you may have to face. Remember that you are ALWAYS preparing for greater and greater challenges and responsibilities. It is an infinite journey of expansion within The One Light—Creator Source.

I am Lady Nada, come in response to the petitions of those of you who call upon the Light for Guidance and Insights. I am sent by our Father who monitors closely the intents and hearts of all involved in bringing forth these messages to the world. May you find the answers you are looking for—and hopefully MUCH MORE!

Salu.

# CHAPTER FORTY-SEVEN

# Forgiveness And Manifestation Go Hand-In-Hand

## *Violinio Saint Germain*

### January 4, 1997

As the new year unfolds in all its wondrousness and all its uncertainty, there is one thing which is absolutely certain. The subject has been glazed over so lightly and the word is tossed about with no understanding of the fullness of meaning or intent. That word is FORGIVENESS.

Good afternoon. It is I, Violinio St. Germain, here to speak on the subject of forgiveness and manifestation, for they do, you know, go very much hand-in-hand. Without the forgiveness from the very center of your being, you will never experience the wonders of manifestation in the Light. As long as there is any unforgiveness within your soul, you will continue to manifest the same garbage you have been experiencing for thousands of years.

By the way, I, Germain, the Seventh Ray, the Violet Ray, do come unto you this day in the Radiant White Light of Holy God of Creation. The White Light is the completeness of the spectrum of all Light frequencies, and manifests itself in many forms. The universe was born out of this Light, divided so that all its frequencies might experience in their own fullness, but not one of these frequencies could exist without the complementary other frequencies, for such would simply not be possible in the physical universe. Creator is about balance and pure equality, and so the lower frequencies must, by necessity, be given the same equality as the higher frequencies, for all expressions of Light are necessary for the fullness of the Light.

No, I am not speaking mumbo-jumbo. It's all quite simple in concept and application. If Creator is about balance, then all must be equally experienced, for if one were to have a greater experience than the other, then all would be out of balance. All that exists everywhere is but an expression of that same Light, regardless of what that expression might be.

Likewise, you too are all expressions of that same Light, as is your world, and all that you experience upon that world. Whether plant, animal, or mineral, all are but different aspects of the Light, and each aspect interacts with and complements all other aspects (or frequencies) of that Light.

But you say, "What does all this have to do with forgiveness and manifestation?" Well, we are getting to that, but first we must lay down the foundation upon which to build. Anything built without benefit of a foundation is a weak structure, destined only to crumble and fall.

Your dictionary defines forgiveness as: "The act of forgiving; pardon." The word forgive is defined as: "To grant pardon for. To grant freedom from penalty to (someone). To cease to blame or feel resentment against. To remit as a debt. To show forgiveness; grant pardon."

All these definitions are precisely what forgiveness has been all about, yet I wish to explore the deeper meaning, effects, and impacts that TRUE forgiveness has upon one's own spiritual nature, for as I stated earlier, we have tossed the word around without experiencing the EMOTIONAL impact of real forgiveness, and the emotional impact is wherein lies the power behind forgiveness. Without experiencing forgiveness on an emotional level, you will never truly purge the hurt or anger, or any other emotional response from yourself.

**Forgiveness is not about lip service, but about heart service. For, you see, true forgiveness comes not from the head, but from the heart, wherein lies true love. This love is not the love you express through your physical being, but rather the love you express through the emotional gut of your being. You experience this kind of love on the deepest of all levels, and it has little or nothing to do with the physical act of love making.**

In your world, you have been taught that there is good and bad. Yet, how would you describe each of these things? Good is pleasant and bad is unpleasant, and basically that is all that you have to base your judgment upon—true? And yet, how would you know a good thing if you had no concept of bad? How would you be able to discern bad if you had no concept of good? You see, it works both ways, does it not? Remember, it's all about balance.

**A state of unforgiveness is like living in all your own garbage—it's dirty, it smells bad, and it's unhealthy, and the only way to remedy the problem is to clean up the garbage. Spiritually, unforgiveness is dirty, it smells bad, and it is very unhealthy, and the only way to remedy this problem is to clean up the mess—that is, to experience the cleansing of TRUE forgiveness.**

Unforgiveness will clog up the manifestation pipeline quicker than anything, so most of you live in a world in which you are never able to achieve and experience the GOODNESS of manifestation, but rather, you have a bountiful harvest of the other side of manifestation.

Forgiveness, then, is also about balance. If you judge a thing to be bad, how then do you deal with it? Do you harbor the unpleasantness of an experience within yourself, or do you experience it and go on? How do you deal with the ones who offended you?    Do you harbor resentment and anger, or do you experience the emotions and go on?   What happens to the offenders? Have you chosen to ignore them, or do you confront them?   If you confront them, how do you handle the confrontation and how do you resolve same within self?   Will you choose to truly forgive another for an offense, or will you just mutter the words without feeling?

Feelings?   YES, FEELINGS—EMOTIONS!   You have them, but how do you handle them?   If you were really offended, then you experienced the offense not only on an intellectual level, but also on an emotional level.   You, therefore, cannot forgive only on the intellectual level alone, but must also forgive on the emotional level.   And forgiveness does not mean putting the thing out of your mind and hoping you will simply forget about it. That's not forgiveness—it's forgetfulness, and it simply will not work to purge the offense.   For, you see, forgiveness, when it comes from your emotional depths (heart-felt), is a purification of sorts, and though you may never intellectually forget the act which offended you, the emotional attachments and ties to that offense will no longer exist.   For you see, it is not the act you forgive, but rather the person.

**Let us remember what emotions are: emotions are energy in motion.   ENERGY IN *MOTION*—not energy in stagnation! Emotional energy reproduces after its own kind and, like it or not, every emotional response will create!   It's your choice what it is you create, and it is your RESPONSIBILITY.**

In truth, you cannot blame anyone else for your "good luck" or "bad luck".   You have but to go look in the mirror to find the one responsible.   But, by your heart-felt emotional responses you create your own reality, be it good or bad by your judgment.

It may not even have been in this current life where the energy first manifested, for unforgiveness can and does follow from lifetime to lifetime. You will continue to carry it forward with you until you recognize it, deal with it, and finally purge it from your very being.

Most people on your world are dealing with mountains of unforgiveness accumulated over numerous life streams. Why do you think you have such an angry world—a world in which legal litigations are run amuck? And, until such time as each and every individual understands and has a knowing about what unforgiveness has manifested in their lives, and how it has interacted with so many others, over and over and over again, you will continue to experience the present state of affairs on your planet.

Look at the amount of racial anger and hostility present. Look at the amount of national anger and hostility—nation against nation. Look at the amount of divorce, abortion, senseless acts of violence, legal suits, etc. All have their basis in unforgiveness, and lifetimes of harboring the anger and the resentment. And, after all, all are but lessons—albeit some end up being pretty good-sized and far reaching. Wars, lawsuits, acts of violence—all these emotionally driven energies are about to come to a head, and when they do, your world will erupt into such a mess as you have not ever seen or even imagined possible.

Everyone is growing weary of the struggle to just survive, and yet if the truth were to be known, the resolution lies within the very soul of each person on the planet. Once true forgiveness occurs, then there is no more desire to seek out retribution, and that is what all the unrest is about. Each one wants what they feel is their own just reward. Well, chelas, you are getting your own just rewards, for you are manifesting exactly what you have put the energy into.

**True forgiveness is born out of love—love for each other and love for all things, regardless of what color or shape they come in. Each and every one of you is related to everything else that exists in the universe, and each and every one of you is but a part of everything else. So, to hold unforgiveness of anyone or**

**anything, is to hold unforgiveness of self. Think about it, chelas. You are holding yourselves hostages in your own realities, and you have no one to blame for your state of affairs and your "good luck" or "bad luck" except yourselves.**

You are not victims of anything except your own hard-heartedness, and it is far beyond the time to get past it. This year, each and every one of you should take it upon yourselves to examine just who and what you are harboring ill-will against, and purge it from within—NOT IN YOUR HEADS, BUT IN YOUR HEARTS!

No, you cannot change another's heart, but you can change yours, and you can change from this point forward just how you react to an experience.

Do you feel that someone owes you something? Ask yourself why. Why put the responsibility off onto someone else? Why not start with the enemy within? And how, may I ask, do you expect another to forgive you when you still have unforgiveness within? Remember: like energy manifests like energy. Stop preaching to another about their unforgiveness, their problems, when you are holding onto unforgiveness yourself.

You also tend to forgive based upon the degree of the "crime". You have developed levels of forgiveness, such as, "Well, okay, I'll forgive you this time, but now you have to do something for me in retribution." Come on, that's not forgiveness! True forgiveness is absolute, and requires nothing from the offender except the heart-felt apology. To forgive in degrees of severity is the same thing as judgment, and you all know what that is about, do you not? Whose job is it to judge? It is not yours to judge another, I will tell that straight up. What you are, in essence, saying here is: "Well, all right, I hear your apology, but because I'm better than you (in this instance), I will decide just how I will forgive you, and I've decided that you owe me!" In this case, there is no forgiveness, and the darkness is still present and will continue to grow inside, extinguishing the Light within.

Without that Light, you will never achieve the ability to manifest through Light.   All your manifestations are going to be done through the darkness, for like reproduces like.

Keep in mind, also, that it is not your place to judge the sincerity of another's apology.   The only judgment you are responsible for is whether you choose to accept the apology and forgive them.   They will have to deal with and live with their emotions, just as you must deal with and live with yours.   If you ones spent less time judging another's integrity and more time judging your own integrity, you would have a lot less bickering and violent behavior.   If the truth were to be known, you would be so busy cleaning out your own house that you would not have time to notice that another's house might be dirty.

Unforgiveness is like a parasite.   It requires a host to feed on, to live and grow.   It will continue to eat away at the host until it has fully consumed the host.

Anger or resentment will grow and grow and grow until you become angered at everything and everyone for some reason or another.   This is the tactic of the enemy of God.   Anger, resentment, and unforgiveness create a gap between you and God, for these things are from the heart as well.

**The world is a very angry place today, because you live in a world of emotional denial.   You want to handle everything on a mental level, but anger is not mental, it is emotional, and you cannot deal with an emotion on the mental level, for the mind is not emotional.   You can rationalize it; you can logically deal with it and file it (the anger from perceived hurts) away in some memory bank, but that is not ridding yourself of it.**

In order to grow past the negative emotional responses, you have to get rid of them, not just tuck them away in some dark corner of your mind. Emotional responses come from deep within your very beings, and must be dealt with on that level. You can spend countless hours on the psychiatrist's couch talking about your emotions, but until you go within your own closets, so to speak, and honestly take these emotions out and look at them and deal with them, face to face, you are never going to rid yourself of the negative ones. And without ridding yourself of them, you are never going to get past where you are, right this very moment.

No, it's not easy—nothing worthwhile is ever easy! You are in this third-dimensional expression to learn and to grow. Neither of these things come easy, especially if you are to get the most out of the experience. But until you open your eyes to the reality of what you are doing, what you are feeling, and what you are creating, you will stay right where you are.

Forgiveness is one of the "biggie" lessons of your third-dimensional experience, and yes, one of the most difficult to resolve. Most of you have so much unforgiveness within that it has become confused and convoluted to the point that you don't even remember exactly who it is you are angry with—you are just plain angry with nearly everything and everyone! Now multiply that by five billion and see what you have—see the reality you have manifested!

It is not going to remedy itself overnight because you did not get to this point overnight. But, all things are possible in the Light, and all forgiveness lies in the Light. When you pray, pray that you might find forgiveness for everyone whom you might be holding anger or resentment against. Then, and only then, can you approach a state of peace and hope to achieve forgiveness. It is all about balance, chelas.

Approach the Light and you will find that, within that Light, there is no anger, no tears, no ill-will, only Light—and no darkness can enter into the Light without being completely extinguished.

**If you want to rid yourself of anger, sadness, all those "negative" emotions, then begin by forgiving first. Forgiveness is one of the greatest weapons you have in your arsenal against the enemy.**

I can see you ones rolling your eyes and yawning and thinking, "Oh boy, more touchy-feely, New-Age gobble-de-goop." Call it what you will. It is not New-Age anything—the concept of forgiveness is as old as the universe. And as for touchy-feely—it's a lot better and much healthier than hatred and murder!

No one says you have to forget, all I am telling you is that you must learn to forgive. And guess what? Once you have true forgiveness, the forget part just happens!

If you like the mess you have on your planet, just continue down the path you are on now. If you are tired of the mess, as you all are saying you are, then do something about it, and stop whimpering and whining and waiting for the ships to come and bail you out.

YOU made your messes, and YOU are responsible for cleaning them up. So stop the pity parties, stop the sniveling, stop the complaining, and start doing something about it. Quit pointing your finger at someone else and saying they're picking on you and you don't deserve it. You ones have spent far more time chasing after the devil—when in reality the devil has been right there within those dark, negative emotions all the time.

Thank you for your time and for your attention to these matters. These are the days of your final lessons in third-dimensional school, and you are in the hardest of all lessons yet. However, know also that you have the ability and the tools with which to get through these lessons, and you are not experiencing more than you are capable of handling. The lessons are only as difficult as you expect them to be, and you achieve by the same degree as you put energy into them.

Each of you are important and blessed to us. We would not strive with you if there was not hope and knowing that you can succeed. The closer you are to finishing, the more difficult become the challenges. The Light is ever with you, and we are ever with you, as well. When you find yourselves backed into the proverbial corner, look up, for you are never alone.

Now go get to work—and go in peace, go in love, go in Light, and go in FORGIVENESS.

**Make your re-SOUL-ution this year be to truly forgive those for whom you hold anger and resentment. Forgive those who have hurt you, and in so doing, you will find your own healing of heart!**

I am Germain. Salu.

# CHAPTER FORTY-EIGHT

# May Your Life Never
# Be Without A Good Challenge!

### *Sanat Kumara*

### January 18, 1997

Good morning, my friend. It is I, Sanat Kumara. You know me as "Grandfather"; others may recognize me as Tonkashila. I come now to you as the representative of the Silver Ray of Creator Source. Many associate me with your Sun and resonate with my life-giving Light. Please do NOT get overly fixated upon the label, for if you do, you will surely miss the message.

The label is to identify to you ones who need such in order to not be overwhelmed with who or what we, from the Higher Realms, really are. We are Co-Creators who have walked the paths that you are on and have learned our lessons. We are what you are— thought projections of Creator. We are Light. We are One in that we are all connected to Source and we project outward in many dimensions simultaneously from this One Light.

**You and I are Creator experiencing and growing. We all have a common purpose—it is to go forth and experience and GROW. We only differ in the approach to this basic directive which is encoded into the "genetic" makeup of our soul.**

If one creates a wheel, then would it not be better to go forth and create a use for the wheel than to have everyone going through the process of creating a wheel? See the elegance and wisdom of that which is before you, and use the tools that you are given in order to move an idea forward.

We of the Lighted Brotherhood do not have need for ones to reinvent the wheel over and over again. Stop asking for the secrets of Tesla. Take that which you know and use the gifts that you have to create a new and better "soul-ution" to the challenges that you are currently being faced with. In doing so, you will realize the joy that you have been looking for, yet missing, all these years.

**Creating is JOY manifesting!**

For example, look to a small child and give them finger paints or colored pencils, and you will see them play with them for hours. Yes, eventually they will get bored with them for they will have experimented and realized the limitations of their current abilities.

For another example, consider the simple act of giving. When you give to another spontaneously, do you not, in effect, create surprise and pleasure within the recipient? How does this make you feel? Even if you give to a complete stranger who you may never see again, you will feel, at some level, the emotional acknowledgment of the appreciation which that one feels within when they realize the value of the object or kind act.

**Look for opportunities to express in a creative manner and you will be well on your way to creating the joy you desire.**

If you feel that your life is full of misery and grief, then I would suggest you take a long, hard look at what it is that you are doing. This is not as easy a task as it first may seem, for it will not be plain to see the overall impact of your actions as a whole.

Many perceive that they are helping others "ALL" of the time. Yet, these ones may not realize that they have to let others grow and experience for themselves. This is quite common of overprotective parents who are actually stifling the creativity of their children, all the while thinking that they are doing the "best thing" for the child. This, in turn, will cause the children to rebel and distance themselves from those who are actually suppressing the children's ability to fulfill their innate inner directive—to experience and grow.

The hardest thing for a person to do is to allow another, whether it be friend or relative, to experience for themselves the "pitfalls" of life. Ones will yell at, beat, and mentally abuse the ones they love in order to reinforce their love and to "protect" these ones from going out and fulfilling their inner desire to experience and GROW.

Look at your actions. Are you trying to control another by making them conform to your way of doing things, or are you allowing the uniqueness of the individual to grow in its own way? What right do you have to interfere with another? We are, here, talking of adults, and NOT small children who are not well adjusted to their body or the environment in which they are experiencing.

Allow even the small children to express their creativity. For instance, if you are going to rearrange the furniture in the child's room, maybe you can give them a choice as to where they might like to put their bed. This will help them to feel a sense of worth and pride in having helped to create the change in the appearance of the room. Even a two-year-old child will find this fun! You will also be helping the child to learn that they can think for themselves—and CREATE.

Look for opportunities to give others the chance to create. Stop trying to control everything and everyone, for in doing so you will have usurped the opportunity of another to experience and grow. You may feel uncomfortable doing this at first, but the repercussions of not doing this will be quite a bit more uncomfortable to you in the long run.

Look at where you are this day and at how you feel. Take PERSONAL responsibility for your condition and look at those things that you are preoccupied with or otherwise worried about.

What hold have they on you?

Do you worry about whether or not your teenage child is having sex? Did you ever stop to wonder if the teenager is worried about whether or not he or she is having sex? Be assured that they probably are, especially growing up in this "modern" society. Now, ask yourself: "Why don't I have better communication with this child?"

Have you pushed this person away from you through your attempts to protect them? Do you always find faults in their young, "inexperienced" logic? Can you make suggestions without insisting that they do a thing YOUR way? You should offer to them guidance and give them your reasons for offering same. But above all—allow them to experience and grow!

If you are concerned about whether or not your child is doing drugs or having sex, then talk to them and explain to them your feelings on these matters and acknowledge to them that they will have to eventually be responsible for their actions and choices.

No parent wishes to bury a child, but who are you really burying? You are burying the body, not the person. The soul, who was wearing the body, shall eventually realize that their actions were destructive and that they cannot blame another for their choices.

Understand that you can only offer assistance and, if it is refused, then you will have to release such God-fragments of Light to their own destiny of choice.

See where you might have made mistakes; find forgiveness within for self, and then release the past, lest it consume you in the present. YOU HAVE ALL MADE SUCH MISTAKES!

Many have learned these lessons late in life and wish that they could go back and do it over. You cannot go back, and if you did, you would make the same mistake again, for in going back you only would have that which you had then. You need these experiences;

be thankful that you have grown to the point of NOW being able to spot your errors. Allow others to have the same opportunities to grow as well.

When you are able to help another in this manner, you will find that friends and family members will actually come TO you, seeking advice, for you are unassuming and they will see that you DO know what you are talking about. But, allow them to come into this realization for themselves. In this way you will have gained the respect you deserve and you will be heard instead of being ignored. Do not be the one who must always interject an overbearing opinion.

Allow for others to solve their own problems in their own way—and they will probably include you in the problem solving, if and when they feel it is appropriate.

**Inasmuch as you clean the garbage out of YOUR life, you will help others to do the same. In the process of creating new answers to YOUR problems, you will begin, again, to feel the joy you long for within.**

Many can remember back to a point in their life where they did not have much to really worry about, to a time when everything seemed new and interesting. Your life could be this way again IF you were to but realize that you do not need to place the restrictions and burdens upon yourself that you currently do.

Again: What is so important that you must continue to beat yourself up, over and over again, day after day?

When you can honestly realize that the answer to this question is "NOTHING!", then you will have learned the first step to overcoming all that may be bothering and annoying you.

You will now have to evaluate, for yourself, what it is that you are doing, and realize that there is probably a better (new to you or untried) manner in which to handle the "problem" that you are faced with.

Let us take, for example, that you are in a relationship with another and you are constantly yelling at one another in your attempts to be understood. You may wish to experiment with different manners of getting your point across. Perhaps a quiet whisper, or even, perhaps, giving in, for a change, to the suggestions of the one who is probably "only trying to help".

Put aside your ego long enough to realize when you are being stubborn just because you hate it when others are right. Are the things that you argue over REALLY very important in the overall scope of the experiencing down there?

Do you argue over who should do the "menial" chores? Can you not share the chores and be grateful that you have someone to share with and talk to, instead? Work with one another and you will be surprised at what two (or more) Aspects of Creator's Light can come up with when focused on the same problem.

If your old routines are leaving you unfulfilled inside, can you not break free from the programing of the routine enough to create a better way—perhaps a "routine" of evolving?

All things are in a constant state of change! When you hold onto the past or freeze a moment in the present (which is actually, again, holding onto the past), you are resisting the prime directive within. You are then, in effect, causing unnecessary pressures in your life by resisting the natural flow of experiencing. Like a boulder stuck in the midst of a flowing stream, you create backpressures and "ripples" in the otherwise natural flow of Experience. It is most difficult to simply proceed forward and not try to go back and make a different choice and see where that one leads you.

You are where you are because you need the challenge of the new experience. With each new challenge, you are presented with an opportunity to create a soul-ution that has never been tried before. You may not always be successful in each attempt, but you will eventually be quite successful at experiencing and growing, and this will gradually lead you to the answers you seek and the joy you desire. Be forever persistent and you will NOT know failure!

I am Sanat Kumara, your Elder Brother, offering assistance to those who may desire same. I come in the Light of the One Light, Creator Source. May your life NEVER be without a good challenge, lest you stop growing completely!

Salu!

# CHAPTER FORTY-NINE

# Focusing
# Your Emotional (Heart) Desires

### *Master Hilarion*
### January 25, 1997

Good afternoon, my friend. It is I, Hilarion, of the Emerald Ray of Creator's spectrum of Light-Thought projection. I have come this day that a needed message be penned for there are many in need of The Truth regarding the nature of their current condition.

Many are faced with the bombardments of the physical environment at this time. One major way of distracting a person is to get them focused on the physical body in which they are housed. You are being bombarded from every direction imaginable at this time and, for some, these directions are UN-imaginable. Let us simply list a few of these serious distractions:

(1) Your food supplies are depleted of the necessary nutrients.

(2) You are being attacked with various lethal viruses that, on top of the physical dangers and discomforts, cause further mental anxiety (FEAR!) of the possibilities that you or a loved one "might" contract such a disease.

(3) Your medical doctors lack true healing knowledge, and thus the treatments lack depth and understanding, and thus fail in most cases.

(4) You are being heavily attacked with electronic "pulse" weapons that cause disrupted sleep, so that no matter how much sleep you get, you never seem quite rested.

Throughout all of this, you ones attracted to these messages are trying to maintain a focus on the spiritual aspect of "why" you might be there.

I have been asked to assist in the understanding of who you are and the purpose of the physical experience. I am known as the Healer because the frequency and wavelength of my energy field most often will cause a triggering of the heart energy center within ones. I only CAUSE the triggering; the person or entity will do the rest, if it is to be done at all.

The GREATEST killer of mankind is the inner mental programming of the mind. Put in other terms for clarification: man creates and holds onto the past pains, and allows them to grow until they literally manifest in the physical. For example, ones will hold onto the pain of past emotional trauma that resulted from the "lost" love that they felt for another. They continue to grind on this past emotional trauma until it manifests in the physical domain as an "incurable" cancer. The condition may even respond—at first—to treatments, but it will come back stronger than ever, for you have decided that you do not want to get better and that you, somehow, need to punish self.

The only way for this type of condition to be healed is from the inside (inner mind) out. Treating the body in this case is of little-to-no value unless and until the MIND is in a balanced mental state *AND* the HEART is in a balanced emotional state. There is an important distinction to be emphasized here: ones can MENTALLY tell themselves to heal—BUT—if the HEART is in conflict, the healing shall not occur. IT IS POSSIBLE FOR ONES TO HEAL *ANY* CONDITION THAT AILS THEM *IF* THERE IS TRUE HEART DESIRE TO DO SO!

Many will simply say that they do not wish to die—yet they will, in actuality, create a condition in which they will suffer for years and be a burden for others as they fight with a mental desire (USUALLY FEAR OF DEATH) to live and an emotional desire to escape the pain.

**When these ones can learn to forgive themselves with the heart, and not with the mouth, they will begin to turn around the condition in which they find themselves, and the miraculous healing will have begun!**

This condition is becoming a plague on your planet at this time and will continue to grow in the coming years due to the impact of that which is to come—from the process of the cleansing of the planet herself.

You live on a Sentient, Living Being who has a right to mentally and emotionally heal herself of the "cancers" that have been allowed to fester and grow. She will not be denied this right, and those who cannot withstand the cleansing process (a frequency shift into a higher dimensional existence) shall be the ones who will not survive the impact of this shift!

This will, in effect, be a lot like what your biological scientists call Natural Selection, wherein only the strongest survive. In this case it will be only the strongest emotionally and mentally—those who have their heart and mind in balance enough to keep up with the frequency shifts. The chaos of unbalance will not be tolerated. Those who refuse to pursue the personal responsibility to BALANCE their thoughts and actions, and thereby maintain the emotional wattage (power) that they give these unbalanced thoughts, will simply weed themselves from the play!

The choice is always left up to the individual in these cases. Each must make their own choice as to what is the more important heart desire:

(1)  to grow beyond what you are this day and explore further your potential as a souled being; or

(2)   to succumb, as you are, without knowing what you could have accomplished if you had chosen to overcome the limitations that you have placed upon self.

**Keep in mind that the journeys of the soul are infinite and that you will again be faced with the same choice, again, in upcoming experiences and you will have to face the inner battle, again and again, until you can find a deeper purpose in making a more daring choice.**

This same general phenomenon applies to ALL your choices in life, regardless of whether or not it is a terminal disease or going through abusive relationships, one after another. Unless and until you decide that you have punished self enough, you will continue to subject self to these tortures.

**WHO, exactly, might you think would help you to stay in this state of self punishment? The adversary (that which is in opposition to Creator God) knows that he cannot be victorious, and thus behaves somewhat like an immature child in that, if he cannot win, then he will make the game as difficult for everyone as possible.**

What causes you to hold on to these past pains and traumas? Why is it that you can MENTALLY see the absurdity of doing so, yet you cannot seem to EMOTIONALLY break free?

Could it be that you are lying to self and holding onto a fallacy that only exists in your mind—or heart? You must get honest with yourself! This is done by looking within and seeing yourself as you REALLY are, and NOT how you "think" you are.

For example, we see those who will run around loudly complaining about others, such as how this or that person gossips too much, etc. Yet, all the while, these complainers do not ever stop to notice that they do the same exact thing which they claim to despise in these others.

If you are not willing to confront your SELF, then you are insuring that you will be repeating the same unbalanced conditions, over and over again. These experiences are for SELF discovery! God knows your inner potential. It is YOU who do not realize this, for you are too busy with your emotional guilt and mental anxieties to realize that these are the challenges you have to face in order to grow into the responsibility of the position as a co-creator in the infinite expanse of everything that is.

HEALING BEGINS WITH THE HEART DESIRE TO DO SO! This is the emotional feeling that precedes the mental desire.

This brings us to a most important point: What comes first, the thought or the emotion?

EMOTION IS ENERGY!

Emotion is the energy that precipitates the thought! Emotion has potential that is focused with the thoughts. Thus, you will have greater success in healing if you can become impassioned about the healing. When you feel "down and depressed" over your condition, you are utilizing very basic (low frequency) emotional energy. This energy is NOT very conducive to healing!

Returning now to the point I was introducing at the beginning of this writing: **the ones who are trying to control your societies are aware that if they can keep you in an off-balance condition, with great mental distractions which precipitate these lower emotional states, then they will keep you sick, mentally stressed, and thus in a drained condition that is most conducive to the suggestive nature of their mind-control techniques.**

You can override these traps when you realize that you do not have to dwell long in these lower emotional states. DO allow the honest emotional reactions to a situation to play out, but DO NOT dwell, for very long, down in those low frequency depressions.

For instance, you ones have heard that "laughter is the best medicine". Why can this be quite true?

When you laugh, you are altering (raising) the frequency of not just your brain waves, but of every cell in your body! This, in turn, will allow for better, more efficient communication among ALL of the various parts and systems in the body.

The body will begin to operate more efficiently and you will begin to eliminate the toxins, poisons, and other foreign agents that will otherwise accumulate due to poor communication between the various organ-coordinating energy centers of the body.

It is like revving up an internal combustion engine (like your automobile motor) and blowing out the carbon deposits that will otherwise just sit there and accumulate around the cylinder walls and exhaust ports, to the continual detriment of engine performance. In a mechanical sense, you can think of the revving-up process as akin to "raising the frequency" of the engine.

**There shall come a time when you ones will not feel much like laughing about anything. You must effort to keep in mind that the upcoming, massive cleansing cycle is as natural as sneezing. When your planet sneezes, coughs, and otherwise shakes with the tremors of a fever, she is doing this out of a NATURAL healing cycle that will lead her back into balance. YOU may perceive this as a very destructive occurrence, but let me assure you that it is quite necessary and quite beneficial in the long run.**

When you are sick and trying to rid yourselves of a viral infection, do you give consideration to the very germs or conditions that allow for this sickness to persist? If the raising of your body temperature a few degrees, for a short period of time, will burn out the viral infestation, is it not acceptable to do so without regard for the well-being of the life forms (viruses) causing the conditions that allow for the disease to grow?

Your planet shall have the balance that she seeks, for she is entering a high-frequency light field (what you ones have named "The Photon Belt") that will help facilitate this healing and transformation. In the process, those who are adding to the problem (by not putting their houses in order) shall be "out of sync" with the cleansing and will, in effect, remove themselves from the playing field.

Remaining in ignorance will not be acceptable, either, because the emotional frequency and vibration of "fear that is borne out of ignorance" shall likewise cause these ones to remove themselves from the playing field.

**Under the purging conditions of this high-frequency Light field, holding onto ANY lower-frequency emotions will cause a very rapid deterioration in the physical body. Thus ones will have to deal with these lower emotions in short order. NOTICEABLE DETERIORATION WILL TAKE PLACE IN A MATTER OF WEEKS INSTEAD OF YEARS!**

Please know that you CAN survive the upcoming changes. You will have to learn to release the garbage (the emotional baggage) that you hold onto so closely.

You will need to be more consciously aware of how YOUR emotional state affects your health—as well as affecting the health of others AND the very planet upon which you live. These emotional energies are focused with the mind and can add to or subtract from those around you.

The general, overall result is a collective frequency or tonal vibration of the planet and her occupants. You EACH contribute to this overall average and you EACH have a choice in whether you add to or subtract from this average.

Find something that you can be thankful for and happy about, and you will have taken the first steps toward healing. Get impassioned about something worth living for, and you will almost undoubtedly heal. Keep up the "woe is me" attitude, and you will almost certainly create a condition that is most unpleasant.

Choose wisely that upon which you focus your emotional energies, for you will ALWAYS manifest your heart's desire! Your actions will always reflect this desire.

I am the Cohan of the Emerald Ray. I am Hilarion, Teacher and Wayshower. I come in the Radiance of Creator's One Light, which is infinite and eternal. Blessings to you all, from my heart to yours!

Salu.

# – CHAPTER FIFTY –

# Restless Time
# Of Choices And Challenges

## *Lord Michael, Archangel*
### February 2, 1997

Good afternoon, my scribe. It is I, Lord Michael, of the Archangelic Realms as recognized by you ones down there in the physical. I come as a Messenger of Creator's Light so that you and others may have the Guidance promised to you.

You sense the familiarity of my energy field. This is fine, for I am around you constantly. Be at peace, my friend! Take my hand and allow me to guide you through these trying times.

Your world is being starved for the things that provide sustenance at all levels. Ones are becoming restless as to what it is that is happening (or about to happen) to them at this time. This restlessness is, in part, due to the imminent changes that are trickling into the consciousness of the masses.

The restlessness is also due to the fact that ones know Truth when they hear it. This means that ones sense, at some level, that they are being lied to. This causes ones to not trust one another, for each can sense The Truth. Each can discern whether or not the person they are interacting with is indeed duped, along with the rest of the masses, or if they have insights which can lead ones out of the confusion which lies behind the restlessness.

You can only maintain a façade for so long before it crumbles in the Light of Truth!  Allow for The Truth to reveal itself to you.

Find and cultivate the Inner Voice (your direct Light connection to Source) that will give you the inner discernment necessary to see The Truth and cast off the lies.  You must all learn to discern for selves!  No one will be allowed to do your learning for you.

**This does not mean that you cannot ask advice or assistance from another.  I am saying that it is still YOUR responsibility to discern for yourself the correct path for you!  You ones are so afraid of making a wrong choice that you will give over your personal responsibility at the "drop of a hat" in order to not have to face the responsibility of making a bad choice.**

There are no wrong choices in the larger picture.  Any choice will lead you to new and different circumstances and, eventually, to a point wherein you will be faced squarely with the OPPORTUNITY to make another choice.  Each time you encounter such an event, you will have grown and learned from your past experiences.

These experiences can be viewed as either good or bad.  Let me assure you that, just because YOU view an experience as bad, it does not mean we of the Hosts view the experience as bad!

We can see farther and in depth that which will play out in sequence of events.  You may need what is perceived to be a bad or traumatic event in order to wake you up and cause you to search deeper for your answers.

Your Higher Self (the SOUL you) will pull in to you the necessary experiences that you need in order to fulfill your purpose for going down there in the first place.  If you have agreed to participate in order to balance out past indiscretions, then you can EXPECT to be faced with similar circumstances to those with which you had difficulties in the past.  You should expect to be faced with the kinds of challenges that "tripped you up" before.  This is part of the rebalancing that will free you from the self-imposed karmic guilt and will lead you into a higher level of awareness and understanding.

There are NO victims down there! You each have your reasons for participating. So, stop the "poor me" victim attitude and realize that, if you are overwhelmed with inner emotional turmoil, then perhaps you are making the SAME mistakes over AGAIN and your Higher (KNOWING) Self is trying to get you back on a path that will lead you into balance. The inner frustration usually comes when you resist these changes in perception or direction.

**You each would be wise to take a humble, self-introspective look at what it is that you resist in the way of accepting change on a personal level. You all are in a battle, at some level, with the acceptance of the next higher step in responsibility, regardless of who you are or where you are this day in terms of growth.**

You are each provided with the individual insights that you need in order to see that you have a choice before you. Note: I did not say that the answers lie before you. I said a CHOICE!

When you are faced with a choice, do you effort to reason out each option as to long-term potential impact on your personal growth, or do you go for the short-term gratification of the physical comfort?

When you find yourself angry with someone or with a set of circumstances, do you look first for a means of retaliation or do you look first for a means of forgiveness?

The retaliation approach MAY provide you with a measure of short-term gratification, but the forgiveness approach will provide you with a long-term peace as well as avoiding the generation of future guilt.

We who are your Elder Brothers have walked the path upon which you now experience. We have faced the trying challenges of the physical and have been successful in overcoming the self-imposed restrictions of the mind.

You may take these messages and use them, or discard them, as you wish. We, as Messengers of God, are sent to provide you with the insights that your inner self desires. What you DO with them is your choice. May you act in wisdom while considering all your options prior to discounting that which you have a hard time accepting as real.

Do you believe in Angels of Light (Angels of Creator God)? What do you think is our purpose?

**We are Messengers of Truth! We counsel directly with Creator Source and act within the wisdom of that counsel and guidance.**

How could we fulfill our purpose if we just sat around and did NOTHING? "Messenger" implies communication! We must have means of communicating directly with you ones, else we cannot carry out our purpose. Remember that all-important Inner Voice.

Allow for the Inner Voice within to guide you. Be cautious and keep the adversary (that which is in opposition to Creator God) out of the mental and emotional energy space in which you function. Many a great entity has stumbled due to the trickery and subtle nature of the adversary. Be respectful of your enemy, else he will "mop the floor" with you.

Please realize that it is acceptable to stumble. Just remember to get back up! When you just lay there, licking your wounds and feeling embarrassed that you stumbled, and worrying about whether or not anyone saw you—be assured that God saw!

He is more interested in what you will DO (what choices you will make because of the experience) than He is that you stumbled.

You can be more today than you were yesterday, but only if you get up and move forward. Or, you can lay there in your stagnation and embarrassment, waiting for all the stumbling blocks to be removed. They will not be removed until YOU remove them!

Allow for the input from Higher Source to flow through to your conscious understanding—from whatever direction may be effective. For instance, insights may come from complete strangers who are Guided to do or say something that they themselves don't even understand. Or, a small child may even have an Inspired Insight for you, if you but listen and pay attention to the circumstances. Again: you have to choose for yourself what you DO with the "Helping Hand" once such is presented to you.

**Be not long in your deciding that you can get back up and take another step forward. Then hold in your heart and in your mind that which you have experienced and learned, and take the next step forward. Set as your goal the understanding of who you really are—if you can see no other goal to work toward—and persist through the challenges that may have you stumbling again and again. Soon you will see that you have learned to recognize and overcome the stumbling blocks and their subtle clues that are ALWAYS there for you to see if you but look and pay attention.**

The answers are there that will satisfy the long-term restlessness that you feel, but you have to come into the realization of and recognition of those answers FOR YOURSELF, and in your own unique way. What may work quite well for one may not work at all for another. Remember: you are EACH a unique aspect of Creator's thought projections and you will EACH return to Creator on your own UNIQUE path.

May this writing find understanding within your heart, wherein lies the restlessness that calls out for assistance.

I am Lord Michael, come in the One Light of Creator God as a Messenger of Truth so that His promise to you is fulfilled.

With love and respect, blessings to you ALL!

# CHAPTER FIFTY-ONE

# *Preparation* Includes
# Listening To Your Guides

### *Ceres Anthonious Soltec*

#### February 9, 1997

Good morning, my friend! It is I, Ceres Anthonious Soltec, come in the Radiant One Light of Creator God. Thank you for again sitting this day to write for we of the Hosts.

There is a need at this time to issue yet another warning concerning the geological INstability of your planet. Your planet is under severe stress this day and she is in great need of relief. She shall have her relief! You ones need to be prepared for the upcoming changes. Whether they be from man's tampering with forces that he does not understand, or from natural balancing of pressures within the body of Earth-Shan is of little consequence when the walls of your dwelling are coming apart!

Your elite controllers feel they are running out of time—when they perceive the extent of their progress toward world control and compare that to where they think they should be according to their blueprint agenda. This is cause for sounding an alarm because there are horrendous plans to counteract this "time" discrepancy in their schedule. There are several plans developed to counter this perceived problem and each plan has a set of back-up plans. We could discuss any number of these plans, but most of them have already been touched upon in previous writings.

However, at this point in the unfolding "play", you who are going to be prepared have already done so, and those who are still sitting on the fence will continue to do so until the fence is literally shaken out from beneath them.

You are well into serious times down there, and most know it not. The fox is in the hen house and has you convinced that he belongs there and that you should have to feed and support him in his efforts to destroy all that for which you have worked.

Many down there will blindly continue to support the dark ones who drain the life force from the very being of these unsuspecting ones—until this blind majority completely succumbs to the elite controllers' parasitic condition. The ignorance and naiveté of these clueless ones will enable the elite controllers to pull off the massive annihilation on your planet.

**It is only through knowledge and understanding that you can divert these catastrophic plans for your planet. As always, the masses will refuse to listen, for it causes them great discomfort to have to feel responsible for their part in the overall drama of life.**

These are the ones who will refuse to hear the messages of Truth. These are the ones who will say, "What's the use? I am only one small person; I can't change anything." These are the ones who are frightened by the thought of taking an action that might lead them into a position of responsibility. These are the ones who will choose to remain in ignorance and thus go along with "Big Brother" as he uses them, and then discards them when they are of no further value. These are the ones who shall have to recycle through this sort of experience, again and again, until they "get it right". These are the "young" ones whose growth we stand ready to assist!

By contrast, many of you who diligently read these messages are the Ground Crew members who have volunteered (Oh, yes you did!) to come at this time, in the physical form, in order to re-give that which others before you have given to you. Inasmuch as you prepare now, you will find that your job will be easier to accomplish in the years to come.

When catastrophe strikes and YOU are prepared, those who are not prepared will come to you asking, "How is it that you knew to prepare for these things?" At that time you will probably have the undivided attention of the ones you have been trying to help all these years. It is at that time when a larger part of your mission will be recognized! You are teachers and wayshowers for the ones who are in need of realizing who they are and why they are going through such horrendous experiences.

You are part of the Hosts who have been sent at this time so that God's promise would be fulfilled to those who are seeking diligently to find the answers to the questions that demand an answer. These are questions like: "Why am I here?" and "Why has all this (catastrophe) happened?"

**God promised that The Truth shall be known and that people would be given to know WHY the great tragedy has befallen them. YOU are the answer to this promise! You shall stand as a beacon of Light during very dark times. Your job is to assist your brothers in their understanding of WHY all of what will transpire has transpired.**

Inasmuch as you prepare NOW for your future survival, you will capture the attention of those around you for having greater insight than they, because your very actions will have proven this to be so!

There are many reasons why we of the non-physical expression suggest that you do the things that we ask. We will, however, always wait to see where you are at, in ability to discern for yourselves, prior to just giving you the answers.

So, if you're just sitting out there all alone, and you are thinking that you do not need to prepare, for you have no real responsibilities to attend such as children or family, then I would suggest that you consider your choices most carefully prior to dismissing preparation as a course of action. To those of you who have prepared for yourselves, you may wish to consider adding to your food supplies so that you have extra to offer those in need. [*See* Appendix A *in this book for a* 72-Hour Kit Checklist *of emergency items.*]

Know that you ALL have a purpose to fulfill. Realize also that, though we may not always respond to the individual question in this forum, we WILL most certainly respond to individual questions on an individual basis, for the call compels the answer. But that means making the effort to go within and be attentive to the response!

With this said, I will ask that this morning's earlier "private" writing to this scribe be attached following this message, for there are many who can benefit from the words and we simply do not have the time to re-write the message again.

*PREPARATION* **IS THE KEY TO FULFILLING YOUR INDIVIDUAL PURPOSE and we will assist you in ALL your efforts—when YOU take conscious action to meet us part way!**

I am Ceres Anthonious "Toniose" Soltec come in the Light of Creator Source. May you *SEE* beyond the words and *FEEL* the Love with which these messages are sent! Salu.

[*Editor's note: The following writing was scribed just before the message above. It is the "private" message which geophysical Commander Soltec suggested was worthy of general attention and sharing in conjunction with the advice penned already.*

*Indeed, in any imaginable capacity of teaching or wayshowing under the chaotic conditions we are about to experience, connection to Source for Guidance is a most prudent first step toward fruitful later action—don't you agree?!*]

Good morning, my friend; it is I, Toniose Soltec, come in the One Light of Creator God. Thank you for hearing the call and responding. We have work to get done, so please get comfortable and find balance within.

We shall stand with you throughout all of the challenges that you will face down there. Call upon the Light whenever you feel the desire to do so. Please do NOT hesitate to do this! We can assist you more when a conscious call is made.

Allow for the changes in perception to unfold within your mind as well as within your heart. You will be Guided to the answers you desire. Be patient and persistent, for the answers are there when YOU take the proper focus in order to perceive them.

We shall assist you, when and where we can. You can help us by keeping your space cleared and by calling in the Light for assistance. Once the call is made, you can KNOW that an answer WILL present itself to you. But—YOU must recognize the clues and follow your Inner Nudgings in order to help manifest the answer in physical space (or in the physical consciousness).

Many times we send you ones the answers you desire, or a clue that will lead you to the answers, only to have the opportunity lost due to a lack of cognitive recognition of the subtle nudges that we are sending to you in response to your call for assistance. Be attentive to the nudges and learn to recognize the thoughts that seem to "pop" into your head.

In time you will come to greatly appreciate the communications and insights that manifest because of this developed perception that you ones call INTUITION. We shall continue to work with you ones in order to strengthen this sort of communication cycle.

It always helps to have a reminder, such as this one, to help you to remain focused upon the training cycles that you are experiencing almost non-stop every day. However, this is also to caution that, when you are being constantly Guided throughout your life, you will sometimes become complacent with the whole process and thus begin to ignore the suggestions that we are making to you.

When you remain focused and place the proper amplification on a thought, then you will have done YOUR part. You will soon more fully realize the value of maintaining a conscious mental awareness of our Higher Presence within your mind, as thoughts come and go throughout the day. You will also be able to connect more easily to the Higher Consciousness of we of the Higher Energy Realms as you consciously practice becoming attuned, and then effort toward amplifying those thoughts.

As always, you must maintain your guard at all times, for the adversary will most certainly try to influence this process IF you give him the opportunity to do so! Keep your Light shielding up at all times, and if a thought causes you concern, then clear your space and ask for clarification.

Act always in wisdom for you are responsible for all that you dwell upon, and thus manifest in the physical experience. Release the thoughts that will only serve to distract you for they are just that—DISTRACTIONS!

You are under constant barrage from all directions in order to slow you up or even stop you if the adversary is able to "pull it off". Again, there is nothing new here—just a reminder to you to keep an "ear open" to our nudges and follow your Inner Guidance.

**Recognize when we are there working with you. Even the small, seemingly unimportant or mundane tasks can be turned into a training session IF you but call us in and then pay attention to the clues that we will provide.**

As always, the choice is yours and YOU must have desire to participate, else there is little value that we can add. Thank you for receiving my energy this day. We shall walk through the challenges together, if you but ask.

I am Toniose Soltec—Friend, Guide, and Teacher, in Light and Service to Creator Source.

Salu!

## – CHAPTER FIFTY-TWO –

# Watch Japan For
# Earthquake Timing Clues

### *Ceres Anthonious Soltec*
### February 11, 1997

Good morning. I am Ceres Anthonious "Toniose" Soltec, present with you this day in the Radiant Light of Holy God of Creation. Thank you for sitting with me this morning, as we undertake a most tedious writing.

I have been assigned, as you ones all know, the task of geophysicist. My main duties of late have been scurrying about attempting to keep tabs on the changes which your planet is undergoing at present time.

I understand some of you in your skepticism at my ongoing dialog on the subject of Earth Changes. In fact, I, too, weary of the task of always bringing you these sorts of messages, and I am well aware of the fact that the subject has probably received so much press of late that most feel as though we are but "crying wolf" and saying, once again, that "the sky is falling". But, facts is facts.

Believe me when I tell you that I would much rather bring you spiritual messages of Growth and Manifestation and Transition. Well, I suppose this writing actually does deal with all of the above—however, in a little different vein.

The reason your planet is undergoing the present changes is because of the presently occurring transition of your little blue planet from the heavier, denser, third dimension into the lighter, less dense, fourth dimension. As for growth and manifestation: well, these two naturally go hand-in-hand because, as you traverse through the transition, you will, of necessity, grow, and when there is growth, there will naturally occur manifestation. As I have so often said, it all hangs together, does it not?

But for now, let us turn to serious geophysical business as it is developing this day upon your planet:

**Watch Japan VERY closely during the next several weeks. Watch for POSSIBLE activity to occur in this place— beginning with many small quakes, followed by an earthquake which could well register up to 9.5 on your present scales.**

As the Pacific Plate continues to grind against all adjacent plates, watch next for POSSIBLE quake activity to begin along the coastlines of the Americas—both South and North. There is indication at this time that, should quakes occur in Japan, there would follow, within three to five days time, some significant shaking along the coastal areas of the Americas.

This shaking will be what I would label, in technical terms, as "sympathetic vibrations". In other words, as one edge of the moving plate moves in one direction, the opposite side of the plate will likewise move, and that energy will manifest itself, full-up, in approximately 72 to 120 hours, or three to five days of your counting, from the FIRST large incident in Japan.

It is not as easy to estimate how large these quakes would be, and I cannot precisely pinpoint location, except to say that (1) the weakest points, and (2) the points at which the most energy is stored, are the most likely candidates for seismic activity.

*[Editor's note: Since this information came to my attention just after our last issue of CONTACT went to press the night of February 10, 1997, almost two weeks ago now, I (E.Y.) have been*

*more carefully monitoring the Pacific Rim earthquake map data, in case there appeared evidence warranting this message be quickly placed on our* CONTACT *Telephone Hotline, 1-805-822-0202. That turned out to not be necessary so far, but do be aware of what is happening as I write this:*

*To begin with, let us again picture looking down on the Pacific Plate, from up in the sky, as approximately a clock face. What I observed, from the date of Soltec's writing until a few days ago, was heavy quake activity at the 12 o'clock position of Alaska's Aleutian Islands, as well as down to about the 11 o'clock position in the region of Russia's Kamchatka Peninsula and Kuril Islands, just above Japan.*

*Suddenly, however, at this present moment, quake activity in the 5-to-6 magnitude range is creeping on down toward the 10 o'clock position—that is, into Japan proper! This ought to be prudently interpreted as a significant preliminary warning sign for possible things to come.*

*SO PLEASE, EVERYBODY—WATCH JAPAN CLOSELY AND WATCH FOR NEWS, EVEN RELUCTANTLY LEAKED OUT ON THE NON-NEWS PROGRAMS, ABOUT NEW SEISMIC ACTIVITY IN JAPAN. AND THEN TAKE APPROPRIATE ACTION IF YOU RESIDE ALONG THE WESTERN COASTAL AREAS OF THE AMERICAS OR FEEL THAT YOU MAY BE OTHERWISE IMPACTED BY SUCH SEISMIC EVENTS—SUCH AS WITH THE UNEXPECTED APPEARANCE OF FRIGHTENED AND CONFUSED RELATIVES OR FRIENDS NEEDING A PLACE TO STAY AND POSSIBLE MEDICAL ATTENTION FOR BUMPS, BRUISES AND BROKEN BONES.]*

We have been preaching and preaching until we are all but blue in the face for years now, and most have chosen to ignore our messages. So be it. Those who are going to hear, have heard, and we have awakened just about all who are going to be awakened.

Yes, I know that many across your world rely upon the *CONTACT* for their information and Guidance. However, what are these ones going to do when there can be no paper printed because of the so-called infrastructure of your world being in a state of great disarray and destruction?

The paper was to be a means of reaching and awakening those who would be awakened. We have been down this Earthquake & Earth Changes subject road so often that I could easily rerun tapes of previous messages, and save the bother to you ones who must process these messages, as well as to myself. Yet, this message will stand as confirmation *AFTER* the fact.

Yes, we are arrived at very tough times. Our Ground Crewmembers can attest to this fact, can they not?

Stop and look over your lives in the last couple of weeks. How many of you can actually stand up and say you have not been down a rocky road of late? If you can, then you have obviously been doing something wrong, for ALL of our people have fallen under attack of late, and the attacks are all targeted upon those who have the greatest tasks at hand to attend.

So, if you are one of the "lucky" ones who feel you are about ready to "throw in the towel", stand back and examine what you are doing that is so important as to warrant all this attention from the adversary! The greater the attacks, the better the job you ones are doing.

(I am reminded by this scribe that the above comment is one hell of a back-handed compliment!)

Returning now to the condition of your world:

I would like to urge all of you who have animals near you to watch them very closely. They are telling you that the Earth is about to give a great heave. Watch for abnormal migrations and animals showing up in odd places. Watch your house pets, as well, for many of them are exhibiting odd symptoms of apparent illness or they may be just acting "weird".

You see, these creatures are more attuned to the frequencies of the planet than are their two-legged counterparts, and they will begin to react long before earthquakes and other geophysical events take place. Watch them also for out-of-the-ordinary behavior, such as dogs biting who normally don't bite—that sort of thing. Those of you at the coastal edges, watch the tidal activity, for there are many, many small earthquakes occurring within the depths of your oceans and the tidal activity will reflect these occurrences.

Listen also to sounds within your own heads. Many of you are earthquake sensitives, and you will begin to, if you get yourselves quiet, find that you are hearing some very-low-frequency pulsing sounds. Those of you who feel your nerves are literally about to split at the ends will find that you have been hearing these low frequency sounds in conjunction with a greater and more intense array of high-pitched tones within your heads. These sounds—or more accurately, the conditions which are producing them—are what you can consider the main source of your nervous or agitated conditions. Watch for strange pains, itching, muscle twitching, unexpected digestive problems, etc.

Take time to listen to the sounds. I can nearly guarantee you that they will be present—but you must get quiet to hear them.

You ones are not as removed from the connection with your world as you would like to think you are. You have simply found very effective ways of ignoring and over-riding these sounds and sensations and so you think you are immune to these things.

Those of you who know you are going to be leaving your area, should shaking begin, would serve yourselves well to prepare in SERIOUSNESS for your journeys. You all have had many dry runs of preparation for this event, so you should have it down quite pat by now. Practice does perfect, after all. You ones all know who you are, so if the message here rings within you a note of recognition, then know that it is meant for you and plan to act on the message, please.

**For all of you who live in the earthquake-prone places, I can but give you one word of advice: *BRACE!* Prepare for that which is about to descend upon you.**

It is time to recycle your water and food supplies, replenish your first-aid kits, check for such things as bandages, aspirin, antibiotics, rubbing alcohol, hydrogen peroxide, anti-bacterial cremes and salves, and anti-nausea and anti-diarrhea aids, etc. For small children, lots of baby food, diapers, bottles, blankets, electrolyte balancers, children's aspirin, ibuprofen, etc. For your pets, make sure you have plenty of food and water and any of their medications. Pet cages, carriers, etc., will come in quite handy.

Do not forget such things as eyeglasses and sanitary products, bathroom tissue, paper towels, wet-wipes, etc. Ready-to-eat foods such as high-protein bars, granola bars, etc., will come in very handy because many of you will find yourselves with no means for preparing cooked meals, and these types of things will at least keep you going. Do not overlook candy bars, either, because though they are generally quite empty of nutrients, they will help to temporarily boost sagging energy levels and will be quite soothing to the children, from time to time. AND, FOR GOODNESS SAKE, DON'T FORGET A CAN OPENER! Also make sure you can locate the sleeping bags, tents, lanterns, flashlights, and lots of extra batteries.

A portable radio, preferably one that is of the old-style crank type, will come in very handy for receiving information. This type of radio requires no batteries or electricity outlet. The radio plays for about a half-hour for each few minutes of winding up the spring-powered generator, just as you would wind-up a non-electric clock or wristwatch. (Remember what those are?!)

Have on hand extra blankets and pillows for comfort and additional warmth. Sensible, warm, and rugged clothing should be considered a must. You would do well with a heavy type of shoe such as a pair of hiking boots.

There is no way that we could take the time right now to list everything which you should have in your emergency closet, but most of you already know what you need. I simply gave you a short list to prompt you to go take a look at what you have and don't have, and take an immediate inventory of the condition of your supplies. DO NOT HESITATE, HOWEVER, TO RESTOCK OR ADD ANY ITEMS YOU FEEL YOU WILL NEED. [*See Appendix A in this book for a* 72-Hour Kit Checklist *of emergency items.*]

**Now is the time for preparation. However, TIME is the critical word here, from your reference point, because TIME is run out! Once the little shakers begin, it will be too late, because the little shakers will quickly be the prelude to more violent activity.**

I ask you ones to take this message VERY SERIOUSLY, because there are too many indicators manifesting at present for us to ignore them or for us to not inform you of probabilities. Your scientific world is not about to be accused of being fear-mongers, and they also know upon which side of the bread is their butter. Their very livelihoods depend on them understanding just how to play the game of well-paid silence.

**I am not going to give you a science lesson at this time because it really doesn't matter what might be subducting and what might be slipping. When the seismic activity begins, you are going to shake, shake, shake—regardless of the cause. Know only that the handwriting would appear to be on the wall,**

and you ones are—as usual—not being forewarned through your "normal" "news" channels. So take appropriate action, whatever that action might be.

As your levels of agitation and irritation increase, you will know that not only is the Earth ready to make a very large shift, but also that you are under serious adversarial attack, because the time frame is such that things are ramping up because of the transition period you are now within.

Yes, indeed, these are definitely heavy-duty times you are encountering. But understand also that, the more you experience, the greater becomes your knowledge and wisdom. You are into the experiencing of some big-time lessons, and those of you who are working day and night with us are experiencing some of the biggest lessons. You also have the greater burdens, and the adversary is working very hard to distract you and deflect you from your appointed missions.

You are ALL quite able, although you need to take the time to support one another, from time to time, for each of you do experience your weak moments, and need just a few minutes of breather time to regather strength and stamina. Allow yourselves those times of recuperation.

Examine your priorities carefully, for you are finding yourselves being tossed to and fro, for much is being hurled your way to take time away from the mission at hand. If you know what your primary tasks are, then see to them, and don't fall for the distractions. There is much to be done in a very short period of time, and your time is being gobbled up by the adversarial forces trying to take you off your path and divert you from your goal.

**You see, the adversarial forces have much to lose if you succeed, and so they are working very diligently at trying to cause you to not succeed. You need to be constantly aware of**

**these sometimes subtle tactics and respectfully treat them as the growth challenges that they are.**

We are continually with you, and you designated receivers are going to be very, very busy in the coming days. That too should be a flag for you ones to know just where you are in the overall picture.

Let us draw this message to a close, for you are going to be plenty busy in the coming days with our business with you. Your life is changing—do not resist the change. We have need of all of you right where you are, and that need is growing. Please think upon these things. In no way will you ever be forced to do anything you wish not to do; however, we would request that you examine wherein lies your dedication and your priorities.

Do not spread yourself too thin and expect to give your best to anything if you are pulled in a hundred different directions. Think upon this, chelas. You are loved, you are honored, and you are appreciated for your diligence; however, you will be of little or no use to anyone if you try to do five jobs at once. Many of you are unable to stay focused because you are going in so many directions. Learn to simply say, "Thank you, but no thank you" when avoidable distractions present themselves.

These instructions apply to most all of our Ground Crewmembers at this time. You are going in too many directions and, instead of moving forward, you are running around in very large circles. Take a deep breath and examine what it is you are doing and why you are doing it.

Thank you for your attention. I shall take my leave at present, but I shall move only to standby, for it is quite possible that there shall be more needing to come through at a moment's notice.

I am Toniose Soltec of the Hosts of God of Light and Creation. Peace to you who heed these warnings and stand prepared.

Salu.

## A Later Update
## On Soltec's Recent Japan Earthquake Alert

*Editor's note (from the March 11, 1997 issue of* CONTACT*):
In his writing of February 11, 1997, which we printed on page 25 of
the February 25, 1997 issue of* CONTACT *(because of the insipid
legal distractions, you may remember, which kept us from printing
an issue the week of February 18, 1997), Commander Soltec
ominously cautioned that we watch Japan for timing clues to
dangerous earthquake activity along the western coastal areas of
the Americas.*

*Well, since the time of that writing, and an Editor's note which I
(E.Y.) included closer to publication time that included the news of
stepped-up activity coming down from Alaska's Aleutian Islands
area toward Japan, there has indeed been a great increase in
"smaller" quake activity around Japan. I say "smaller" because,
what used to be considered  moderate-to-large earthquakes only a
few years ago, have become so commonplace that such are now
considered rather "small"—especially when one takes into account
the newer "K-mart" (discount) measuring scales in use now to
"ease our worries" about the significance of such events.*

*And then we have the following little news item tucked away in a
small corner of those newspapers even willing to print it.  This one
comes from the* Arizona Republic *for Saturday, March 8, 1997, and
is headlined:*

*[QUOTING:]*

## 6,432 Quakes Tremble Tokyo Area

*TOKYO —Several moderate earthquakes hit a popular spa resort
near Tokyo today, bringing to more than 6,000 the number of quakes in the
area in less than a week.*

*One of the larger ones was a 4.7 magnitude quake that hit the Izu Peninsula area this afternoon. There were no reports of serious damage.*

*Since Sunday night, the Central Meteorological Agency recorded 6,432 quakes—most of them too weak to be felt—off the east coast of Izu, 60 miles southwest of Tokyo. A few of the quakes have been felt in the capital.*

*[END OF QUOTING]*

*A nail-biting number of the quakes around Japan have actually been in the 5-to-6 magnitude range, despite the "not to worry" tone prevailing in the above little gem of distortion. And, as Soltec said would happen, quake activity along western coastal areas of South America has really increased today (March 10, 1997)!*

*Meanwhile, quake activity in the Middle East has also escalated with, for instance, over 40,000 people living in tents in a very cold, snowstormy region of northwestern Iran right now, since a "6.1 magnitude" quake clobbered (was detonated in?) that area on February 28, 1997.*

*Stay alert!*

# CHAPTER FIFTY-THREE

# Soaring With The Inner Joy Of Creating

## *El Morya, The Statesman*
### February 22, 1997

Good Morning and thank you for sitting to write this day! I am El Morya, Master of the First Ray. I come in the Radiant One Light of Creator God so that His promise to your world will be fulfilled.

As you each go forth in your experiences of day-to-day living, you are bombarded with many mind-influencing suggestions. You are constantly receiving data from all directions. This information is continually being updated and processed within you so that you might have that which you are seeking. You each are seeking that which will provide you with comfort—basically with "soul peace" and "soul joy". This will be different for each of you, for no two beings are created exactly the same in composition of attributes, nor were you created for the exact same purpose.

As you go through your life's experience, you are faced with choices and decisions as to what you will do from one moment to the next. Many of you have decided to just sit back and see what will happen next. This is a PASSIVE role, yet you will still make progress along the lines of growth. However, this progress will be somewhat slowed.

By contrast, when you take an ACTIVE role in the creating cycle, you will find that your life will be much more interesting and—surprise!—you will find the elusive "hidden" joy you are so desperately seeking in your day-to-day living. This joy lies

WITHIN YOU, awaiting your recognition and utilization of this Divine Connection in the conscious state. Those of you who are busy DOING those things that will bring forth positive change around you, are the ones who are indeed on the forefront of creating the Larger Change that will transform your world into Radiance.

This is where I, El Morya, fit in! I represent the First Ray of Creation and I work closely with my Brother Germain, Master of the Seventh Ray of Creation. Through the Seventh Ray comes the transformation (transmutation) out of the old and into the NEW! In every ending is a new beginning, for God and Creation are infinite and forever evolving.

**Each of you have the opportunity to assist in this transformation process in that you can help create the New Beginning by consciously focusing your mind on those things that fulfill your Higher Purpose for being there. You can know what these things are, for they will inspire you with emotional passion, excitement, and an inner sense of fulfillment.**

Again, this will not be the same for any two individuals. YOU must find those things which fulfill YOU! Follow your heart, for it will tell you where to look if you but pay attention. In doing so, you will be actively setting forth into motion the forces of your soul (soul: that which is in direct connection to Creator Source), forces which will draw to you the circumstances that will help you to recognize your own personal purpose, and thus the emotional satisfaction that you are wanting.

You must do your own part. We of the Higher Energy Realms observe that most of you sit and wait for another to be daring enough to put their neck on the line, while you sit back in your comfortable idea of reality, where you can feel safe, while stating with your mouth the things another should or should not do. All the while you are restless, seeking more, and wanting to do those things that your fears will not allow you to do. Remember those are

YOUR fears and you must overcome them, or you will continue to want more while wallowing in dissatisfaction that can lead to bitterness.

Those who have their necks out on the line will usually ask you your opinion if they think that they need it. If they are not asking, it is probably because they are too busy creating their own circumstances that will lead them to the answers and joy that they are seeking, with or without those of you who play "armchair quarterback".

When you are ready to help contribute to the transformation process, you will first recognize that you have FEARS that have been and STILL ARE keeping you from participating in the excitement of the whole evolutionary process. When you overcome these fears, you will stop hiding behind assumed identities, for you will have recognized that your fears of embarrassment are indeed unfounded, and that you can go against the accepted "norm" and be different.

What is normal? Normal is a "mob rules" mentality which states that you have to follow the crowd in order to be perceived as one who fits in. You are each unique and different; you do not have to "fit in". You are driven by your fears of not being liked, or of being laughed at, or of being the "odd ball", or whatever. You are going against the very inner desires of your soul when you try to be that which you are not.

When you can learn to express yourself without the worry of what another will think of you, then you will have taken a major step in finding the inner joy you desire. Those who do not seem to have time for your perception of how YOU think they should "act" are probably of a mindset to not be concerned about what it is that YOU think. This is not to say that these ones perceive of themselves as being better; it is that these ones are too busy to be distracted by YOUR perception of "proper" etiquette.

If you allow another to offend you, then YOU need to grow-up and realize that YOU are the one creating your own frustrations. When you can focus your attention not upon the SELF-CENTERED perception of negative experience, but rather, upon seeking the experiences that will help you to feel fulfilled within, you will find that you will naturally attract the recognition of your intrinsic value or importance that you desire. Your ACTIONS will show the world who you really are—not your words about same or your mental perception of self.

Realize, please, that when you are FEELING the inner joy of creating your life's experiences, you will find yourselves in a state wherein you do not worry about what others think about you. You will allow them to their own ideas and will not be concerned with there personal perception of how they "would have done it differently". If they want to step out and do it differently, then by all means let them lead by EXAMPLE and not by words!

If you are, for instance, not happy with a publisher because they will not publish your materials, then instead of complaining about the publisher, open your own publishing agency and publish your works yourself. If you are waiting upon another to accommodate you, then you will be deserving of your own inner frustrations, for you have created them and allowed them to consume you.

Monitor your emotional state and allow it to show you where to find joy. If you are insistent upon dwelling on the negativity of the past (whether it be ten minutes ago or ten years ago) then you will continue to find yourself in a state of wanting more. You will draw unto yourself those who will feed the fire of your frustrations if you insist on dwelling upon those negative emotions.

**When you can release of those things that cause you to feel hurt, then you will have freed yourself from the past and you will be able to focus more clearly upon that which you DO want—inner sense of satisfaction and JOY!**

The only point in time wherein you can create is in the present. When you allow the past to consume you, you are giving up the only opportunity you have for bringing forth the change that will allow you to find and fulfill your purpose for being there.

You ask, "How do I release the past?" You do this by focusing your thoughts upon the here-and-NOW, upon creating that which will bring forth the joy that your heart desires—and NOT focusing upon that which you don't want.

Say to selves: "I will TODAY experience something in which I will find joy!" Then EXPECT the joyous experience, for it IS coming! Look for those things that will give you pleasure. This process takes active participation on your part in the form of thought and true emotional desire. When you are fulfilling your purpose, you will find that you will not have time to focus on the past, for you will be too busy and too enthused to do so!

Focus clearly upon the joy and fulfillment, not upon the lack of joy or fulfillment. If you focus upon the LACK of a something, you will create MORE of what you are LACKING!

Quit worrying about what you do not have and focus upon that which you desire, and you WILL create it! If you find yourself surrounded with negative people, it is because you draw them to you with your own thoughts that are negative.

Do not give thought to that which you do NOT like or that which causes within you the negative emotions such as anger, fear, and frustration. When you begin manifesting joy in your daily experience, you will attract to you those who will add unto your joy, and you will find the exciting experiences that you desire. You will also find that you are fulfilling your life's purpose!

Allow others to have their own, self-created emotional state. If they are of the intent to force their view upon you, then pay them NO attention and they will eventually go their own way. When you play into the game of "who is right and who is wrong", you are setting yourselves up for a game that is fueled with the negative emotions that spawn wars of massive destruction. You are, in effect, being distracted away from your True Purpose. You will know when you are fulfilling your purpose, for the emotional state will be that of joy and you will experience a genuine sense of accomplishment.

**Everyone's purpose in the physical is one that involves DOING and CREATING—not sitting idle and talking big talk. In ACTIVELY fulfilling your purpose, you will experience a greater joy than you have ever known prior.**

Monitor your emotional state and learn to recognize your thoughts that CAUSE your emotional reactions. Dwell upon those things that cause you to feel uplifted and fulfilled. Use your emotional sensing as the tool for which it is intended. Your emotions can serve to guide you for they come from your Higher (KNOWING) Self.

It is the physical ego that will mentally cause you to fixate upon those negative feelings in an attempt to reinforce the danger or pain of a situation. When it does this, you will draw to yourself more negative reinforcement, and thus you create a dwindling spiral of negative emotion.

Likewise, the converse is also true. When you are feeling uplifted and happy, your enthusiasm will often spread, and you will draw to yourself more and more of the positive emotions. You will soar upward and outward; you will know no limitations.

I am El Morya, Master of the First Ray. As the old slips away into chaos and confusion, the new shall come forth in Radiance to quell the confusion by providing Direction and Truth to those who persist in their desire to understand and grow. In Light of the One Who Is All, blessings and peace to each of you.

Salu!

# CHAPTER FIFTY-FOUR

# Survival Will Depend Upon Finding Inner Balance

## *Serapis Bey*
### March 1, 1997

Good morning, my brother. It is I, Serapis Bey, Cohan (Master Teacher) of the Fourth Spectral Aspect of Creator's thought projections. I come in the Radiance of His Will, that you and your brethren will have the Guidance that you each desire and for which you call out with great heart intensity.

I serve in the capacity that brings forth balance and order. I am the line of demarcation between reasonable logic and passionate emotion (between the yin and the yang). I facilitate either extreme, yet present an opportunity for balance to those who desire and ask.

With EVERY experience you encounter which seems to impact you in a negative manner, please be aware that, with persistence and effort, you CAN find balance within self—and in doing so, you will find the growth that you desire and which your Higher Self (soul self) craves in the primal thrust for expansion toward Perfection.

In the searching for balance, you will find that you will have to reach for that which you are lacking in the way of understanding. This is not easy, for you are usually unaware that you are lacking in understanding until such time as you are confronted with a situation that causes you the discomfort of confusion. This annoyance presents you with the challenge to have to search for the understanding or meaning of its occurrence, if you are to find true balance (relief from the confusion).

Be thankful, in your heart, for the opportunities of growth when they present themselves to you. Your emotional attitude and ability to reason rationally will serve you much better than either extreme—a fit of rage, on the one hand, or a cold and detached separation from the event, on the other. One or the other of these out-of-balance responses usually comes about due to your efforts toward denying the impacting reality of the situation. There IS an in-between balance that can be reached if you KNOW that it IS there, and if you desire, foremost, to find this balance.

**You are ALL going to be faced with impacting traumatic experiences in the weeks, months, and years to come. My intent is not to frighten you or coerce you in any way! My intent is to assist you, as a Teacher, so that you are prepared for the testing and the lessons—that you might grow past the need to experience these things over and over again.**

Prepare yourself mentally in such a manner that you are confident about who you are and about your direct connection to the God-force within. Prepare NOW with a method of problem solving that will help you to maintain both mental AND emotional stability—no matter what the situation you are facing.

This effort is, in effect, writing a script or mental "computer program" that you can access any time you desire and which will outline a series of questions and statements to yourself so that you will always be able to come to a reasonable choice as to what you should do.

**Step 1:** Regardless of the situation, call upon The Light for protection and guidance. This will give us a greater opportunity to connect and work with and through you. This, also, reaffirms your intent and thus will, in effect, center your focus.

**Step 2:** KNOW, with certainty, that you CAN handle ANY situation with which you are presented. God NEVER gives you more than you can handle. In rare cases where the situation seems to be more than you can handle, He will carry you!

In your certainty, you will calm the fear reactions and thus calm the emotional tendency for overwhelm. This equates to clearer, more rational thought and, again, will help us to help you through a clearer communication link.

**Step 3:** Calmly ask yourself, "What are ALL of my options?" and "What can I DO that will be of the most value to EVERYONE involved and not just myself?"

Sometimes you may have to eliminate possibilities by evaluating the actions that would only serve to compound an undesirable situation. Screaming hysterically would be one such option you could decide to eliminate right now as a course of action to take! You could say to yourself: "I will NOT react violently, hysterically, irrationally, or in any manner whatsoever that will cause me to compound an already dire situation!"

**Step 4:** KNOW that you are NOT a victim! All experiences, whether they are perceived as "good" or "bad", are for reason. Know also that YOU are the creator of your experiences and that any and all challenges that you are faced with are for YOUR growth!

**The point here is to PREPARE yourself now so that, if you catch yourself in a condition or state in which you have already decided NOT to be, you will have already in place the rational ideas and thoughts necessary to pull yourself out of a panic and into a more usable and survivable state of reasoning.**

**We can work through you—IF you are not shut down with fear or overwhelmed with hysteria and panic. You can help us the most by taking the time NOW to affirm to yourselves that**

**you will remain calm and open under ALL situations. This can be practiced almost daily if you look to the small irritations around you and catch yourself in this sort of reactionary state.**

For example, let's say that you have an antagonistic relative or co-worker whom you allow to provoke within you the passions of anger or frustration. Catch yourself getting angry and review ALL of your options. (Take a moment to clear your space and reaffirm your Light shielding, and perhaps you could try sending Light to this one who is being antagonistic.)

Now, look at those options that will help BOTH of you to feel better, and NOT just yourself. Expect an answer that will have balance in its completion.

Let's say that, instead of getting in an argument, you decide to smile and tell the person, "I can see that this subject is of great concern to you and that it causes you great emotional discomfort. I do not wish you, or myself, discomfort, so let us please change the subject." The person may respond antagonistically and/or irrationally to this comment, but you can be assured you will have disrupted the rigid self-perception that the person holds, and thus you will have given such a person the opportunity to expand in awareness of self.

If the person is insistent upon fighting or arguing with you, then you can, perhaps, excuse yourself and wish that one well. You do not have to allow another, who is antagonistic toward you, to bring you to a point of anger or grief.

Remember that the point here is to illustrate one example of how you can catch yourself REACTING emotionally instead of addressing a challenge with reason. There could be many examples of this: such as dealing with children, your ex-spouse, the loss of a loved one, or any other condition that may cause you to panic—such as fear of heights, snakes, or water. Learn to recognize your reactions and USE these small experiences to prepare yourselves for larger, more traumatic experiences that could immobilize you if you do not prepare.

**Preparation is the key to surviving the upcoming transition of your planet.   Fear and shock shall be among the greater causes of death.  Ignorance will be the number one cause of loss. We of the Hosts, who have the task of teaching, understand this, and it is why we effort to get our messages heard.**

You who keep up with the constant outflow of information that we offer will find that you are not ignorant, and that you WILL know what to do when confronted with any challenge that may face you.

Be persistent in your efforts to prepare and you will survive this planetary transition with new-found awareness of self and others. After all, these are the very reasons you have chosen to participate at this time!

Thank you for your efforts thus far!   Enjoy these times of relative peace and calm that you now have in order to prepare; they are indeed invaluable.

I am Serapis Bey, keeper at this time of the Fourth Ray, the Clear Crystal Ray of purity and balance.  May your efforts be toward gaining that level of purity and balance which allows the power of the yin and the yang—the reason and the emotion—to work for you and not against you!  My blessing be with you.

Salu.

# CHAPTER FIFTY-FIVE

# Creating "Time" Through Mental Clarity

### *Esu "Jesus" Sananda*
### March 8, 1997

Good morning, my scribe. Be at peace. I am Esu "Jesus" Sananda. I am, as are you all, a product of Creator's magnificent thought. I dwell within the Oneness of His Light that is the Source of ALL. I come now so that His promise to your world shall be carried out. My will is that of my Father, Creator God.

As you each experience, know that you carry Creator's breath of life (Light) with you in all of your travels. It is through Him that you experience, and He through YOU. There are no secrets in His heart that He holds from you. There is only the waiting for you to grow into mature responsibility before you are allowed to come into the understanding of that which you may erroneously call "secrets of the universe".

While you are in the physical aspect of your infinite journey of growth, you should expect to have challenges before you. You are all desiring to expand your awareness of self, for in doing so you are fulfilling a very basic desire of Creator and Creation. Allow for others to grow in their own way and at their own pace. The journey is infinite and "time" is only a physical perception that allows for the detailed examination of your thoughts, and how it is that you use these thoughts in order to create and expand as a being.

Many of you sense that "time" is moving at a faster and faster pace and that you do not seem to have enough of it to get accomplished those things that you are wanting to get done. Please know that you have all the time that you need in order to accomplish those things that you are there to get done.

Know also that, with the proper mental focus, you can get more done than what you currently believe possible. Self-imposed restrictions are what keep you from realizing alternative modes of doing what you want to accomplish. When you can step outside of the restrictions that you hold onto as though they are law, then you will realize that you can actually control the perception of time flow, for yourself, by altering your basic vibrational frequency.

This phenomenon has been utilized by many in the past, and by a few in your present experience. Some of you utilize this gift daily though you fail to recognize the actual phenomenon. You can witness those who go about and seem to get very little done though there is the potential to accomplish much more than that which they are actually completing. These ones are usually living in a past moment and thus are creating miniature "time warps" or "ripples" around themselves.

Others may have such a clear picture of what it is they are wanting to achieve that, in there clarity, they can anticipate future situations that they will eventually need to address, and do so as soon as opportunities arise, thus saving themselves a lot of backtracking later on.

For example, let us say that you have a clear picture that you want to build a wood fence around your yard and you can see the fence in your mind's eye with extreme clarity. You can see every last detail, from the posts that will support the structure, to the nails you will use to hold the boards in place. You will see the exact color you would like it to be and the exact height that you are wanting. You can see that the posts will go into holes and that there is cement holding them anchored to the ground. You will see exactly where you would like to place a gate. You notice the exact hinges that you will use and the latching mechanism that you like.

You see every last detail in your mind and you decide that you are going to build this fence exactly the way you see it in your mind. You see it in such detail that you know exactly how to build it without any prior experience, for you see it already built. You can see yourself actually building the fence, and you're feeling more and more excited all the while you are envisioning the whole process.

Now, you set out to obtain all the pieces that you will need in order to build this fence. Holding the whole picture in your mind, you get all the boards that you will need, all the posts that you will need, the nails, the hardware, the paint, and the cement, and any tools that you saw yourself using that you do not already have.

You now set out and build the fence exactly the way you see it in your mind. Before you know it, you are done and the fence is completed and exactly the way you envisioned it in your mind.

Now let us take another who is wanting a fence. However, this one does not see it in any great detail in his mind because he is not practiced at "seeing within" first, with all of the details, and his mental focus is clouded with the distractions of other things (usually past guilt or worry) that keep the mind from fully focusing in the here-and-now of the present moment.

This person now sets forth to obtain all the materials that he thinks he needs. He goes out and gets the lumber and the posts and some nails, and brings them back. He goes to dig the holes for the posts and realizes that he does not have the proper tool to dig the post holes. Instead of going back and getting the proper tool, he makes use of what he has at hand. Now the holes take longer to dig than necessary and "time" is slipping away.

Eventually the holes are dug and the posts are ready to be

installed.   Now he realizes that he has overlooked the need for cement.  Everything stops while he must backtrack to the hardware store and get the needed item.

The point of this example is to show you how you can more effectively utilize time by properly focusing your mind.   The unorganized one above will make many repeated trips to get more nails and paint and whatever.  All the while frustration builds, the project is stretched from two days into five days, and the motivation to follow through to completion is nearly gone.  In that case, the fence project may sit for another six months before it gets the paint that it needs!  As you might imagine, the entire creation may end up being quite a bit less sturdy than it could have been and it will probably look quite a bit less pleasing than it could have looked.

You ALL have the ability to manifest and control time in this manner.  Many of you have experienced a sense of "slow motion" during events such as a major automobile accident.  The seriousness of the situation will cause you to give your attention fully to the moment at hand, regardless of the mental distractions which were competing for your mental focus only moments before.  This clear focusing of your mind will enable you to capture every last detail. You will be taking in data so fast that you will perceive everything as moving in slow motion compared to your normal viewing of events.

Some athletes experience this phenomenon while playing their sport, for they are so focused upon what is happening that they will begin to take-in sensing data at faster and faster rates.  These ones have their terminology for this; they will call it being "in the zone" or something of that sort.  The actual phenomenon is a clear focus of thought and being more fully (if not fully) in the present moment as events are unfolding.

**You ones can learn to utilize these natural abilities and learn to function in this mode, as you desire.  The key is learning to**

**release the past garbage and other modes of distraction that you cannot change.**

When you can leave behind the small worries or heartaches of the past, and truly forgive yourself for having offended or hurt another, then you will be more fully focused in the present. You will also find that you will naturally become more and more productive as you shed these fears, worries, and guilts that you otherwise hold onto in order to beat yourselves up, over and over again.

And then there are the overt distractions. You are being bombarded with all sorts of distractions every day, just from all of your television and media programing. You may say, "Well, I only watch the news!" Your so-called "news" programs are just that—"programs"—for your mind, and they are the worst offenders, for they project calculated images that you will not so easily dismiss as "Hollywood theatrics". These distractions are designed to keep you wanting more, or keep you in a state of outright shock, or in a state of constant confusion.

You will have to begin to see these distractions (and others) for what they are, else in this life experience you may never recognize your true potential of expression. Please realize that I am NOT saying that you should or should not watch television or read newspapers.

I AM saying that you will have to realize those things that cause you to lose focus (or never find focus) on what it is that you are desiring to accomplish—if you are to recognize who you REALLY are and what your true potential of creating REALLY IS!

This all goes back to understanding how it is that your mind processes information and how it is that you create those things that you are wanting.

All creation begins with thought. Before you existed, there was the thought of Creator, and as the thought was formed, so were you.

You must realize that YOU create in the same manner, for there could be no other way.

**When you come into greater and greater mental clarity, you will find that your emotional state is vibrating at a much higher rate, and thus the uplifting sensations of joy, enthusiasm, and a sense of accomplishment within, will result. This is the inner emotional state that ALL are continually seeking to find. When you can learn to focus your mind in TOTAL clarity, you will set all the forces of the universe into motion for you as your thoughts begin to manifest.**

This is where time comes into play. The perception of time acts as a buffer so that all does not come crashing in upon everyone all at once. The element of time ensures that a proper sequence is adhered to and that no two physical manifestations occupy the same space at any one moment. This gives order to the physical universe.

Your desires spring forth from the need to satisfy the emotional pressures caused by your innate urges to create and grow. Your emotional state thus plays a basic and direct function in facilitating the manifestation of your thoughts into physical reality.

As you focus that great gift of your mind, and begin to SEE, with greater and greater clarity, that which you desire to create, you will notice that there will come an INTENSITY (a multiplication of the emotional component of your desire) associated with what it is that you are focusing upon. This intensity (emotion) is the energy that propels the idea forward. Thus, the greater the intensity of the emotion, the more momentum the idea will have, and the more quickly it will begin to manifest.

**You all have the basic abilities in order to create anything that you may desire—if you but focus upon same with crystal clear clarity. You are in the optimal environment in which to practice these abilities in a responsible and safe manner. Utilize this grand opportunity in the physical plane to continually**

strive toward applying and intensifying your creative abilities in your day-to-day experiences, and you will attain the satisfaction—that is, the knowledge and understanding—that your soul desires and is seeking.

Do not resist your creative (soul) urges, for in doing so you are resisting inner satisfaction. Likewise, learn to recognize those things which, calculated or otherwise, pull your attention in so many different directions. Worry not about what you do not have, and build a clear image of what you want, exactly the way you want it to be.

This can be a most wondrous and fulfilling journey with the proper mental focus. I am Esu Immanuel Sananda, come in the Radiant Light of Creator's thought. May you be in understanding of the message here, for it is the "food" your soul desires.

Salu!

# –CHAPTER FIFTY-SIX–

# Slumber Time Shall
# Come To An Abrupt End!

## *El Morya, The Statesman*

### March 23, 1997

Good afternoon and thank you for sitting this day. I am El Morya, keeper of the First Ray of Creator's spectral expression. I come in that One White Light which permeates and motivates all of Creation. Be at peace for we have work to do!

**The transition time is at hand and your world sleeps on in ignorance. This slumber shall be coming to an abrupt end very soon! As ones are bluntly awakened to the realization that they have been slothful in their efforts to prepare, there shall come an inner sense of horror as the realization of what is taking place around them takes seat within their mind. These ones are the ones who have chosen to ignore the warnings and thus have chosen NOT to prepare.**

Preparation in these times—NOW—is the key to survival. Your world is hanging on by mere threads and you will see that, literally, one day all is well, and the next day ALL is in chaos, confusion, and horror beyond your ability to take in at the moment of realization.

This is not to frighten you; it is to get your attention! What will your excuse be when you are caught off-guard and vulnerable? Will you say, "Oh God! Why are you doing this to me!?"

You who are drawn to the inspired messages of Lighted Truth (from whatever source they come) shall have had the opportunity to make conscious choices and decisions as to what it is that you will do. **The time to prepare is NOW! Did you hear me? THE TIME TO PREPARE IS** *NOW* !

You who sit on the fence and wonder what your friends would say or your family would think, are the ones who are in the process of creating a very painful experience for yourselves—an experience that does not have to happen.  Nonetheless, you are creating it by your inaction.

There are no free rides and God will help those who effort to help themselves, and others, first!  If you are sitting and doing nothing because you are in an apathetic state of denial, because you make excuses that you do not have enough money or time, or you just do not care about yourself, then I would say to you: "Do not later come asking for a miracle when you are not even willing to lift a finger to help yourself, let alone a brother in need—or the children next door."

**When you make an honest effort, with heartfelt intent, to make preparations, you will find doors and opportunities opening up to you.  When you sit and complain to yourself and others that you just don't care or that you would rather not be around anyway, you are creating the very horror that you are constantly denying.**

These experiences are for your education and growth, and that is why you have chosen to participate in the physical at this time.  You want the experiences that will cause you to expand your awareness of self and of the true nature of your spiritual heritage.

Our mission, as Messengers of God, is to present these messages to you and make them available to any who are honestly seeking.  Those who even have the slightest desire, shall be given every opportunity to find information that will resonate and thus spark an inner emotional desire to look deeper into that which is taking place at this time.

We of the Hosts of God work through many sources in the physical.  We will help your scientists, geophysicists, medical doctors, and even your religious leaders put together the information that they have, in such a way as to come to the same conclusion (but for "different" reasons) as those who bring forth these more direct messages.

If a geophysicist tells you that your planet is in for a major geological shift that will cause great earthquakes and volcanos, many will heed the warning and prepare.  These same ones might read one of Commander Soltec's discourses on the same subject, but dismiss the information, for it came (to their thinking) by way of "mysticism" or "hocus-pocus" instead of science.  Yes, we know there are those who actually take Soltec's messages more seriously than they let on, but that is another matter—one of wrestling with the ego, be it self-pride or be it what other professional colleagues might "think" of them should these colleagues become aware of from where ones acquire some of their technical input!

Let me tell you right here and right now that the communication process by which these messages are being transmitted is quite scientific and your secret governments currently have this scientific technology available to them as we speak.

**It is the ignorance of "intelligent" people which causes them to so easily dismiss that which they do not understand.  You can choose (conveniently?) to believe as you will, but just because you disbelieve something does not mean it is false.  When you cannot allow for the fact that you do NOT know everything there is to know about everything, you set yourselves up for very impacting experiences that will show you that you are in the**

**mere infancy of awakening and that you have quite a bit to learn.**

We will assist any and all who effort to find Truth through any route that ones may choose.  If a scientist wishes to examine one small aspect of Creator's thinking, and wants to know how it is, for instance, that gravity REALLY works, then we will help that one in their quest.  But, they will have to make honest efforts to figure out the answers for themselves.  These ones will be drawn to seek out all information written on the subject and will have a strong EMOTIONAL DESIRE to understand the phenomenon.

When the emotional component is strong enough, therein lies the secret to bridging the gap between the knowledge that has already been presented and the knowledge that lies on the peripheral edge of planetary awareness.  Keep in mind here that there are great technologies available on your planet at this time, and that such have been secreted away from the masses by the greedy, elite power brokers on your planet.

Much of this technology would be considered ancient and primitive by we of the Ascended Realms.  However, it would be considered advanced and "mind-blowing" by the average person of average education on your planet.  There is a kind of "safety factor" built-in for the elite controllers, who desire that YOU remain ignorant of technologies at THEIR disposal.  This safety factor exists because so many would simply laugh at anyone trying to even suggest the existence of such great technology.  The fairly recent movie called *Chain Reaction* is a deceptively accurate example of this situation.

You live in a world of illusion and mind manipulation, and it takes a strong emotional desire to pull oneself up out of the mind-numbing culture that is prevalent on your planet.  Those of you who are reading this now, can look back in your life and find a turning point experience when you were presented with information that sparked a curiosity that needed to be satisfied. If you recall that experience, you will see that there was a strong emotional desire to learn more, to find that which causes emotional satisfaction, and thus your journey of discovery started. Perhaps this happened the first time you encountered the Edgar Cayce material, or the Seth material, or the *Phoenix Journals*.

Whatever your path, you took in the new information and realized that, the more you learned, the more questions you had, for your realization was that there is much more unseen than there is seen. This is to say that the spiritual side of your existence (unseen but FELT) was where the answers are found, and those answers in turn helped to explain the reasons for the physical experiences.

**As you have been growing, somewhere along the way you realized that the "coincidences" along the way were in actuality your Guides helping you along your way. Remember always that when your *heart* desires something, you are in effect calling in your spiritual side for the creation and manifestation of the desire. When you mouth the words, but there is not enough emotional desire to even cause you to take physical action toward finding your answers, then you will not have any real expediency in manifesting your desires. This is to say that the rate at which a creative thought will manifest in your life experience is directly proportional to the emotional content (power) of the desire.**

**Those who sit back (usually on a "fence") and wait for life to happen, and take no real effort at creating or manifesting their desires, will find that their life is somewhat un-fulfilling. These ones are so consumed by the distractions (such as television, movies, sex, food, and illness) that they give up the moment, the here and now, on such a regular frequency that**

**their thoughts are fragmented, and thus their focus and desires lack any real emotional energy. This sort of passive existence is what keeps you in a controlled state and thus powerless to change your current life experience.**

When you can realize that you have a choice in this matter, you will begin to break free from those things that you choose to do on a habitual basis, and thus free up the HERE AND NOW so that change can take place. For instance, for those of you who spend a large portion of your free time watching television, I would suggest you turn it off for a month or two and spend the time focusing your mind on the way you would like your life to be.

If you have difficulty finding something to focus on, then focus on the desire to know what it is that you are wanting. Say to self, "I am wanting to know what it is that will help me to create the fulfillment I desire!" Take five minutes to affirm this statement to yourself every day. Write down any ideas you may have and monitor your emotional response to each. If at first nothing comes, do not worry. For some this may take a few days or weeks in order to really get your emotional side focused. With persistence you WILL have success! Once you find an idea that really causes an emotional response, then follow up on the idea. Spend the five minutes focusing upon that idea and continue to write down any thoughts or ideas that come.

At some point, when the emotional desire is strong enough, you will be compelled to take action on these thoughts. When you take action you are reaffirming, in the physical, your thoughts and thus have started to manifest the thoughts into physical reality. The physical experience is a school for learning how to responsibly create. You have a desire within to want to do this, else you would not be in the physical. The key word is RESPONSIBLY!

**All of your experience is a result of your thoughts**

(non-physical) manifesting into the physical. When you live in a passive mode and wait for life to "just happen", you are not actively fulfilling your Higher Spiritual Desire to learn how to RESPONSIBLY create, and thus the feelings of unfulfillment. When you begin to take the active role and leave behind the excuses, you will then be creating the excitement of living for which you yearn.

So, get off the "fence" and start creating your future and you will find that you will naturally be preparing for those things of the future that may impact your experience. Perhaps YOU will be the one who feeds your neighborhood children when they are hungry?!

I am El Morya, keeper of the First Ray of New Beginnings, come in the Radiant Light of Infinite Source, so that you have the insights that were promised.

Salu!

# CHAPTER FIFTY-SEVEN

# Epilog To The Messages

## *Aton, The One Light*
### March 29, 1997

Be at peace, my son. It is I, Aton, The One Light. Do not be concerned for you shall do just fine. Relax and allow the message to come forth.

My children are many and are but an extension of Me. Each has an innate purpose for being, and each will have an innate desire to fulfill this purpose. Ones have chosen to explore specific aspects of their being at this time and thus fulfill very specific roles at this time.

There are many levels of expressing that are dependent upon each other for guidance and balance. Each level is designed to assist one another toward growth of the individual fragment, and this, in turn, will cause growth in ALL.

At this time in your experience there are the ones you refer to as the "Masters of the Rays" or the "Ascended Teachers". These ones have chosen to specialize in a particular aspect of expressing so that they can explore in depth, with great detail, a single tonal vibrational emanation of Light.

You could liken this choice to a dedicated focus toward studying a single chromosome pair in a strand of DNA and trying to understand every last bit of the meaning and reason for its function and existence. Or, in terms of the tonal concept I utilized above, you might think of these Masters as dedicated to exploring and "mastering" all of the possibilities of one particular instrument in the ensemble you call an orchestra.

These Masters have chosen to focus in this manner, in a COMBINED effort, just like the combining of dedicated, individually-focused musicians comprising the orchestra, in order to expand awareness of self and all of Creation—so that ALL will have opportunity to expand in like manner. You each will resonate with one (more so than the others) of the various aspects of The Whole which these Masters represent. And yet, due to the interconnectedness of all, you will find a part of each within you.

By contrast, all will resonate with the Golden-White Light of the "Christ" energy, for it is a balanced blending of all the Energy Spectrum. It is perceived as slightly golden, to you in the physical, for it has great emotional warmth for ALL, and this is the byproduct of slowing down the vibrational frequency enough to be perceived by physical sensing man.

Each of the Masters represent Me (Creator) in their various fields of expertise and they receive of their lessons directly from ME! These ones, in turn, re-give the lessons to you ones in their own unique, responsible manner, so that they can both measure their level of understanding, and assist those of you who desire to understand.

As Teachers, they are constantly challenged to find any and all manners in which to create circumstances and present ideas in such a manner that you will come into realization and understanding of the lesson at hand. This is no small task, for you each will respond differently to different types of communications and varying levels of nudges.

**THE GREATEST CHALLENGE TO THESE ONES IS FINDING THE PATH THAT WILL UNLOCK WITHIN AN INDIVIDUAL, A GROUP, A COUNTRY, OR A PLANET THE SELF REALIZATION OF THE GOD-FORCE WITHIN.**

Each will approach this task in their own characteristic way and with their own unique style, but also in counsel with one another and with other Great Teachers who have gone before and who have stepped aside to allow another to experience the challenge. Such cooperation at the Higher Levels is the usual way, and insures balance in the methodology of their ideas.

Each of the various Rays have gone through great testing. Each have walked the path that you are now on, and they have EARNED the title of Master Teacher. This is a position that they have each proven to have earned and they each deserve.

They too shall one day grow out of that position and into greater and greater levels of responsibility as Co-Creators within the balanced wholeness and oneness of Creation. But, at that time, another will always be ready to accept the responsibility of carrying forward, from that point, the search for greater and greater understanding.

This growth is always taking place, and the evolution and expansion is infinite. One day you each will step up into greater and greater levels of responsibility so that you can re-give that which was given to you. This is the simple balance that allows for continual evolution.

**The messages that have been penned prior in this book are for your growth and shall stand the test of time. They come forth with great LOVE and COMPASSION for those of you who are continually striving to fulfill your inner desire to grow and expand.**

I thank and bless ALL who are involved in the transmitting, the receiving, the editing, the translations, the formatting, and the publishing. You have each received of My Will and have carried it forward as if it were your own! Whether you are in recognition of this fact consciously or not, it is indeed SO!

I also give great blessings to you ones who are compelled to partake of these words, for it is for you that these words are written and it is for you that these ones effort to assist. You are the ones who have need for these words and will derive the greatest value therefrom. What is the point of having such a compilation if there is no one to partake of the gift?!

**You ones who are reading now will, in future experiences, be the ones who will choose to bring forth (re-give) similar messages to societies and planets of similar situation. This is the infinite balance of My thinking!**

And never forget this: You EACH have the ability, right now, to communicate directly (two-way direct communication) with Higher Source (ME!). You need NOT go through another; you have all that you need. Know that it is so and expect the response— AND IT WILL BE!

**The messages here provide you with the basic tools that you need in order to overcome the self-imposed limitations and beliefs that keep you from this realization of inherent God-connectedness. Go beyond the current beliefs! Reach for that which your heart truly desires, and step out of ignorance and into inner Knowing and Balance.**

You are My children and none is greater than another! It is that some come into this awareness of their Potential sooner than others, and that gives the perception of seeming greatness of one relative to another.

You are ALL great! You ALL carry a part of ME! It is the "Spark of Life" within! It is the seed of KNOWLEDGE and KNOWING that gives and re-gives into infinity. You are infinite, for MY thoughts cannot perish lest I so desire. I desire that you each persist into infinity and grow all the while! Therefore you SHALL!

A book is a very finite object which, at best, will encapsulate an idea or inspiration of the author. This book could be trillions of pages long and still not say everything that these Authors could teach you. At some point there has to be a termination point, else the book would never be completed. This is where WE will end this current outlay of information. But the inspired words will never stop coming forth; they will continue into infinity. When one stops or retires, another will ALWAYS be there to carry forward THE WORD!

I PLACE MY BLESSINGS UPON THESE WORDS AS BEING OF MY WILL.

I AM THY CREATOR.

I AM "THE ONE LIGHT"—ATON.

I AM!

# Afterword

# Twinkle, Twinkle, Little Star

## *Kali*
### September 5, 1994

*Editor's note: As we come to the end of the series of messages or lessons for this volume, a sense of overwhelm is possible since so much is addressed in such a deceptively simple, compact style. Time to sit back, relax, maybe pour a cup of tea, and think over the suggestions and insights herein. But where to begin? Perhaps with the following.*

*This writing was first shared with CONTACT readers in the September 20, 1994 issue. It is by "Kali" who, besides receiving for others Upstairs when the need arises, is one of geophysicist Commander Soltec's longtime scribes and speakers. She is one of the seven receivers who contributed to the content of this volume. There goes that number seven again—like the seven Authors from Central Upper Management, plus the seven Authors known as the Rainbow Masters. Hmmm.*

*Anyway, sitting on her back porch in Arizona, looking up at the stars one night, "Kali" (a name given to her by Soltec and meaning "one who has the strength to keep a clear head despite the surrounding chaos") began to reflect on matters that so many of us contemplate in quiet moments of self-assessment about our place in God's awesome universe.*

*Maybe the most challenging test we face, in this physical "schoolroom" existence on planet Earth, is simply to remember to recognize the God-power that resides within each of us, quietly waiting to be acknowledged and called upon.*

*Keeping that idea in mind, we close this volume with a most delightful musing, offered with the prayer that you, who are sincerely efforting to digest what has been presented herein, shall truly feel a greater confidence about your connection to the Infinite—for indeed, The Miracle resides within each of us. And so shall He manifest from each of us, for the greater glory of All That Is.*

I sit in wonder as I look into the nighttime sky and view all the splendor and magnificence. In the air, there is the first hint of the change of the seasons. Soon the hot and sunny days will be gone and in their place, crisp, cool mornings and nights, and the beauty of the wintertime skies.

The "Seven Sisters" of the Pleiades Constellation are visible once again after their summer vacation. As I look heavenward, they are like sparkling sapphires that stand out in the dark sky. They are as old friends, returned again for their seasonal visit and I greet them warmly and long to again return home.

Then, gazing upon the strobing star-ships, a childhood memory of many days long past comes into mind and I recite the rhyme once more:

"Twinkle, twinkle, little star, how I wonder where you are, up above the world so high, like a diamond in the sky."

It still carries with it a magical tone of wonderment, but now even more so, for I truly *DO* wonder where they might be and what they might be seeing from their vantage point, way up there among the stars and planets. Is there more peace and love and contentment there? I certainly hope so.

All the beauty of the sky at night, such splendor to behold, and I wonder: *HOW* was it all brought forth from nothingness? Then I hear the answer: "By thoughts of Love—a Love so great that it could not be contained and it exploded outward, ever growing, ever expanding."

Then I begin to realize that I am a part of that expansion, of that love so great that it could not be contained and, moreover, that within me is a fragment of that *SAME* love and the *SAME* thoughts which brought all forth!

And then: if I be a part of the whole, then I too must have the *SAME* ability to be filled to such an overflowing that I could not contain it and that I, too, would have to release it and send it on its way, allowing it to ever grow and expand!

So then: if that be the case, why do I sit here, waiting for my ship to come in? Why do I not go out there and find that ship? What's stopping me? Who can stop a thought of love so great? The answer: only me, only me. I am the only one standing in my own way because, out of fear and unbelief, I stand still—waiting, waiting, waiting.

But what if Columbus had waited because he was afraid; or if Immanuel had run the other way because he was fearful; or what if Thomas Jefferson had doubted his beliefs? What did these souls possess that I do not? Were they any more a part of The Whole than I? What made these ones so great?

Could it be courage? And where does courage come from? How do I get some? What makes one man develop it and not another? Is there some magical formula that I just don't know about? Where did they find it? Was it there all the time, waiting for them to call upon it? Is it within me, waiting, waiting, waiting.

Perhaps great men aren't born courageous; perhaps they become courageous simply because they have a passion so great, a love-thought so great that it cannot be contained within them and it explodes forth, growing and expanding.

Is that how it all is in this universe?  Do we lack the passion of men of days gone by, or have we taken passion and turned it into a lust—a lust for the physical pleasures?

Have we forgotten what life is really all about and why we are here?  Have we been seduced, just as those in the days of Sodom & Gomorrah were seduced, by the physical lusts?

And if that be the case, then what is our destiny?  What is our legacy?  Are we destined for the same end, the same judgement as were those two cities?  What an utter waste of the magnificence of the civilization that could be.

So I have to ask myself whether I shall stand proud before the Almighty for the part I have played, or shall I hang my head in shame?  Will I be told, "Well done, my good and faithful servant!" Or shall I hear, "Go to the left, for I knew you not."

I must ask myself, with each thought I think, each word I speak, each thing that I do: "Am I benefiting civilization, *OR* am I benefiting anti-civilization?"

There is so much of my past that I am not proud of, yet the Creator still continues to bestow blessing after blessing upon me, even when I feel the most unworthy.  And if that is not Love, then I do not know what is.  Then comes the reminder: "To whom much is given, much is required."

With this knowledge, no longer am I able to sit back and wait for another to do it, for I am responsible for all that I have thought, all that I have spoken, and all that I have done.  I—and I alone— shall be held accountable for *MY* life.

And if I err, then I must have the courage to admit the error; and if I should hurt another, then I must have the courage to ask their forgiveness.

And, above all, I must have the courage to stand up for that which I believe in, and allow the passion to grow beyond containment, regardless of the ridicule that will come.

Then and only then will I truly be able to say that I am a part of the overall plan of Creation and that I have played my role to the best of my ability—and will be able to stand before our Creator with my head up and hear the words, "Well done, my good and faithful servant!"

It is amazing, the thoughts that come from "nowhere" when we simply get quiet for a few moments, put aside all the worries and cares of our lives, and sit open-eyed in wonderment beneath a starry night sky and sing, "Twinkle, twinkle little star...."

# Appendices

# 72-Hour Kit Checklist

## *Kali*

### March 15, 1997

Everyone knows that the time to plan for an emergency is before the emergency occurs. Unfortunately, few people have taken the time to plan and make emergency preparations. Most people don't even have an evacuation plan in case of a fire in their home.

Thinking about emergency preparedness is not pleasant, but it could save the lives of you and your family, or at least make getting along a lot more pleasant during an emergency. Sometimes it is the fear associated with unpleasant happenings that keeps people from even considering how they would handle such events as natural disaster emergencies. Sometimes it is simple laziness. At best these are excuses to procrastinate; at worst they are running away from responsibility—responsibility that may include the care of a family, some members of which may be dependent on someone(s) in that nucleus of interaction having good sense and a level head.

You need only talk to any of those people who were directly affected in recent-years' earthquakes, hurricanes, floods, or tornados, and they will be the first to tell you that some items are ESSENTIAL. When they were left without shelter, food, clothing, water, or cash, many wished they had taken the time, prior to the emergency, to put together a kit of survival items. Even if you do not have to leave your residence, having some basic essentials will make the difference between being miserable, cold, hungry, thirsty, etc., and being able to satisfy these basic needs. And, should you have to leave your home in a hurry, having a pack pre-prepared allows you more time and peace of mind to plan your journey.

It is only common sense to plan for your own survival. Your neighbors, nearby friends and relatives, etc., will be more than busy taking care of themselves in a large-scale emergency, and do not need any other burdens. So, you can't expect to depend upon anyone but yourself and maybe your immediate family.

However, if several families elected to get together in an organized way, then you could pool your supplies. Moreover, it can be quite helpful to be able to draw upon the moral support of others in any type of emergency. Thus, should you find yourselves together with some others, then recognize the possibilities of cooperative action and sharing of resources—so long as ALL are "BRINGING something to the party" rather than simply TAKING.

On the following two pages is listed a 72-Hour Kit Checklist of items you should consider assembling together in some form of a portable pack. These items are basic bare essentials, and you may add to them as you have space and funds. Each family will have their own specific, personal needs to customize this general list.

With any luck, you will never need these all-important items; but isn't it better to be prepared and not need them, than to be unprepared and left stranded, wishing you did have them?!

We are in a time of massive changes everywhere upon our beautiful little planet, and you do not need to be a psychic or "receiver of Higher Sources" to be aware that something unprecedented is occurring upon our world. These changes are only going to continue to accelerate, the further we proceed into the planetary transformation, and we would all be wise to get ready and remain in a state of preparedness.

REMEMBER, IT'S TOO LATE TO PREPARE *AFTER* THE EMERGENCY! SO TAKE RESPONSIBLE ACTION NOW!

# 72-Hour Kit Checklist

☐ **Water**
Stored in a portable container; at least three gallons per person (for a three-day supply).   Rotate regularly. Have water purification method(s) such as 10-12 drops (per gallon of stored water) of 35% food-grade hydrogen peroxide, plus water filtration equipment.

☐ **Food**
Suitably packaged for long-term storage.   Also cups, utensils, paper plates, can opener if needed.

☐ **Extra Clothing**
A complete outfit of warm clothing for each family member.  Include socks, underwear, walking shoes.

☐ **Warmth and Shelter**
Coats, hats, scarves, and gloves for everyone.  Include warm blankets (wool or emergency blankets are best). Rain ponchos, garbage bags, umbrellas to keep off the rain.  Warm packs or other heat sources.  Tent or tarp.

☐ **Light Sources**
Flashlights with extra batteries, or chemical lightsticks. Flames from kerosene, propane lanterns require caution.  Have at least two quick and safe light sources.

☐ **Tools**
Pocket knife, camping shovel, duct tape, matches, pocket sewing kit, screwdriver, pry bar, hammer, etc.

☐ **Important Papers**
Important documents (birth and marriage certificates, insurance forms, wills, etc.), addresses and phone numbers of relatives, and places to meet if separated.

☐ **Money**
Store at least $20.00 (CASH) per person.  Be sure to include change, such as quarters for phone calls, etc.

# 72-Hour Kit Checklist
## (continued)

☐ **First Aid Supplies**
Pain relievers, bandages, antiseptics, clean cloths, burn ointment, rubbing alcohol, first-aid instruction manual. Include personal medications and prescriptions.

☐ **Special Needs**
For babies: diapers, ointment, bottles, pacifiers, hand towels, special foods, other supplies. Consider needs of elderly, handicapped, or other special cases.
Don't forget pets. Include pet foods and any medications they need. A pet carrier will be handy.

☐ **Stress Relievers**
Card games, books, small hobbies, audio (music) tapes and player. For children: small toys, paper and pen, and favorite security items (blanket, stuffed toy or doll).

☐ **Communications**
Portable radio with batteries (one requiring no batteries is best), signal mirrors, whistles, red flags, signal flares.

☐ **Personal Sanitation**
Toothbrushes, antiseptic mouth wash, hand soap, dish soap, razors, sanitary napkins, towels, toilet paper.

☐ **Portable Container(s)**
Backpacks and duffel bags are ideal. Container should be light-weight, sturdy, water-proof, and easy to carry. Shoulder straps are best for traveling long distances.

☐ **Additional Items**
Add as carrying weight and budget for kit will allow. Extra food, camp stove, cooking equipment, tents, sleeping bags, sun block, insect repellant, portable toilet, additional tools (like axe for clearing fallen branches) and more sophisticated first-aid items including the *US Army Survival Manual* (FM 21-76, available from Barnes & Noble Books).

# Listening With Your "Inner Ears"

### Ceres Anthonious Soltec
#### October 26, 1997

*Editor's note: The following writing is what is called a "squeaker" in the publishing world; it just barely squeaked-in under the wire! You can see from the date how chronologically out-of-sequence it is with respect to the termination point for the other writings included in this volume. And yet, here it is. Why?*

*Well, first of all, a large number of the writings herein—maybe ALL of them, in one way or another—encourage each of us to achieve our own direct "hook-up" with the God Source within. As ones take their first consciously directed learning steps into this realm, all kinds of questions get generated. (Since nearly all of the writings collected in Part II of this volume have already been presented in the CONTACT newspaper, the questions have been streaming back for some time now, along with wonderful "thank you" notes.) Lots and lots of questions, like: "Am I doing this right?" and "Really, how do I know this is not just me, making things up?" and then, finally, "I can't believe this could be so easy!" That last one probably makes God smile.*

*Understand that any Lighted being conscientiously efforting to make this personal connection with God is going to have moments of doubt and uncertainty and, always, feelings of inadequacy (due to our cultural programming) toward this awesome yet very basic gift. In addition to the political arena, all of the religion clubs depend heavily upon you turning over to the "Chosen Ones" most all of your personal responsibility toward any interaction with God. It is ok for the pastor to assert to do the interfacing with God FOR you, as well as doing any important speaking or interpreting on behalf of God, but it's very much NOT ok for little ol' uncredentialed you to do the same—ahem—else what would THEY do for a job?!*

*This subject of "receiving" has been directly addressed in Chapter 6, in the biographical sketch about communications Commander Korton, and then moreso in Chapter 29, by Commander Korton himself. It has also been indirectly discussed at many scattered locations within other writings throughout this volume.*

*However, when the following writing appeared on the scene recently, during the final editing work for this volume, it begged for inclusion since it addresses issues, possibly not already covered very well, that naturally come up when ones effort to recognize and then develop this most direct connection to God. At least this writing should provide additional perspective to go along with what has been discussed already within the pages of this volume.*

*As Lanto, The Sage said in Chapter 24: "It is not everyone's task to write public messages for the masses. It is, however, YOUR God-given right to connect-up to Higher Source and receive your own personal instructions." Or, as Commander Korton expanded upon that thought in Chapter 29: "First of all, KNOW that it is YOUR God-given RIGHT to receive directly from Creator Source (as well as from we of the Lighted Brotherhood) any time you so desire." And a bit later: "...know that receiving is as natural as thinking...." What a "loaded" sentence that last statement is!*

*With that said, it is hoped the following may assist those of you who are sincerely efforting to do what Commander Korton so poetically calls "awakening the 'sleeping giant' within".*

Good morning. Toniose Soltec present in Light, here to advise on matters the heart requests—sometimes subconsciously, at other times more expressively.

The first "item" on the agenda today deals with connecting or listening with your "inner ears" to those subtle nudges we send from time to time throughout the day. These can sometimes be misinterpreted as emanating from your own thought processes, but in reality they originate from outside of you and are transmitted into your head.

This is a large subject to attempt to cover briefly because of the degree to which thoughts can be placed into your head that DO NOT originate from we of the Lighted Brotherhood. Those of you who have been regular readers of the *CONTACT* newspaper are well aware of the secret technologies available to your elite controllers and would-be kings for achieving such perverted mind-control, mass-people-manipulation goals.

This is where the maintaining of your Light shielding becomes imperative. For the parameters of this discussion, I shall assume you have called in The Light for protection (with great emotional sincerity), and possibly even asked Commander Korton for assistance with the communication link-up. So we are henceforth focusing mostly upon the process of the receiving of Lighted input rather than adversarial thoughts possibly injected from, say, the nearest military installation.

I must digress here briefly to address the subject of your personal Lighted Guides. All Lighted beings who have elected to enter into the challenging learning environment of planet Earth have personal Guides specifically assigned to assist them. In the Catholic Church these Guides have long been referred to as Guardian Angels. Over the centuries, this terminology has become generally familiar on your planet. The Native Americans would refer to these same Dedicated Beings from the Angelic Realms as Spirit Guides.

There is even a popular (and in some ways quite accurate) current television show on your place called *Touched By An Angel* which, along with the many popular books and magazine articles available on this subject, full of personal testimony of "miraculous" occurrences, are more than ample evidence for the VERY REAL presence of these Angelic Guides. Moreover the current popularity surge about the general subject of Angels is one strong indicator of the great spiritual hunger and spiritual searching being undertaken by so many on your place at this time. (Again, as Dr. Young first mentioned in the Preface, and then near the end of the Introduction, these are also the main reasons why we have guided the appearance of this current volume at this exact time—as well as why the volumes called *The Celestine Prophecy* and then *Conversations With God* have, as recent stepping-stones along an evolutionary path of awakening, struck such resonant chords of popularity with so many on your planet.)

My point here is simply to give these most gracious Lighted Guides some much-deserved "publicity" because we watch so many of you go through your entire lives without ever so much as even acknowledging their constant presence, much less actively seeking communion and counsel with them on a regular basis. So when I refer, in the following discussion, to the subject of communing with God, take that to ALSO include any Lighted Messengers of God!

With that said, I return now to the most commonly asked question: "How does one really tell the difference between internally-generated and externally-generated thoughts and ideas?"

Bear in mind that the process of receiving is hampered by the injection of one's own interpretation and possible modification of, as well as by mis-perception or non-attunement with, our signal. When ones *think* they are receiving undiluted messages, only to have overlaid one's own personal imprint at the time of receiving, the result is an admixture of words that only approximates "the real thing". And again, this is, of course, assuming your space has been cleared to begin with, otherwise the message will be contaminated, not only by self-generated opinion or interpretation, but also by false and misleading matter interjected by the dark ones always ready to interfere with a Lighted project.

It is neither comforting nor encouraging to be reminded of these avenues for distortion, especially when one has been receiving for any great amount of time, but the point is to always effort to receive BETTER, and not dwell overly upon past errors. Sloppiness has no place when ones strive to perfect their receiving skills, and ALWAYS you must be vigilant in detecting incongruous or nonsensical interference from either the lower self or from outside dark agents.

While it is true that the higher the receiver's body frequency, the easier and more fluent is the likely state of the communication connection with us, unfortunately there is little that can be done to increase the receiver's body frequency beyond a certain level. Above a certain point, discomfort sets in. So it is best for you ones to maintain a balanced, joyous mental state and allow us to deal with the adjusting to whatever resultant frequency level you comfortably maintain due to the "positive attitude" condition.

Ones should remain relaxed at all times throughout the receiving session, so as not to grow tense or irritable, and thus lower one's frequency and also cause the draining of nervous system energy from the project at hand. Comfortable surroundings do help, such as a comfortable chair and back support. Otherwise the situation makes for discomfort and agitation, which can cause distraction and thus break the signal flow.

Let me reiterate again that A JOYOUS ATTITUDE should guarantee a productive and engaging discussion, free of unnecessary strain upon the nervous system, which is called into action during receiving, both on the mental and the physical levels of function.

Actually, the physics of the receiving process is quite a bit more complicated than the way I refer to it here, but for the sake of this discussion, picture your nervous system as an inter-linking "antenna" between activities in play at the physical, mental, and emotional levels of energy interaction.

Back to distinguishing one's own thoughts from those received from us. We generally cause you ones to search for the corresponding word that describes the non-verbal idea we are sending. You will, to the best of your cognitive ability, find a suitable word description that, when once completed and coupled with other words composing a sentence, should make perfect sense to YOU.

A writing can always be "cleaned up" afterwards for better clarity and more readable sentence structure, so long as, of course, the original concepts or ideas, as transmitted, are not distorted or eroded. Some perform this task quite well and the most successful technique for doing so is simply to again call-in the writing's Author for assistance with the clarification of "rough" passages.

Unfortunately, some ones are given to altering our Lighted input to suit their own "I know better" needs, simultaneously with the writing in progress, which only adds to the resulting confusion of the finished product. Even in the very best-intentioned cases, seldom are writings perfectly free of minor distortions; but the more you allow our signal to come through, and not focus upon yourself responding or reacting to our statements, the greater will be the accuracy of your writing.

Never get either too lax or too involved with a writing as you take it down. Again, a relaxed, joyous, but emotionally detached attitude is best, clearing your space from time to time, and always asking (to ensure authenticity) for confirmation of the receiving coming from an Author of Lighted Source.

This may sound redundant to emphasize, but make sure also to be in a calm and serene mood. Seldom do stressed, anxious, exhausted, or angry people receive properly. When the body is made to lower its frequency, then the range of accuracy diminishes accordingly. At that point, it is usually best NOT to write and to set aside communing with us for another time.

Most ones feel more refreshed and "inspired" upon awakening, so it may be best to sit during this period of the day. In any event, receiving can take place at ANY time of the day or night, depending on your schedule and mood. Daily writing sessions, at the same time each day, can be an optimum approach to strengthening your accumulated skill, but this will vary from person to person and upon one's schedule. Of course, it is better to write once a week under relaxed conditions, than to effort to write every day in a stressed mode.

An empty stomach usually works best, simply because the nervous energy can be reserved to assist the mental aspects of receiving, rather than be diverted to and used up in the process of digestion. Again, it is a matter of balance and comfort, for if one feels, say, intense hunger, then that alone acts as a most annoying distraction, and thus a light snack before beginning the receiving session becomes advantageous.

The rate at which one receives is also a variable. Some prefer audio taping their voice due to the rapidity with which they receive our signal (this denotes a close frequency match between receiver and Sender), or writing shorthand for the same reason. The advantage of speed is that there is less chance for tampering with the message through such as the injection of personal elaboration.

Most will do just fine at "normal" speed through the process of ordinary writing. This rate can usually be speeded up or slowed down, depending on how one is feeling on that particular day, the motivational level, and can vary with the subject matter under discussion, as well as many other factors.

A reasonable test to help one evaluate the "hearing" accuracy of what one is taking down is to set aside the document to later return to it when its contents are forgotten (or nearly so). Then ask yourself, "Could I have stated this alone?" If you answer "yes", then it MAY be more your own thoughts than an accurate rendering of our signal. If you answer a definite "no" or even an emotional "no way!", then in all likelihood, providing you cleared your space, what is written down is your translation of our signal.

Again, what others think of your work is irrelevant. If it sheds light or understanding on some uncertainty that you wished to have clarified, or brought insight and learning, or gave you another perspective, perhaps gave you clues to solving a problem, then the writing you received is a declared success—from "Whom" is seldom important!

Note that this evaluation process is fundamentally an exercise in discernment, which is itself a kind of internal "compass" measurement with respect to what you know, in your conscience or heart, to be true. All Lighted beings possess this inner knowing of right and wrong, for such derives from the God-Source within!

It is when there are confusing declarations, unqualified comments, contradictory statements within the same writing, that one must exercise a higher degree of cautionary discernment. This is not to be taken as a point of discouragement, but rather, a safeguard to guide you toward more accurate receiving.

It is seldom necessary to *effort* to receive, so much as one should mentally, physically, and emotionally relax mind and body, let go as it were, and tap into the cosmic vibrational field where the ideas and messages originate. Most "blocks" occur when ones "try" too hard and become fixated on the mechanism, rather than the message.

We hope this is of some value, as more and more come into these abilities through desire to communicate directly with their Higher Guidance. Thank you for sitting this day. Soltec to clear. Salu!

# Look Up, Among The
# Clouds And Stars

### *Dr. Edwin M. Young*
**Editor-In-Chief, *CONTACT* Newspaper**

For those of you who may be reading for the first time material such as is presented in this volume, it is a perfectly natural reaction to pause at some point and say to yourself "I must be nuts!" Or maybe worse yet, have someone whose opinion you usually respect say something like that TO you, especially when you try to talk with them about what you feel inside that drew you to this information.

Maybe you can even accept the possibility of some Angelic Messengers from somewhere "up there" writing inspired words of wisdom through otherwise normal people "down here". But—its just a bit too much to accept the idea of an Intergalactic Federation Fleet, of a Space Command and Elder Brothers from those ranks, running around watching over us and this planet. Or is it?

The next time someone whose opinion you generally trust says to you, "Ah, your head's up in the clouds!"—don't be offended. As a matter of fact, take their advice and DO LOOK UP, AMONG THE CLOUDS. You may be surprised by what you see there.

Back in Chapter 6 mention was made of both the "spectrum-strobing" starships often visible in the night sky, as well as the "cloud ships" often visible in the daytime sky. Then, again, in Chapter 7, there was a comment made about the "cloud ships" you may observe as part of Commander Soltec's geophysical monitoring teams. These "cloud ships" are quite real.

When craft desire, they can stand out, sometimes in a pronounced manner, without actually stepping down in frequency enough to become visible (and thus vulnerable to attack) themselves, by accumulating water vapor around their outer surface. Sometimes these shows are personal communications for YOU!

In some instances these can become quite humorous presentations, especially when these craft (which may have been there all the time, but in an invisible state) just appear "out of nowhere", and sit there as the only "cloud" present in an otherwise clear and dry sky. Or when they remain in place (or worse yet, go the wrong way!) in high-wind conditions, while other clouds move on by as they're supposed to, with the wind.

The following examples were photographed by (and are shared here with the kind and enthusiastic permission of) retired dentist, Dr. Al Overholt. These "cloud ship" photos were taken on many different occasions in the vicinity of a small Southern California desert town located not too far from several major earthquake fault lines, as well as secret underground military installations associated with the nearby, but more visible, Edwards Air Force Base (where the Space Shuttle sometimes lands), the China Lake Naval Weapons Facility, and Lockheed's infamous "skunk works"—biggies among the elite's dark arsenal of "interesting" technical places. In other words, these were taken in a geographic area that is routinely busy with a lot of up-to-no-good stuff going on, and thus a location ripe for a lot of supervision by teams of our Elder Brothers.

Look at these photos should you need some tangible evidence of the very real presence of our Elder Brothers amongst us. Or look up into the sky where, both day and night, they watch over us and may just provide YOU with a few photo opportunities of your own!

AGMV
MARQUIS
Québec, Canada
1997